IN WAR AND PEACE

The Story of Corrymeela

ALF McCREARY is the Religion Correspondent of the *Belfast Telegraph*, and an award-winning journalist and author. He graduated from Queen's University, Belfast, with an honours degree in Modern History, and he is a part-time tutor in writing at the Institute of Lifelong Learning at Queen's, and also at the Irish Writers' Centre in Dublin. The first of his thirty-five titles, *Corrymeela: The Search for Peace*, was published in 1975. His recent books include the acclaimed biographies of Senator Gordon Wilson, published by Harper Collins, and Archbishop Robin Eames, published by Hodder and Stoughton. He was appointed MBE in the 2004 New Year Honours List.

IN WAR AND PEACE
The Story of Corrymeela

Alf McCreary

THE BREHON PRESS
BELFAST

First published 2007 by The Brehon Press Ltd
1A Bryson Street, Belfast BT5 4ES, Northern Ireland

ISBN: 978 1 905474 15 8

Design: December Publications
Printed and bound by J H Haynes & Co Ltd, Sparkford

CONTENTS

Dedicated to
THOMAS JOSEPH McCREARY

FOREWORD

IT GIVES ME GREAT PLEASURE to write the foreword to this book outlining the history of the Corrymeela Community. My friend, Alf McCreary, whom I have known for more than forty years, has long been supportive of the work of the Community, both in his writing and his public speaking.

However, he has retained his individuality and integrity as an author and a journalist, and he is ideally placed to take an independent view of Corrymeela over the past forty years. What a great story he has to tell! It is particularly fitting that he has undertaken this latest task, because he worked with me closely on his original book about Corrymeela which was published over thirty years ago.

Much has taken place since Corrymeela was established in 1965. I look back with immense gratitude to the many people who have helped the Community and who have accompanied us on the long journey. It has never been easy, but the achievements have been humbling and yet reassuring, and we are all indebted to Almighty God for His guidance and sustenance during every step of the way.

There are so many people whom I would like to thank personally, but I am inhibited in doing so because, inadvertently, I would almost certainly leave somebody out! However, in extending my sincere thanks to you all, I know that you will remember our journey together, and what we learned from one another. Nevertheless, there is one person whom I want to mention especially, with deep love, affection and gratitude. My wife Kathleen has meant the world to me, and she has contributed so much to Corrymeela in her own way.

The Community has learned much over the years, not least from our individual and collective failures, and yet I believe that

Corrymeela has much still to teach others and to contribute to the wider world. I am confident that the Community will continue to show the faith, hope, determination and open-mindedness which have marked out the journey so far, and which will enable it to make the best of the future.

I wish you well, and God bless you all.

Ray Davey

INTRODUCTION

THIS NEW BOOK OUTLINING THE STORY of the Corrymeela Community since its establishment in 1965 was largely researched and written during and after its fortieth anniversary year, a notable milestone in its history.

The final manuscript was sent to the printers in early 2007, and well before the remarkable agreement which was achieved between the DUP and Sinn Fein, and which made possible a restoration of devolved Government to Northern Ireland. On 8 May the new First Minister, the Reverend Ian Paisley, was pictured at Stormont with the Deputy First Minister, Martin McGuinness of Sinn Fein, together with the then British Prime Minister, Tony Blair, and Taioseach Bertie Ahern. It set the seal on the formation of a new Northern Ireland Executive, and the historic occasion was rightly described by the *Belfast Telegraph* as the "Day No one Thought Would Ever Happen". This included, perhaps, the main participants themselves. It was a good day for peace and democracy in Ireland, and it was also the beginning of a new path which Corrymeela and its friends had championed for over four decades. It had been a painful and problematic path for all concerned, and much remained to be done. However it was a belated but welcome birthday present for Corrymeela, which had celebrated its fortieth anniversary some time previously.

My earlier and first book on Corrymeela was published in 1975, and it has been fascinating to study the developments since then, as well as to revisit the Community's early beginnings. In some ways Corrymeela has not changed much. The familiar Ballycastle site is as dramatic and as beautiful as ever, and apart from the new and refurbished buildings, the ambience has changed little in the past four decades or so.

However, much has changed in Northern Ireland and worldwide since 1965, and the following pages attempt to chart not only Corrymeela's reaction to these events but also its own development. It is a fascinating and complex story, but one that is by no means finished.

In the meantime, this book is an attempt to relate some of the worst and the best of the past in Ireland, and also to underline some of the achievements which may lead to a better future. Coincidentally, as I write these words I am reminded of an article in the *Belfast Telegraph* earlier this year by a young writer, Lucy Caldwell, who left during the worst of the Troubles but who returned in 2006 and was "dumbfounded" by the improvements and lifestyle of her native city. Her reaction, no doubt, is shared by many others.

The story of Corrymeela is the story of a Christian Community trying to come to terms with a society at war with itself for so many years and which is also learning to live with an imperfect peace. Significantly, the lessons learned by Corrymeela could apply to other parts of the world where there is chronic violence and misunderstanding. One of the central themes of this book is that Corrymeela has not been just an "Irish solution for an Irish problem", and that others might study with benefit the lessons learned here. These lessons are hard-edged, because reconciliation is not a soft option and it is difficult to achieve.

As many people in this book will testify, Corrymeela is a special place which offers a unique experience. I first encountered it through the Community's founder, the Reverend Dr Ray Davey, and his wife Kathleen, whom I met during my undergraduate days at Queen's University, and who have remained lifelong friends, though I have never been a member of the Corrymeela Community.

During my work involved in writing this book, I reminded myself of two important turning points in my career which had a connection with Corrymeela. The first was in the mid-Sixties when I returned from an extended visit to Canada, where I actively sought employment at a time when Northern Ireland was apparently heading for what appeared to be a full scale civil war, and it seemed not to be the place for a young couple to bring up their children. I returned, however, convinced that any ability I possessed as a writer would be more productively used in my native province, however deep its trauma. One of the first tangible results arising from this decision was the production of my earlier book on Corrymeela.

Much later, in the mid-Eighties, I left journalism to work in the newly-created post as Director of Information and Head of Information Services at Queen's University in Belfast. After nearly fourteen years in that stimulating job, where I nevertheless continued to write about Northern Ireland and its challenges, I began to feel a desire to move back into the world of journalism.

One afternoon in 1996, when I had sought out some space to think things over, I parked my car in a lay-by beneath the Corrymeela Centre at Ballycastle to look at the gorgeous view of Rathlin Island. Suddenly my reverie was interrupted by a sharp knock on my car window, which I wound down to encounter a somewhat fraught lady. She asked, "Can you help me, mister? I've got a mini-bus full of children staying at Corrymeela and I've run out of petrol. Would you drive me up to the Centre to get some assistance?" I replied, "Hop in", and off we went.

On the way up she said to me, "Aren't you the man who wrote that book on Corrymeela?" I was surprised, and to be honest, a bit flattered to be recognised as the author of a book which had been written some years previously; but more important than that, I was given the unexpected opportunity once again to watch Corrymeela in action. I shared a meal of sausages and somewhat soggy chips with an enthusiastic and noisy group of young people in the Centre, and afterwards I talked at length with a mature co-worker from West Belfast.

During our conversation I was impressed, as I have been before and since, with the sheer dedication of the volunteers, and I asked her, "What sustains you?" She paused and said to me, matter-of-factly, "Each night my family knows that when I go into our front room, I go there to pray. That's what sustains me." There was nothing more to be said. I left Corrymeela with a fresh reminder of the motivation of the Community, and also some of their values which had sustained me as the author of the first book on Corrymeela.

Not long afterwards, I left Queen's University to resume a career as a full-time writer. Some people might regard this as a coincidence with regard to my unexpected visit to Corrymeela, but while many other factors were involved, I believe that my experience at Corrymeela on that day also reinforced a deep instinct as to the direction of my future career. During the research for this book, others have told me how Corrymeela also touched their lives in unexpected ways, though they never became members of the Community.

Finally, there are many people whom I wish to thank for their help during the production of this book. They include Dr David Stevens, the Leader of Corrymeela and his colleagues; Brehon Press, the publishers; all those people who took time to talk to me or to write background papers on Corrymeela; the editors of those publications referred to in the narrative, and who are duly acknowledged; and the individuals not mentioned by name but whose contributions are known to me and are deeply appreciated.

In particular there are two people whom I would like to thank especially: Anne McDonagh from the Corrymeela office in Belfast, who typed the transcripts of my audio tapes and who was cheerfully and patiently helpful in every way; and my wife Hilary, who yet again supported me at all stages of this latest literary journey.

Alf McCreary MBE

ONE

HEAVEN AND HELL

"GOODBYE SEA, GOODBYE SHORE, GOODBYE HEAVEN." This description of the Corrymeela Centre at Ballycastle by a girl of seven who was returning to her home in a troubled area of Belfast sums up the reality and the vision of the early days of this unique religious community in Ireland.

The little girl was correct in describing so concisely the beautiful scene she was leaving. The restless sea was ever-changing as the strong currents swirled through the channel between the rugged North Antrim coastline and Rathlin Island, with its depth of history and sometimes quirky people, not unlike Northern Ireland itself. The shore along which she had most probably walked during her stay at Corrymeela would have given her a sense of freedom and safety which she would not have found in the dangerous streets of a troubled Belfast.

It was no wonder that Corrymeela seemed like heaven to her, and to so many others who came to discover the special qualities of the Community in such beautiful surroundings. Behind the vision, however, there was the earthy reality of this small group of people who, against the most difficult odds, were trying to live out the example of Christian reconciliation in a deeply-divided community. For many people caught up in the Troubles an idea of heaven was scarcely imaginable as they struggled with the daily hell of violence and hatred.

The story of Corrymeela is the story of a Community working between heaven and hell. Some people might find this description too extreme – but are there better words to describe the Corrymeela vision of a better world, or the hell of a society torn apart by violence and political and religious tribalism, and apparently intent on self-destruction?

Corrymeela faced not only the challenges of conflict in the wider society, but also its own internal divisions and failures. In trying to deal with all of these challenges it made mistakes, but it also helped to show that reconciliation is more than a pious aspiration. In certain ways and in particular circumstances it can become a reality, and the working out of that difficult path has characterised the role of Corrymeela over the past forty years.

The original concept seems to belong to a totally different age, to a world before the September 11 attacks on the USA in 2001 and the advance of militant Islam, before the invasions of Afghanistan and Iraq, and before the bombs in Madrid, London and elsewhere, with their implications of bringing a war to the heart of a civilian society. Yet the early Corrymeela witnessed a similar violent invasion of civilian non-involvement through the terrorism of the Provisional IRA and Loyalist paramilitaries, who inflicted on a small population one of the most destructive campaigns of indiscriminate violence in Europe since the end of the Second World War.

The violence in Northern Ireland, and the resultant suffering, had become unfashionable topics for discussion. The headlines were moving elsewhere, and reference to the Troubles had produced boredom among the policy-makers and the media in capital cities who wished that the messy Ulster conflict would end – as it seems to be doing. Nevertheless, the experience of Northern Ireland has important lessons for others caught up in civil strife, if they wish to learn from it.

These include governments as well as armies and security forces trying to deal with huge crowd demonstrations, rioting, and counter-security measures. There are also hard lessons for peacemakers, and the experience of Corrymeela goes far beyond that of a small group caught up in a remote Irish war. It has much wider implications which are still being worked out, and which others might study with benefit. The story of Corrymeela, forty years on, is reminiscent of the lines from the poet TS Eliot:

> We shall not cease from exploration
> And the end of all our exploring
> Will be to arrive where we started
> And know the place for the first time.[1]

The Corrymeela Centre for Reconciliation was opened in Ballycastle on Saturday 30 October, 1965 but the concept began much earlier in the minds of those who felt that such a Community was necessary. To that extent it is difficult to know where or even when the idea of Corrymeela really began, and the main evidence lies in the notes and recollections of some of those who were the prime movers in such an ambitious project.

It is widely acknowledged that one of the main visionaries was Ray Davey, the urbane and gentle but tough-minded Presbyterian minister who became Corrymeela's first Leader and Founder. Davey had a conventional upbringing as a son of the manse, and he may well have ended up as a mainstream Presbyterian minister in Northern Ireland.

It is conceivable that he might have had a quietly fulfilling and productive ministry like many of his contemporaries. He was good with people, he was doctrinally orthodox, and he had a strong sporting background, which would have given him an opportunity to relate to a wide range of people who might not usually have crossed the path of a budding cleric. One of his main claims to fame in the early days was his outstanding ability as a rugby player, and he was an impressive full-back for Ulster.

Today he would probably be part of an Irish "squad" if he were a professional player. Even at ninety-two years of age, he fondly claimed that one of his finest achievements was to have played for an Ulster side which drew with the mighty New Zealand All-Blacks touring team in 1935. If he had actually scored the drop-goal to clinch victory, he might well have been tempted to feel that his life's purpose had been already been achieved.

Yet Davey proved that he was no conventional Ulster minister in the making, though he had followed the familiar preparatory path of an education at the Royal Belfast Academical Institution, Queen's University and the Presbyterian Assembly's College. However, the outbreak of the Second World War changed his life utterly, as it did the lives of so many others. He was an assistant minister in First Bangor, but after some heart-searching he decided to join the war as a member of the YMCA and to bring practical and spiritual help to the front-line combatants.

He reflected later, "We at the college hated war, but when I heard what was going on, I asked myself, 'How could I really stay out of it?' I would have been a pacifist if I hadn't had the opportunity to work with the YMCA, which provided services for the soldiers such as canteens and sending messages home. It also enabled men of all denominations to come together in an atmosphere of community. Looking after both material and spiritual well-being was at the heart of our mission."[2]

Davey was sent to the Middle East, and he initially had a "good war" in the conventional sense that he fulfilled an important role in bringing material and spiritual help to his colleagues in great need. However, his war was cut short when he was captured by the Germans at Tobruk, and he spent the rest of the conflict as a prisoner-of-war in Italy and later in Germany. In several of Ray Davey's books he has documented this seminal experience of creating and sustaining community within a situation of sustained conflict, but he rarely spoke in detail about the horrors of his war experiences. However, his innate courage and powers of survival in battle were most clearly described in his war diaries, which were written painstakingly in longhand during his wartime incarceration in the prison camps and published in 2005.[3]

In an entry dated 23 February, 1942, he describes the dangers he faced at the height of the Desert War, and his understated writing style adds considerably to the mood of tension and the extreme dangers of those days:

"A most unsettling day. Visibility was restricted by low clouds, and several planes darted in, dumped their load and got off just as AA got into action. This process got us all quite jumpy. Then 'Tank' arrived back with his wagon in tow and peppered with shrapnel holes. He has four small pieces in his body, fortunately not serious, two in the leg, one in the seat and one in the chest. 'Tiny' was very badly shaken. They were attacked by a Stuka, which dropped a stick of bombs across them. Both were below the car. One of the drivers in a nearby vehicle was killed outright.

"At night I went to the first of the mission services. It was an experience I'll never forget being at a mission service with a heavy air raid on. We could hear some of the bombs crunching and the tremendous noise of the harbour barrage and the beat of the enemy bombers, which seemed right above. I did admire old Padre Leyland, who went on unperturbed. I certainly did not feel too good. Quinn's eye was in a bad mess, as a landmine had blown up in his face."[4]

Ray Davey as the eventual first Leader and Founder of Corrymeela has been often portrayed as a saintly figure, and rightly so. However, it is easy to overlook his inner steel which was tempered in the fierce heat of war and which gave him the single-mindedness and strength of character to help establish the Community and to guide it through its own considerable battles for survival. The challenges of community life were imbedded deeply in his psyche by his prisoner-of-war experience, as he reveals tellingly in the following description of life in an Italian camp near the Adriatic coastal town of Porto San Giorgio:

"Here in these few acres was the concentrated life and energy of a goodly-sized town, with men drawn from every walk of life. It was revealing to see what a vital force life is and how, when it is dammed and blocked in one direction, it will eventually find outlet and expression in another. Nearly everyone found some little ploy to keep himself going. Living was three times faster than normal. Here one had all the problems of communal life. It was an ideal laboratory for the psychologist, the moralist, the philosopher and the theologian. As one prisoner said, 'If one could settle the problems of a prisoner-of-war camp, he would settle the problems of the world.'"[5]

A particularly shattering experience was the Allied bombing of

Dresden. As a prisoner in a nearby camp, he witnessed the destruction of that beautiful and historic city, and he later wrote with clarity and deep sensitivity about his feeling of sadness, loss and even suppressed anger at such destruction. He noted: "Dresden was something I could never forget. It underlined to me the futility of all conflict, and when I returned back home, the challenge of trying to do something about conflict stayed with me, especially in my own society which was so polarised."

One of the most striking revelations about what had been shaping the inner man is contained in one of Davey's final entries in the war diaries, shortly before his release from prison camp. On 6 December, 1944 he wrote:

"How will I react after all this time away from home, this unsettled irresponsible life? Four-and-a-quarter years away now. Who would have thought so? September 1940! But at present there is a deep sense of satisfaction, in that I did get out of the rut of orthodox clerical life and find an experience like this. I feel in many ways a rebel and hope for the courage to live out a true religion and faith. May reality, simplicity and service be ever my guiding stars."[6]

When he eventually returned to Northern Ireland, it was no surprise that this apparently orthodox "rebel" seized the opportunity to become the first Presbyterian Dean of Residence at Queen's University, Belfast. This was an exciting time for Queen's which was welcoming an influx of ex-Service men and women who helped to give the university a more cosmopolitan outlook.

Around the same period, Queen's was fortunate to appoint the eminent Dr Eric (later Lord) Ashby as its new Vice-Chancellor, and under his inspired leadership the university developed from being a small provincial institution to become a nationally-recognised seat of learning. It was within this exciting new atmosphere that Davey was able to develop his idea of community, and he did so quietly and effectively, as Ashby himself later noted. He wrote:

"For nine years Ray and I were colleagues at Queen's University. I was occupied with the management of its secular life; he was concerned with the spiritual life of its members. Quietly – so quietly that some of us didn't know about it until we saw the results – he created a community within Queen's. It was primarily a community of Christians, not just Presbyterian, but (with co-operation from chaplains of other denominations) truly ecumenical. All of us at Queen's are deeply in his debt."[7]

Ashby, who was one of the most successful and shrewdest Vice-Chancellors in the University's history, made the important point that Davey had created at Queen's not just a Presbyterian "ghetto", but in fact an ecumenical community. This was a considerable achievement in a Northern Ireland which was still suffering deeply from religious and political apartheid. It was no surprise that the seeds of a wider religious community developed from the experience at Queen's, and that some of the other main Corrymeela visionaries had learned a great deal as undergraduates, and later graduates, of the university.

However, no history of Corrymeela would be credible without an in-depth explanation of the genesis of the idea of community as lived through the early life of Ray Davey, in war and peace. Sometimes, when the story of Corrymeela is related in its various forms, the role of Ray Davey becomes almost muted by sheer repetition of the details. It is a salutary experience, therefore, to retrace the steps and to realise how much is owed to one man, whose time had come, and to pay due tribute to him. Tribute is also due to Kathleen Davey, Ray's wife, who has been his tower of strength and who has also made an inestimable contribution to Corrymeela.

Ray has never been a man to seek tributes, however, and one of his most attractive qualities has been his self-effacement and his ability to give the credit to others. Above all, he has been a supreme catalyst and a leader who has been able to attract people and to mould them into a creative team. As a later Leader, Dr David Stevens, noted perceptively, "Ray spoke the language of reconciliation and the importance of relationships, when this was unfashionable. Today, that language is mainstream; it is on the lips of church leaders, politicians and government ministers. This is a mark of Ray's success. He is a prophet of a shared future."[8]

It is important, however, that a prophet (however heavenly-minded) should have his or her feet on the ground, and the concept of Corrymeela began to coalesce from a series of meetings with like-minded people who thought that such a Christian Community was not only necessary, but that it could work. Davey recalls the first meeting in his office at Queen's University in 1964 with two Presbyterian ministers – the Reverend John Morrow, who was later to make an important contribution to Corrymeela as Leader, and the Reverend Alex Watson, minister of Harmony Hill Presbyterian Church at Derriaghy, near Lisburn.

Significantly, both men were members of the Iona Community in Scotland, and they were impressed by its spirituality and practicality, as well as the leadership of the Reverend George MacLeod. Morrow later wrote that MacLeod impressed him with his "robust humanity. The spiritual power he exuded had an earthiness about it which communicated to me. He knew about life in the raw: he knew about the experience of 20th century humanity, in its suffering and its lostness. He knew that the Church was often out of touch with the realities of the time.

"For an Irish Presbyterian like me, this movement awakened a new consciousness on a number of frontiers... In the renewed worship on Iona we recognised the richness of that holistic Celtic tradition with which many Irish Protestants had lost contact. Also the challenge to recover a shared common life was there in the Benedictine tradition of the Abbey even though the Community knew that they must search for different ways of expressing that in the secular world of the 20th century."[9]

Ray Davey knew George MacLeod, and he greatly admired the Iona Community. The gifts of John Morrow and Alex Watson and their experience at Iona were complementary to that of Davey and added greatly to the Corrymeela vision. Craig Cameron, another founder-member of Corrymeela, described it thus:

"Alex was like a farmer with a dog collar, a big Ulsterman with a shock of white hair and a lovely smiling face, a wonderful warm personality, and just a pleasure to be around. John was probably more of a thinker, more of an idealist, and Alex was probably more a feet on the ground, practical man. The help that both of them gave to Corrymeela from their Iona experience was invaluable."[10]

The first meeting between Davey, Morrow and Watson led to another meeting attended by some fifty people from widely differing backgrounds. It was clear that there was an impetus for a Christian Community, but not yet sufficient consensus as to what shape it should take. Ray Davey recalls: "We knew that we had to take time so that we continued to meet and to pray together, that we should be shown the way."

The discussions, and the philosophies, were wide-ranging. The group included those who had visited Iona, as well as Taizé in France and Agape in Italy. Craig Cameron summarises the early full flush of the group's ambitions:

"We had the vision of an ecumenical Christian group in Ireland dedicated to the reconciliation between God and men and women, Catholic and Protestant, religious and laity, believer and unbeliever, and young and old. The idea was to live a more integrated life while remaining grounded in (and not apart from) normal family life, work, Church, society and politics. We wanted to be open to new ideas, to catalysing change, while learning and teaching by doing."

In early 1965, the group was told that a Holiday Fellowship Centre near Ballycastle was up for sale. Ray remembers that the news immediately concentrated their thinking. He wrote: "No longer could we indulge in rather abstract discussions on the nature of Christian community. Now we had to face a real choice, and our ideas and our visions were put to the test."

The Centre had real possibilities. It had superb cliff-top settings, and the potential for expansion. Even though the group had no money, Davey was encouraged with the others to make an offer, and he put down a deposit of £1,000, which seemed a small fortune in those days. Cameron, and others, were deputed to raise funds of some £9,000. He says, "Some of the people I thought I might get money from, gave us nothing, and some of the others whom I thought were no-hopers, gave generously. It was a tremendous learning experience, and we raised the money within ten days."

Nevertheless, some people had honest, though temporary, misgivings. John Morrow remembers:

"We had to put up the money for a deposit, and each of us was asked to raise a minimum of £10. I was living as a minister on a minimum income with three children, and £10 at that time was quite a lot. However I was reassured when I looked at the site and I felt that, even if it went all wrong, we could sell the place. When you think of prices now, all that was meaningless.

"Anyhow, I was always very filled with hope because I had great faith in Ray, and I had also the Iona experience. I really felt that there was a need for something similar here. We could learn from Iona but we had to do our own thing. I really felt that the time was ripe, and that we were onto something."

Meanwhile Davey was so excited by the prospect of buying the Centre, and so worried that they might lose it, that he went into the estate agent's office on the Friday of a holiday weekend. He said, "I could stand the anxiety no longer, and pressed the estate agent very strongly to accept our offer, which he finally did. I came home very excited with the prospects that began to open up for our embryonic community."

In some ways that was the easy bit. The Centre was derelict, and an army of volunteers was required to make it habitable. This was done through a series of work camps, where people discovered the virtues of hard work, and the welcome surprise of developing skills which they did not believe they possessed. The pioneering, cheerful nature of this adventure was well captured by the recollections of Desney Cromey, née Kempston:

"The first work camp was in June 1965, when six of us – Joyce Nice, Agnes Kirkpatrick, Billy McAllister, Glen Rowan, Roger Cromey and I – moved into a very sad and neglected Corrymeela site. The main buildings and chalets were a rather horrible shade of green. The kitchen was antiquated but lively; a massive wooden sink dominated the scene, but the eye was distracted by the racing activities of numerous mice busy in the open cupboards below.

Sanitary arrangements were quite primitive, as there was no running water for the first few days, and many a bucket of water was transported down the hill by our own Jack and Jill. There was little furniture downstairs, and none at all upstairs. New work campers were welcomed with cries of 'Come on it. You'll have to make your own bed. Here's some wood, and ask Billy for a hammer and nails.'

What times we had; often rising at 6am for first breakfast and morning worship, followed by hard physical work until lunchtime. The rest of the day was devoted to exploring the local countryside, solving the world's problems, cooking and washing-up. Close friendships were made, and many a romance, including my own, flourished in the work camp setting."[11]

One of the key figures was Billy McAllister, who seemed literally to be God's gift to Corrymeela. He was a deeply spiritual but practical man who had the important skills of a clerk of works, and could keep a professional eye on the many activities which were taking place on the site. While this important work was going on, the Community's loose structure was formalised. Ray Davey was confirmed as Leader, and a Council was elected as the central governing body – Ray, Craig Cameron, Bill Breakey, Basil Glass, Robert Carson, Joyce Nice, Angela Breakey, Tom Patterson, and Bill Boyd.

Even before the renovation and rehabilitation of the site had been completed, the first Corrymeela "event" took place; Ray Davey described it well:

"In June 1965 a group of some forty to fifty people entered the lounge at Corrymeela. It was a Saturday afternoon, and the purchase of the premises had just been completed. This was indeed the first Corrymeela event and somehow it almost took us by surprise, as the building itself was undergoing some long overdue renovations and much obviously needed to be done before it would be fully functional. I don't think there were even enough chairs to go around, and some had to stand. It seemed so much a non-event, with no Press and television coverage. Yet it was a first step, and something had happened."[12]

What had taken place was little short of a minor miracle. Looking back on those events of more than forty years ago, it seems incredible that this small group of people had such a clear vision of reconciliation in a society which was still so burdened by the past. Subsequent developments, if only the Corrymeela founders had known it at the time, would test the Community's resolve and ingenuity to the utmost in the midst of a gathering storm. The establishment of Corrymeela was a brave, almost naïve, step in its well-meaning intensity; yet it was also practical, timely and visionary. Much would need to be done, but something important had really happened.

TWO

MAKING HEADLINES

THE OFFICIAL OPENING of the Corrymeela Centre for Reconciliation on 30 October 1965 was a memorable occasion. On a blustery but bright Saturday afternoon around 200 people gathered together in the main building on the cliff-top "Hill of Harmony", with its magnificent views across the sea to Scotland. The building itself was originally green, but a decision had been made to paint it white. This simple but effective step somehow underlined the brightness, the freshness and the purity of the new project.

Wisely, the founders had decided on a simple opening ceremony, rather than staging a formal ecclesiastical occasion, burdened down by heavy clerical robes and even heavier liturgy. If Corrymeela was to make a difference, it had to look and sound different from the very start. This it did, in its own way.

There was a wide mixture of people present, in terms of age, background and religious traditions. Ray Davey described the atmosphere thus:

"It was a happy and relaxed day, beginning with the procession of work campers cheerfully winding their way up from the coast road. They were dressed in their jeans and T-shirts, and carried all the various tools they had used in the restoration of the House. They were a noisy and colourful procession, brandishing not only spades, shovels, picks and paint-brushes, but also kettles, pots and pans, recognising that everyone had a part to play."[1]

These young people symbolised the theology of practicality, in the everyday world of buckets and spades, of drains and plumbing, of lighting and heating – all of which was vital in the down-to-earth success of this Christian undertaking. The opening ceremony also provided much material for deep reflection. Dr Bill Breakey led an act of worship, and Desney Kempston, another founder-member, read a passage from Ephesians which was the hallmark of the Corrymeela challenge: "For He is our peace, who has made us both one and has broken down the dividing wall of hostility."

The simple Litany of Dedication was spoken by the Leader, the Reverend Ray Davey, and responded to by all who were present. It summarised neatly the thinking and philosophy of the group over so many months previously, and helped to focus on the main challenges facing the Community. No doubt a more exhaustive set of challenges might have been produced, but in 1965 there was more than enough challenge in the opening dedication ceremony.

The Litany brought together a number of main themes: Corrymeela needed to focus on Christian training, particularly of lay people. The Centre was to provide a space for quietness and retreat, for respite and for renewal. It was also to be a place of conference and study "for the meeting of men and women from industry, commerce and professional life". Corrymeela was to be a location for work camps "of craftsmen and voluntary helpers in a realistic Christian fellowship" and also to provide an international dimension and "the increase of friendship and understanding". Finally, Corrymeela was to provide for "the ministry of reconciliation in working and community life and in the church". In effect, nothing of major importance was left out, or implicitly ruled out. Like the Apostles' Creed, the Litany of Declaration read well, and it was able to encompass the widest possible mandate in apparently the fewest possible words.

Ray Davey formally welcomed Pastor Tullio Vinay from Agape, who had been asked officially to open the Centre. It was a wise choice, not only because of what Vinay said, but also because of the authority with which he spoke. He was not just a welcome visitor from a similar project on the European mainland which had inspired the founders of Corrymeela, but also a man who had risked his life in sheltering Jews from Nazi persecution, and helping them to escape.

During the Second World War, Tullio Vinay had been the Waldensian pastor in Turin, where there had been a large colony of Jews. To help rescue as many as he could from the Gestapo, Vinay built a secret room under his study where he sheltered individual Jews until they could escape to the comparative safety of the Italian countryside. As an Italian Protestant from a community which had also known in their history the injustice of marginalisation and victimhood, he could identify all too easily with those he was trying to help.

Following his war experience Vinay was appointed as a youth pastor for the north of Italy, and with a group of war veterans founded the beautiful mountain village of Agape, which was dedicated to Christian reconciliation. Vinay's presence at the opening of the Corrymeela Centre had an added dimension – his experience of reconciliation, like that of the former prisoner-of-war Ray Davey, and also in common with Iona's George MacLeod, who had been awarded the Military Cross in the First World War, had been grounded in the depths of violence and suffering. This was also part of the reason for the foundation of the Taizé community by Brother Roger – originally a Swiss layman, Roger Schutz – in helping people who were fleeing from Nazi persecution in France, including Jews. After the war Taizé looked after orphans of the conflict, and also former German prisoners-of-war. The example of Taizé had been another inspiration to the Corrymeela founders.

Corrymeela was not just a new Community for Northern Ireland, but rather a part of a wider European outreach, in its aspirations for a better world. In his address at the official opening, Tullio Vinay asked that the Centre should be "a question-mark to the Church everywhere in Europe so that it may review its structures and task, and may be free from this instinct of preservation, to hear the time of God for its mission in the world".

Forty years on, those words sound even more prophetic, and it is perhaps only now that some of the churches are beginning to understand more fully what Vinay was trying to convey so long ago. Significantly, however, in asking Corrymeela to be a question-mark, Vinay himself, by his commitment and lifestyle, had earned the authority to do so. As a later Leader, Dr David Stevens, noted, "You have to earn the right to be a question mark."[2]

Tullio Vinay's address, though delivered in halting English at the official opening in 1965, has been reprinted many times within the wide range of the Community's literature. Yet it is still worth studying as a consistent challenge through changing times and circumstances. Vinay stressed that Corrymeela should be a place of "preaching the New World as we see it in the person of Jesus Christ. The world needs to see this message in the real world of men. Here, living in the New World together in work and prayer, you may point it to all categories of men and push them to the same research, be they politicians, economists, sociologists, technicians, workers or students." Incidentally, it is interesting to note how Vinay was a man of his time when the contemporary language was non-inclusive of women.

In his address Vinay also challenged Corrymeela to be a place of encounter and dialogue, with believers or unbelievers. He said, "The believers need the presence of unbelievers because they represent a criticism on your faith and life, the unbelievers need us if we have real news to bring. A member of the Italian Parliament once said to me, 'I am not religious but I am terribly attracted by Christ.'" It is not difficult to imagine the cool reaction to Vinay's challenge from many of the Christians in the Northern Ireland of 1965, whose only reaction to unbelievers would have been the New Testament injunction, "Come ye out from among them."

Tullio Vinay's challenge to Corrymeela about being a "question mark" has already been mentioned, but the final part of his address was, in his own words, "more than all that" which had gone before. He said, "You – being together – have always open eyes and ears to understand when the Lord is passing nearby, to be ready to follow the way He shall indicate to you. As a Church we should not have an inferiority complex, not because we are or have something, but because every possibility is given to us as his instruments."

Even today this speech is remarkably prescient, and it should remain the bedrock of the Corrymeela challenge. Of necessity the Community has produced numerous papers and developing liturgies, and it has organised many conferences and workshops full of eloquence and high-mindedness, as well as necessary realism and, in some cases, froth. Almost to a fault among peacemakers, and community and religious bridge-builders in general, there is a tendency at times to over-elaborate and almost to talk a concept to death. The Corrymeela Community and its associates and friends would do well to keep before them the simple but profound words of Tullio Vinay in his historic address of 1965, and also the shorter but equally prophetic challenge from their Leader, Ray Davey.

He said, "We know there is no cheap and easy route to unity. We cherish and respect the separate traditions of each Church, but we are convinced that there are multitudes of things that are crying out to be done together, and it is high time we got on with them." Davey expressed the hope that Corrymeela would be known as "the Open Village", open to all of goodwill who were willing to meet one another, to learn from each other and to work together for the good of all.

He also emphasised that Corrymeela should be "open for all sorts of new ventures and experiences in fellowship, and study and worship; open to all sorts of people, from industry, the professions, agriculture and commerce". He concluded, with characteristic realism, "This is at least part of our vision. We know that we are only at the beginning, and there is so much to be done."

It was a tall order, and those who went home after that simple but impressive official opening ceremony at Ballycastle were aware that there was indeed much to be done. The challenge to "openness" was quickly tested by the Community's attitude to an important historical anniversary which was being marked only a few months later.

This would be the fiftieth anniversary of the Easter Rising of 1916 which ultimately led to the partition of Ireland and to the formation of the Irish Republic. In theory Corrymeela had a choice either to leave this important commemoration to those on both sides who wished to make political capital out of the event, or it could use the occasion to remind the world that it had arrived and that there could be a more inclusive and peaceful way ahead for all the people of the island.

It chose the latter course, and organised the important "Community 1966" Conference which was addressed by the then Northern Ireland Prime Minister, Captain Terence O'Neill. The event, which was seen by O'Neill and his advisers as a suitable occasion on which to put forward their important bridge-building policies, helped to place Corrymeela on the map.

It was no mean achievement for such a fledgling community to provide such a forum at the centre of the major political developments of the day. Brian Walker, the conference chairman, said that it would be a witness "that Protestant and Roman Catholic groups can meet together to think about the common good of the community at a time when they might be expected to stay apart".

From this point in time, it is perhaps difficult to recall the tensions which underlay the 1966 commemoration of the Easter Rising. Nationalists and Republicans who retained their vision of Irish unity, despite the creation and continued existence of Northern Ireland, saw the commemoration as an important reminder of the sacrifice of those who had fought and died to create the new Irish Republic. Unionists, not surprisingly, saw the commemoration as a reminder that many people did not accept partition and that Northern Ireland, in the words of a later Irish Prime Minister, Charles Haughey, was a "failed political entity".

There was the added complication that 1966 also marked the fiftieth anniversary of the Battle of the Somme, in which the 36th (Ulster) Division had a huge number of casualties among the dead and wounded, precisely at a time when "traitorous" Irishmen in Dublin had struck a savage blow to the heart of a British Empire engaged in a major European conflict. There were also considerable casualties among the Irish soldiers serving with the British in the First

World War, but the official recognition of this politically inconvenient sacrifice in an emerging Republican state took nearly ninety years to be recognised. Any commemoration of the fiftieth anniversary of the major events of 1916, or implicitly linked to the significance of the anniversary, posed problems for the governments, and for institutions, in both parts of Ireland, including the newly-established Corrymeela.

In the event, the Community got it right. The Conference was acknowledged as a success, and the speech by O'Neill on Good Friday symbolised not only the pain of past inter-community divisions which had held back the proper development of Northern Ireland as a state, but also the hope of new life and a better political and social future for all. O'Neill was a shy man with an aloof manner, which did not help him to make friends at a time when he needed all the political help he could get. Significantly, he was not a good communicator, either within his own Unionist Party or to the public at large, and this was a contributory factor in his eventual downfall. However, at Corrymeela he not only said the right things, but he had also shown politically that he was trying to practise what he was preaching.

To that extent he had the authority to offer a few home truths to a Community which was just setting out on the difficult road of reconciliation. He said, "The conference will not achieve its potential without frank speaking, and an admission of differences of principle. The avoidance of controversial issues may be comfortable, but it makes no real contribution to better understanding." This indeed was a neat summary of the philosophy of the liberal Unionism which he and too few of his colleagues espoused, and which continues to challenge the politicians and communities in Northern Ireland.

O'Neill had the advantage of employing particularly good speech-writers, and his Corrymeela address confronted the major issues in an elegant form of language which slightly softened the stark message he was trying to get across. He said, "The Ulster community is a place in which two traditions meet – the Irish Catholic tradition and the British Protestant tradition. In India the place where two great rivers join together is often considered to have a particular sanctity – but it is also often a place of turbulence, as the currents from opposite directions swirl around each other. By and large these religious traditions have also been synonymous with political views."

O'Neill may have thought inwardly "A plague on both your houses", but he was too polite a man to say so in public. He and his advisers also knew that there was little political capital in calling an agricultural instrument a "spade" at a time when carefully chosen words might have had more effect than a direct condemnation of any group or community. Nevertheless, he stated bluntly that the "correspondence of religion and politics has, in the past, created certain peculiar frictions in our public affairs, and prevented us from mounting a united effort to surmount the other social and economic problems". Little did O'Neill know that these "peculiar frictions", by which he euphemistically described the political stagnation of Northern Ireland, would soon develop into a political and social revolution.

At Corrymeela, Prime Minister O'Neill did not avoid the prickly question of segregated education, and he made the pointed observation that "Many people have questioned, however, whether the maintenance of two distinct educational systems side by side is not wasteful of human and financial resources, and a major barrier to the promotion of communal understanding."

Predictably, he later received a testy retort from the Roman Catholic Primate Archbishop William Conway, who said that he welcomed O'Neill's appeal for goodwill and Christian charity, but that he found "this continuing pressure on Catholic schools, by the head of the Government, very surprising and, indeed, disquieting". In other words, ecumenism was all very well, but "hands off our Catholic schools". No doubt, some Protestants would have felt the same about their own institutions.

The centre-point of O'Neill's speech at Corrymeela was a powerful appeal to both main communities in Northern Ireland. He said, "If we cannot be united in all things, let us at least be united in working together in a Christian spirit – to create better opportunities for our children, whether they come from the Falls Road or from Finaghy. In the enlightenment of education, in the dignity of work, in the scrutiny of home and family, there are aims which all of us can pursue. As we advance to meet the promise of the future, let us shed the burdens of traditional grievances and ancient resentments. There is much we can do together. It must – and God willing – it will be done."

It was a brave and visionary speech, and those people present who were of like mind may well have felt that this was political leadership of a high order. With the virtual demise of the Official Unionist Party in recent times, and the absence of a local Primate Minister for nearly twenty-five years (apart from the brief rein of David Trimble as First Minister) it may be difficult for younger generations to understand that, in 1966, a Stormont Prime Minister was a very influential politician indeed. O'Neill was not only Prime Minister, but he was also saying the kind of things that should have been voiced by Unionist leaders many years earlier.

The Corrymeela speech received widespread praise from the liberal newspapers of the day. Jack Sayers, the crusading and liberal Unionist editor of the influential *Belfast Telegraph* wrote, "Through Captain O'Neill and those who organised the community conference, Corrymeela takes its place in Irish history." Privately, Sayers confirmed his public stance in a letter to the conference chairman, Brian Walker: "What a public platform and how very finely the PM rose to the occasion. Given support, his speech takes us a long way forward. But it also means that Corrymeela and all you who belong to it, are just starting."

The Dublin-based *Irish Times* noted that the Corrymeela Conference had taken place "to preserve the good relationships which have grown rapidly in recent years in Northern Ireland". Perhaps the best summary of the O'Neill speech came from the *Corrymeela Bulletin* itself. It stated that "Northern Ireland's self-inflicted wounds are showing signs of healing… the Prime Minister's brave opening speech will be remembered not so much for its content as for the fact that it was made."

It all seemed so hopeful, so "Corrymeela", so right – and sadly, as events were to prove, so optimistic and ahead of its time. Within three years Northern Ireland was engulfed in demonstrations and counter-demonstrations as the civil rights movement gained strength and authority, and later on the Province was sucked into a civil conflict of varying degrees that lasted for practically all of Corrymeela's forty years of existence.

How did it all go so horribly wrong, so quickly – and what would it mean for Corrymeela, almost before it got properly started on the road to reconciliation? Perhaps the seeds of future conflict had been planted already, and too many people had either forgotten them or had underestimated the potential for a further outbreak of violence, or – understandably in human terms – had allowed their hope and faith to over-rule one of the cardinal rules of Irish political and religious life, namely that the more things seem to change, the more they stay the same.

THREE

DOWNWARD SPIRAL

THE EARLY DAYS AND MONTHS following the Corrymeela Conference, which had drawn such publicity to the Community, brought few further headlines. It was a time of consolidation, of building up structures, of completing projects that had not been finished at the time of the official opening of the Centre, and of starting others. Ray Davey recalls the mood and the ethos at the beginning:

"Looking back, we were certainly idealistic and visionary, though we never claimed that we would solve the Irish problem, or bring back peace. We saw our function rather to begin the process of reconciliation; point out the way; and witness to what as a Christian Community we believed peace to be. But there was one thing that was salutary for us as a Christian community. Corrymeela from the start, by its very nature, was about relationships and people. All sorts and conditions of people began to come to Ballycastle."[1]

In the early years a number of other significant conferences were held at the Centre, and these contributed to the development of important voluntary movements and organisations. They included the Northern Ireland Mixed Marriage Association, the Northern Ireland Federation of Housing Associations, the Northern Ireland Hospice Movement, and Integrated Education. Community members also organised and ran Summer Family Weeks at Ballycastle for those who could not afford a holiday by the seaside, or anywhere else. Volunteers led programmes with families, children and pensioners. The tradition of work camps continued, and provided not only valuable friendship and fellowship but also the hard

practical effort required to continue the renovation of the site, and
the upkeep of the buildings.

Corrymeela was thus doing what it had been established to do –
to be a place of encounter, and a place of respite, and also a focus
where the challenge of Christianity could be worked out in practical
and spiritual dimensions suitable for the modern age. Yet, all the
while, the political clouds were gathering across the Province, in
contrast to the bright hopes of the new Christian community on the
cliff-top site in Ballycastle.

At the time, few people in Corrymeela or elsewhere had the
inclination, or the time, or the historical perspective, to analyse the
political events that were taking place elsewhere in Northern Ireland,
and which represented a kind of a parallel universe which was apart
from the daily lives of many people. The emphasis was on hope and
progress, rather than dwelling on the past, or being negative about
the present. With hindsight, there are those who claim that the
wrongs in Northern Ireland were so great, that there was bound to be
an upheaval, sooner or later.

However, it is also right to point to a feeling among most people
that whatever the difficulties of the present, the worst of the violent
past in Ireland seemed to be over, and the continued injustices and
discrimination in society could somehow be worked out peacefully
within the prevailing political framework. This would take time and
patience, but it was felt that after the end of the abortive IRA
campaign from 1956-62, the gun was no longer a force in Irish
politics.

That prevailing mood was neatly summarised by Dr Bill Breakey,
who wrote "before the Troubles erupted throughout Northern
Ireland, it was a time of some optimism among liberally-minded
people because, although we were aware of many of the injustices in
society and the iniquitous divisions among Christians, there was a
sense that we were moving in the right direction, and that things
were going to get better. It was evident to us that bridging the
Protestant-Catholic divide would be an essential part of any attempt
to develop a concept of community in the Church, though this did

not have the central importance that it came to have a few years later."[2]

The mood of general optimism was confirmed by the historian Dr Jonathan Bardon in his authoritative *History of Ulster*. He noted how Captain Terence O'Neill had represented "a new liberal Unionist generation prepared to move away from the siege mentality of those in the turbulent events surrounding the formation of Northern Ireland". However, this brave new world had foundered through political intransigence and the outbreak of violence until Northern Ireland made major international headlines for all the wrong reasons. As Bardon further notes: "Such an outcome was not envisaged by anyone when Captain O'Neill first set out in an optimistic spirit to regenerate the economy of Northern Ireland."[3]

It was the speed of the breakdown which seems so astonishing, from this point in time. O'Neill was not a gifted leader, but he did have some support within broad Unionism for his bridge-building measures, even if he alienated a large number of his party by meeting the Irish Prime Minister Sean Lemass without telling them. On the other hand, if he had told them in advance, the meeting might not have taken place at all. O'Neill, who in retrospect seems a tragic figure, presided over a burgeoning economy, partly through the efforts of his dynamic Minister of Commerce Brian Faulkner, but he was unable to deliver quickly enough the reforms and benefits he had promised to the Roman Catholic minority.

He was thwarted by the resurgence of traditional Unionism, and he was unable to bring with him his key ministers such as Faulkner and William Craig. To add to his difficulties, his attempts to help the Roman Catholic population were seen as a sell-out by many Protestants. He made a brave attempt to save the worst of Unionism from itself and to build a truly cross-community society, but it is difficult to see how he could have succeeded, given the political intransigence and stupidity of mainline Unionism at the time.

Even on the symbolic level the Government made huge mistakes which alienated the Nationalist and Roman Catholic community. Early in 1965 the ill-fated new city in mid-Ulster was named

Craigavon, after the first Unionist Prime Minister, and to add further insult, the Government decided that year to accept the recommendations of the Lockwood Report that the New University should be sited in safely Unionist Coleraine, and not in Nationalist Derry, which had a tradition of higher education at Magee College. The Lockwood Committee no doubt based its controversial and unconvincing rationale on educational factors, but the point was noted widely that it did not have a Catholic among its members.

In 1966 the Belfast Corporation continued the tradition of myopic Unionism when it named a new bridge in Belfast after Lord Carson, one of the founders of Unionism. In a remarkable move the then Governor of Northern Ireland Lord Erskine suggested to the Belfast Town Clerk that the name be changed to "Queen Elizabeth Bridge", and this was accepted. This outraged a great many Unionists, and the young firebrand, the Reverend Ian Paisley, and his followers hurled abuse at Lord and Lady Erskine as they left the Presbyterian General Assembly. It is said that Lady Erskine never recovered from the experience.

Some weeks earlier there were other ominous signs. In May the newly-formed terrorist group, the Ulster Volunteer Force (UVF), declared "war" against the IRA and its associates, and shortly afterwards a Catholic was shot dead in Belfast. This was followed by the shooting of three more Catholics, including Peter Ward, who died from his injuries. Three Loyalists were later arrested and convicted of his murder. All of these may have appeared as isolated incidents, but the outbreak of violence and the continued intransigence of Unionism, despite O'Neill's best efforts, did not bode well for the future.

Significantly, all these events were contemporaneous with the establishment and development of Corrymeela, but few people within or without the Community were aware that Northern Ireland, far from stabilising as a peaceful state, was slipping back into the worst violence since its foundation.

That is not to say that Corrymeela was unaware of contemporary events, and the need to reach out to those with whom it differed.

Craig Cameron recalls some early attempts to build bridges.

"Some of us made a lot of effort trying to involve Ian Paisley and some of his followers, but they were intent on protesting against any form of ecumenical thinking. As a student I went to the old Ravenhill Road Free Presbyterian Church one Sunday evening with a couple of strong-arm fellow-students. We tried to sit near the back where we felt we would be anonymous, but we were marched up to the front, and the sermon was preached at us as much as at the rest of the congregation.

"Ian Paisley preached on the theme 'Tickets for Hell and Where They are Bought'. That was my first contact with him and I've never forgotten it. Years later I appeared with him on a television programme in Dublin, and he was highly defensive and rather scathing of anything that Corrymeela either represented or might represent, and very defensive about any form of open dialogue. Over the years we failed to build links with the Free Presbyterians."[4]

From this perspective, it is interesting to surmise whether the founders of Corrymeela could have done more to reach out in the early stages, or whether the Community should have started its work much earlier – even in the less encouraging period just after the war, when Northern Ireland was locked in the religious and political apartheid of the years when the Unionist leader Lord Brookeborough ran largely a Protestant state for a Protestant people. Equally it is legitimate to ask whether the Corrymeela founders might have been more aware of the trouble that was brewing, even in the apparently peaceful progress of the mid-Sixties.

John Morrow provides a timely reminder, however, that when Corrymeela was established, "the Troubles hadn't really begun in the violent sense. Obviously we were living in a divided society, but even the civil rights movement hadn't begun properly and we thought that the omens were positive, much more positive than they turned out to be. You had Terence O'Neill coming in with some new ideas, you had Vatican II, and we were meeting priests and ministers in various places. We felt that there was an atmosphere in which things would develop, perhaps gradually but positively. It was only later that we realised that the situation was going to be dire, but luckily we had made a few friends and built a few relationships before the whole breakdown in the wider society took place."[5]

The breakdown, when it began, proceeded remarkably quickly. The civil rights movement gained widespread support and the Government was incapable of stemming the tide. There were demonstrations and counter-demonstrations throughout the summer and autumn of 1968, culminating in a civil rights march in Derry on 5 October. The situation was handled badly by the Royal Ulster Constabulary (RUC), and television footage of policemen batoning the protesters, including the nationalist and socialist MP Gerry Fitt, was one of those pivotal moments which changed the course of Northern Ireland's history.

It was clear that Northern Ireland, which had largely been left to its own devices for so long by the British Government, had serious problems, and it became questionable as to whether or not the Stormont Government could handle the situation. On 6 December 1968, Captain Terence O'Neill, in a plaintive television broadcast, made a last, forlorn appeal to both communities and asked, "What kind of Ulster do you want?" The answer, sadly, was to become all too apparent.

The Government lurched from crisis to crisis, and on 28 April 1969, the doomed O'Neill was forced to resign. His successor, Major James Chichester-Clark, was a decent man from one of the Province's older gentry, but he was totally out of his depth, and fared no better than O'Neill had done. In August 1969, there was a prolonged three-day battle between the police and rioters in Derry's Bogside, and the situation continually threatened to spiral out of control. There was shooting and widespread communal rioting in Belfast, as well as serious disturbances in Strabane, Newry and elsewhere, and thousands of Catholics fled across the border to the Irish Republic.

The Irish Prime Minister Jack Lynch, at the height of the Bogside rioting, stated in a television broadcast that his Government could "no longer stand by and see innocent people injured and perhaps worse". Lynch had no intention of invading the North, and even some of his own military personnel were startled by his enigmatic words. One army officer later said, "We had horrible visions of having to commandeer civilian lorries and even bread-vans and move north to our side of the Irish border to help."[6]

The British Government, however, could not afford to "stand by", and on 15 August 1969, it took the momentous decision to send in troops to help the police restore order. The peaceful province of the mid-Sixties had descended into chaos in a remarkably short time, and the Corrymeela Community, after less than four years from its establishment, had to try to handle the crisis as best it could.

The situation became progressively worse. In October 1969 Constable Victor Arbuckle was the first RUC officer to be killed in the Troubles when he was shot by the Loyalist UVF during rioting in the Protestant Shankill area of Belfast. As well as the violence, the underlying political uncertainty continued throughout the next year, and in June 1970, there was further rioting in Derry and Belfast. The British Home Secretary Reginald Maudling visited the Province in the same month, and left the airport with a comment which echoed the Westminster Government's irritation and frustration at being drawn into the Ulster quagmire. He said, "For God's sake, bring me a large Scotch. What a bloody awful country."

By the end of 1970 the disturbances had cost an estimated £5.5 million, and worse was to come. On 6 February 1971, Gunner Robert Curtis of the Royal Artillery became the first British soldier to die in Northern Ireland since extra troops had been called to the Province in 1969. He was killed by a sniper from the Provisional IRA, the vicious and deadly Republican paramilitary group which had been formed in 1969 in the wake of the inter-community upheaval in Belfast, Derry and elsewhere. In March 1971 three young Scottish soldiers were kidnapped and murdered. There were frequent explosions, and numerous gunfights between the Army and the Provisionals as the disorder grew progressively worse. In 1970 alone, 180 people were killed – and more than half were innocent civilians.[7]

On 9 August 1971 the Government made a disastrous miscalculation when it sanctioned an early morning swoop in

Nationalist areas and security forces arrested and interned without trial more than 300 Republican suspects. Much of the intelligence material was faulty, and almost one-third of the prisoners were released shortly afterwards. However, the political and social consequences of this botched operation were incalculable, and it resulted in terrible widespread disorder.

EVEN FROM THIS DISTANCE it is difficult to convey the chaos, fear and panic which gripped Belfast and many parts of Northern Ireland in those days. One seasoned journalist recalls driving across the capital city early on the morning of 9 August to bring his small daughter to be cared for by relatives, while his wife was giving birth to their second child in a hospital at Carrickfergus, north of Belfast. He recalled later:

"I drove past a timber-yard which had been set on fire. The traffic was chaotic, as public transport was cancelled, and there were extensive gun battles between troops and Provisional activists in the north and west of the city. I feared for the safety of my daughter, in a city filled with foreboding and tension. Back in my newspaper office we did our best to report the chaos of the day, with the city in turmoil. Despite the pressures on all our journalists, my editor Eugene Wason very kindly allowed me some time off in the afternoon to visit my wife and new-born son in Carrickfergus hospital. I was never so glad to get out of Belfast in my life. It was terrifying."[8]

Corrymeela, like many other groups and agencies, became heavily involved in trying to cope with the dire consequences in the days following the initial internment swoops when there was widespread disorder. The decision was made by Corrymeela to evacuate children from some of the worst hit areas, but one of the greatest problems was to provide transport. In one tense area of Belfast a Corrymeela minibus appeared in danger of being hi-jacked for use as a barricade, but with the help of some young locals, the driver somehow managed to bring it out safely.

The relief operation lasted around two weeks, and some 300

children were evacuated to Ballycastle. Local schools which were empty during the summer holidays were used for accommodation, with the minimum of bureaucracy. One headmaster said, "We should have the permission of the school committee to do this, but there is no time. Here are the keys."

It is important to underline that Corrymeela had had no preparation, or training, for such an emergency. The Community's volunteers did the best they could in almost impossibly difficult decisions, and demonstrated good sense and ingenuity in the process. There was no time for long discussions or committee resolutions. This was once again the theology of practicality, in bringing help and comfort to those in urgent need.

It was all part of the communal experience over the years of Corrymeela, which was fulfilling part of its role by becoming a place of refuge and also of inspiration. Ray Davey described graphically what that meant in real terms. He wrote:

"Whether you liked it or not, you were brought face to face with the harsh and brutal realities of the situation. You spent several days talking to a family who had been intimidated and forced to flee from their home, and you listened in the course of the mealtime and other endless conversations to accounts of all the different members of the family.

You experienced the agony of the past, the frustration of the present, and the increasing apprehension about the future. Mothers opened their heart to you as they talked about life in the ghetto situation – how they had to shut their children in lest they come to some harm. You heard the children scream with delight as they saw the sea in all its north coast glory, and you heard them say when they came back from Ballycastle town after their first visit, 'Strange place that, no burnt-out shops.' Thank God, Corrymeela was all about people, and we did not have to sit and contrive projects and programmes – they sprang at us from all those real life situations."[9]

The Community realised, however, that they were only touching the tip of the iceberg. Davey recalls:

"We were only treating symptoms – what about causes? So other people began to come – community leaders, politicians, and social and political analysts. Thus began the continuing process of looking at the many social, political and religious issues that lay behind the violence and unrest."[10]

A Community that had been established to build bridges and to be a question mark to the churches and society had no time for arcane theorising. It had no choice but to survive its baptism of fire, and to help others to do the same.

FOUR

KEEPING STEADY

DESPITE THE CONFLICT on the streets of Belfast, Londonderry and other parts of Northern Ireland during the early days of the Troubles, the Corrymeela Community – often with difficulty – continued to remain steady in the face of adversity. Even in the worst of times, there were heart-warming reminders that while Corrymeela was caught up in the widespread human suffering, it also managed to rise "above the conflict" in the best sense of that term.

Significantly, the Community was also receiving recognition outside Northern Ireland for its work. In September 1971, shortly after some of the worst of the disturbances following the Government's internment debacle, Canon Horace Dammers came to Corrymeela to present a replica of the Coventry Cross of Nails. This was confirmation of the Community's membership of an international network of some fifty reconciliation centres all around the world. Each, in association with the Cross of Nails, had a common vision of hope for a better world.

The connection between Corrymeela and Coventry Cathedral had begun when Canon Dammers, who was later Dean of Bristol, met Ray Davey at a conference in St George's House, Windsor. Davey spoke to the conference about Corrymeela's work, and Dammers was so impressed that he struck up a friendship with Ray and later visited Northern Ireland to meet members of the Community. The contacts established had important and positive consequences for Corrymeela, not only in practical ways, but also in association with the Cross of Nails as a recognition of the international significance of its work for reconciliation.

The genesis of the Cross of Nails began in the ruins of Coventry Cathedral, which had been destroyed by the German Luftwaffe during the Second World War. A member of the Cathedral staff was sifting through the debris when he found three long nails of medieval design. With a touch of inspiration he formed them into the shape of a cross, and the idea of the Coventry Cross of Nails was born, as a symbol of reconciliation in the wake of suffering and conflict.

It seemed obvious that the first peacetime contact would be Germany, and appropriately a link was established and nurtured between Coventry and Dresden, which had also suffered disastrously from Allied air raids. The contact was more than symbolic, and with a welcome practicality which underlined that true reconciliation requires action as well as words, a moving reciprocation developed between the two cities. The people of Dresden raised funds and built an International Centre at Coventry Cathedral, and volunteers from Coventry visited Dresden to rebuild a hospital which had been destroyed by Allied bombs.

A number of replicas of the Cross of Nails were created, and the practicality and symbolism of making Corrymeela a part of the international network was irresistible. It was important that Horace Dammers himself took the time to come across to Northern Ireland at a time of such civic upheaval, and to present the symbolic Cross of Nails to the Community, which had gathered at Ballycastle with their friends and other guests.

The handing-over ceremony was typically low-key, but none the less impressive because of that. Several members of the Community read from the Bible, and local Protestant and Roman Catholic clergy shared prayers for peace. Even the symbolism of that simple sharing across the divides was not insignificant in a Province torn apart by religious and political conflict.

The Cross of Nails was carried among the people, and Ray Davey spoke the words of the great Biblical commandment which was dear to all: "You shall love the Lord your God with all your heart, and with all your soul, and with all your mind." Everyone shook hands to symbolise the act of reconciliation, and the short ceremony was over. However, and most importantly, the practical help from Coventry to Corrymeela was only beginning.

The Cathedral made the Coventry House of Reconciliation at Corrymeela one of its main fund-raising appeals and began the important task of building the much-needed volunteer accommodation. The Cathedral set about raising money with zeal, and Canon Dammers and the Education Officer, the Reverend Kenneth Woolhouse, set in motion a worldwide appeal for funds. In a relatively short time, they raised the impressive sum of £30,000, which was a great deal of money in those days. Even more significantly, they touched a deep chord in people all over the world, who could identify with the suffering in Northern Ireland, and who recognised the urgent need for a healing of the nations. These suffering people included members of a Benedictine Monastery in Lima, Peru who wrote to Horace Dammers expressing support for the Corrymeela project, and also outlining their own considerable challenges.

The region had suffered an earthquake which had killed some 75,000 poor people, as well as destroying their monastery. The Superior of the monastery, four Sisters and seven students had also been killed. For a year the survivors had to live in tents some 10,500 feet above sea level. For six months of that period there were heavy rains. Eventually they managed to rebuild a Sisters' Convent and the monastery, and also part of a school. They told Dammers, "Rebuilding has taken all the money we had. We feel very much as St Peter – silver, gold, there is none that I have but in Christ Jesus, a blessing upon you and your good works."

There was no money from Lima, for understandable reasons, but there was something perhaps more precious – the Benedictines in Peru had given a necessary perspective that there was great suffering and human challenge elsewhere. They also demonstrated that Christian charity, prayer and goodwill could cross all the boundaries, not only inside Northern Ireland, but in the rest of the world as well. It was a message not only for Corrymeela but for everyone caught up in the Irish conflict where at times the politicians, the people and the churches behaved as if Northern Ireland was the only place in the world with immense troubles.

Sadly, however, the Irish situation deteriorated further, and 1972 was the worst year of the entire Troubles, with dire consequences for bridge-building and community relations. The year began disastrously, on 30 January, when the Army shot dead thirteen civilians in Londonderry during a civil rights march, and the causes were still being investigated at enormous cost by a Tribunal at this time of writing, some thirty-four years later.

In February, seven people died in a bomb-blast at Aldershot barracks, and shortly afterwards two young women died and many other people were badly injured in a Provisional IRA bomb which exploded in the crowded Abercorn restaurant in the centre of Belfast. In a situation that seemed to be going rapidly out of control, the British Government suspended Stormont and took over the direct rule of the Province from the defunct Northern Ireland Parliament. This was a political watershed, and the Westminster Government spent the next three decades and more trying to restore devolved powers to the local electorate.

Still the violence continued, and on July 21, nine people died during a series of grisly Provisional IRA no-warning explosions throughout Belfast. The year ended as badly as it had begun, and in December, two people were killed and eighty were injured in two bomb-blasts in the city. A total of 496 people died in 1972, and 258 of these were civilians. During the next year another 263 people died, and in the following year, the toll was 303. The Derry MP and civil rights leader John Hume told leading US politicians in Washington on 25 April 1974 that the "equivalent proportion to the population of the USA would be a death rate of 150,000 people in four years of civil strife".

Against such a background of violence and despair, the Corrymeela Community did its best to provide practical help, and also to sustain itself, as well as helping others. Ray Davey and others took the initiative by going into the centres of conflict and bringing people to Corrymeela for respite and renewal. This work also earned Corrymeela a high profile in the Ballycastle area, and local people showed their approval by raising funds for the Community's work.

All kinds of groups came to Ballycastle, including those who were invited to take part in "Family Weeks". They came from both parts of the religious and political divide, and from areas of great tension and conflict. They included one family of an IRA man who had been shot dead by the Army, as well as families of Loyalist paramilitaries. There were also those, young and old, who had been tragically caught up in the crossfire. One Roman Catholic girl wrote to Corrymeela afterwards to express her thanks. She also underlined the opening out which so many on both sides had experienced when she added, "It really was a wonderful time. I changed my attitudes to teachers, and to Protestants."

It soon became obvious that Corrymeela had to expand its facilities to cope with the increasing numbers of people who were coming to Ballycastle. This led to the creation of the Tara Village of chalets, with a common room and kitchen and washing facilities, and this was used all the year round. It was also clear that a full-time director at Ballycastle was needed, and in 1973 the Community appointed a young Methodist minister, the Reverend Harold Good.

Harold's wider family had given remarkable service to the Methodist Church, and his brother Peter left the clothing business to become a full-time minister. Harold was articulate and outgoing, but he also had the cut of a determined and stocky man who meant business. During his varied early career he had served as a Methodist minister in the Irish Republic and the United States. At the beginning of the Troubles he had had a parish in a working-class Protestant area of Belfast, and he – like so many other clerics – had to react as best he could to the horrific violence all around.

He said, "I had come back to Ireland, full of what I thought were the new ideas from America… My church in Belfast's Agnes Street was rough and tough… I was trying to get to grips with the challenges of a twentieth century urban ministry when the Irish Troubles came like a bolt from a clear sky. Once again the Irish problem erupted like a volcano of violence, and we were all swept up in the smoke and the fire and the ashes."[1]

Harold Good also described his trauma when he discovered, at the back of his church, several children trying to make a petrol bomb. He said, "I was aghast. Some of those kids were in my Sunday school. I was furious at the adults who led them to this, but my anger gradually turned towards the whole system that had made people behave in this way."[2]

That evening Good made the same remarks on television, and that caused him further heart-searching. Some of his parishioners, in those fraught and hyper-sensitive days, thought he had let them down. In that tribal society, it was not the business of a Protestant minister to criticise his flock in public, even by implication. However, Harold Good was clear about his own primary responsibility. "My side was the Kingdom of God, not the United Kingdom or a United Ireland. I began to realise more and more how little I and others knew about the people and their basic fears, and how little some of them knew about the real burden and responsibility of the Christian Gospel."[3]

Good determined to do what he could, but his church was being merged with another Methodist parish, and he and his wife seemed destined to return to America. However, the Goods experienced one of those periods in life when postal delays, heart-searching and human uncertainty, turn out later to appear more like Divine guidance. Harold talked to Ray Davey, whose work he had admired greatly, and instead of going to America he ended up as the Director of the Corrymeela Centre in Ballycastle.

It proved to be a wise choice, but the path was not easy. The Community, which had dedicated itself to helping solve community conflict, discovered that it was not always best equipped itself to deal with internal conflict and differences of opinion. It is often a mistake to suppose that a peace-making community or a peace-making individual is constantly at peace with others, or within himself or herself. Harold Good recalls: "I think that I helped to bring structure to the place, and that wasn't easy. When I arrived, I only knew that there were people of goodwill who had a vision which was beyond the average, particularly within the wider community and the churches at that time, and that attracted me. I felt that something was there, and I wanted to be a part of it." [4]

Clearly there was a need for structure. "This was a topsy-turvey organisation which had just 'growed and growed'. The seeds of goodwill and vision had been nurtured by good people, some of whom had moved on, and others who were still there. Ray Davey would be the first to say that he wasn't an organisational person. His special gift was to inspire people and let them get on with it. I felt that it was a challenge to give direction to something which at times seemed to be all over the place."

Harold Good's work began in simple, but important, ways. He received a letter from a Corrymeela supporter whose children refused to go back because they did not like sleeping in the beds at Ballycastle. Some of them, she claimed, were unsanitary. Good says, "I had just arrived at Ballycastle, and I decided immediately take a look at the beds, together with our Bursar, Gerry McCambridge, who reminded me that we did not have a great deal of money. We got as far as the third bed and I said, 'Gerry, I can't stand this any more!' We got rid of the lot."

There were repercussions, however. "I took stick from some people not just for spending money to replace mattresses, but for all kinds of things like crockery that matched, and by insisting that the Community should have a book recording who was in the House on any night at any given time, and also establishing an office. No doubt some people complained that it was the way I went about it, and if only I had taken a bit of time, things might have been easier. However, I had been given the task of Director, and I found myself with a row of pegs on which I had to hang a number of hats, ranging from being a hostel manager to a director of volunteer programmes, and I had to get on with it as best I could."

Harold Good and the others formed a Programme Committee. He says, "Out of this came some very good ideas like the Northern Ireland Mixed Marriage Association, and also 'Police and the

Community'. I was asked to go the police headquarters in Belfast to talk to senior RUC officers. They were keen to come to Corrymeela, but they wanted to do some things which were over the top for Corrymeela, like having steak on Sundays. They also wanted us to employ outsiders to do the dishwashing. This might have been more time-effective, but it was not our style and I told them so. I proved that later by watching them wash the dishes with women from the Bogside, East Belfast and everywhere else."

The spiritual dimension at Corrymeela was also important. "I felt deeply that Corrymeela was called to be a place of prayer, not of sugary piety, but a place where people could pray and meditate in their own way. People were encouraged to lead worship, and they could opt out or in, but it was a dimension that we did not hide, because it was central to the spirit of Corrymeela."

Some of the buildings at Corrymeela needed upgraded, especially in the Village area. During one weekend some of the huts were wrecked by a group of young people from West Belfast. Harold Good phoned a representative of the community association which had sponsored the visit, and she came up to Ballycastle see the damage for herself. When she saw the huts she told Good, "Mister, whatever these young people did was nothing to what I would have done if you had put me in there."

Good told her that she was absolutely right, and that no one would be put in there again. "As a result we closed the huts, and set about providing new accommodation. That does not take away from the vision and the inspiration and the commitment of those who had gone up to Corrymeela weekend after weekend and work camp after work camp and had put it all together with their bare hands. However, if Corrymeela was going to move forward to meet the new challenges, it needed structure and organisation."

Inevitably there was some friction within the Community. Good says, "In doing these things you were standing on the toes of some people who had done things their way, in a different way, and who felt challenged by somebody coming in to direct things, but I ploughed on. I had no alternative."

The Community as a whole also needed to keep its nerve in the midst of the storm of violence that was sweeping over Northern Ireland. A Corrymeela Bulletin of 1972 outlined the Community's determination to keep going. It stated:

"Of course we all feel depressed at times, but as to giving up or giving in – we could never contemplate that… this is a war of nerves, a struggle between naked violence and worse – when we think of the recent outrages against human personality and the way of reason, open discussion and reconciliation."

This was not just whistling in the dark. Corrymeela was also looking ahead to the time when the paramilitaries would have to readjust to a situation where violence would be no longer feasible. The Bulletin ended on a strong note:

"We in Corrymeela must be more courageous and unwearying in seeking new ways of understanding, and new formula for communal co-operation. The qualities supremely needed now are patience, courage, imagination and hope."

How right they were, but the members of the Community in 1972, nor anyone else at the time, could possibly have imagined how long and how difficult that path leading to peace would prove to be.

FIVE

KEEPING ON

On 30 June 1973, a Belfast community worker named Sean Armstrong was shot dead in cold blood by a gunman who had knocked on the door of his apartment in Eglantine Avenue, not far from Queen's University. The murderer, who according to reliable sources belonged to a Loyalist paramilitary group, had brushed past Armstrong's young wife and walked up the hall of the apartment.

"Are you Robert Sean Armstrong?" he asked. Sean answered, "Yes", apparently thinking that this was the parent of one of the children with whom he had been working. The intruder pulled out a gun and began shooting. The first bullet caught Sean in the stomach, and as he tried to escape to the bathroom, the gunman fired two more shots into his back. He fired several more shots into the door-frame, and then turned and ran away. Sean Armstrong died in hospital three hours later. He was only 31.

This killing, even by the Belfast standards of the time, was horrific not only in the callous manner of its execution but also because the victim was an innocent man. Sean Armstrong was an Ulsterman who had been a community volunteer with International Voluntary Service, and several years earlier he had been a popular undergraduate of Queen's University Belfast where he had edited the student "Rag" magazine.

Armstrong was a vociferous and larger-than-life character but he had a deeply caring side to his personality. After university, he worked briefly in London and then set out on a journey to discover more about the world, and possibly himself, as many young people of that age still do. He travelled widely to Israel, America, the Greek Islands and many other places, and the journey took about six years.

Eventually that worldwide odyssey took him back to Ireland, but before returning to his roots in Ulster, he spent a short time in Scotland with his new wife Marie, an American from Indiana who had attended the University of California. They had been married only a week. Shortly after Sean's death, his wife discovered that she was pregnant. Some nine months later their son was born. It was a story of trauma and tragedy, but out of that pit of despair new hope was born, in more ways than one.

Sean's mother, Hylda Armstrong, was also a remarkable human being. Her husband had died from cancer at the age of 38, leaving her with two small children. A niece died in a car crash, and she herself was badly injured in a motor accident. During this period she had a vivid "near death" experience which was similar to one she had several years earlier when she was seriously ill after major surgery.

Despite her considerable hardships and the challenges she had faced, Hylda Armstrong displayed enormous resilience and inspiration. Sean had been carrying on reconciliation work with children from both sides of the community divide, and his mother later became a founder member of the Harmony Community Trust, which was established to help Roman Catholic and Protestant children to get to know one another better.

Hylda talked movingly about Sean and his work. She said, "In a way I was left alone, and I began to ask myself, 'Can you carry the torch that Sean was forced to leave down?' It was up to me to do something, even a little bit because if all the little bits are put together they will add up to something. I felt that Sean had been doing what was right. He hadn't been the only one, and I just felt that this lovely dream of his had to be carried on."[1]

Mrs Armstrong had shown great leadership ability in becoming World President of Inner Wheel, and she also had a deeply spiritual core. She said, "I really do believe there is value in prayer. Maybe it's thought transfer, but I believe that when I'm struggling with the hurdles someone thinks of me. I get that little push, and I'm on my way again. I do the same for others, and I believe it works. Some people might say, 'Why do you believe?' or 'How do you believe?' I do not know, certainly I find it hard to explain. I just know there is a God because he has given me strength, though there must be more to it than that."[2] Significantly, Hylda did not allow the heartbreak of Sean's murder to develop into corrosive bitterness.

She said, "I am convinced that if we can all go through the tough experiences of life without becoming bitter, we emerge as a strong, better person. I would rather be the mother of Sean than the mother of the man who shot him. It must be dreadful to be the mother or the wife of someone who has done something terrible. That really is a harder cross to bear."[3]

The inspiration of her son Sean lived on. "Looking back, I feel terribly glad to have known him as a person, as well as him being my son. I could see his faults as well as his good points, even allowing for a mother's bias. But I still see him as he really was. Just as a big oak tree that was cut down, and around the root of that tree all these little saplings are growing. He is remembered not just by his family and friends. He is remembered by some of the children who thought the world of him."[4]

Hylda Armstrong's work continued with the Harmony Community Trust, and with the establishment of the Glebe House Centre in Northern Ireland, where Protestant and Roman Catholic children could meet together and to learn from each other. Hylda was also a strong supporter of the work of the Corrymeela Community, and it was entirely appropriate that in 1973 a playground in memory of Sean Armstrong was opened on the Ballycastle site, and refurbished and extended several years later. It was a reminder to all of the service and sacrifice of just one Ulster family among so many during the years of indiscriminate murder and mayhem that so disfigured the face of Northern Ireland.

As part of the 25th Anniversary celebrations at Corrymeela later, members of the Community undertook a pilgrimage around the Ballycastle site, and they paused at the new Sean Armstrong Memorial Playground which had been opened in May 1986, some thirteen years after the establishment of the original structure. Ray Davey remarked, "Here we are reminded of the terrible cost of these years of violence and killing, and the pain and sorrow so many in Corrymeela, and in the wider community, continue to endure. Sean's assassination, in a very special way, represents the awesome tragedy and futility of the conflict. He was a most attractive and gifted person, representing what was best and most creative in our society. He inspired the establishment of Glebe House, a mini-Corrymeela, in Strangford, County Down, and had given all his talents and energy to underprivileged children, in organizing cross-community work camps, holidays and exchange programmes. This children's programme reminds us of the price so many have to pay, and Sean's life and example will always remain to inspire and challenge us, as we pass by."[5]

On that occasion Ray also paid tribute to the Coventry Cross of Nails network which had helped to fund Coventry House. This was completed and opened in 1976 to accommodate the international volunteer team. Around the same time the Youth Village at Ballycastle was completed to help to provide necessary facilities for those involved in the expanding programme of youth work.

In 1977 a new wing to the Main House and a workshop were completed, and in the following year the Cottages were opened on the site. These new facilities, together with fifty places in the House and thirty-two in the Village, provided crucial accommodation to enable the Community to host several programmes for different groups at the same time.

During the next year another important meeting-place was completed and opened in Ballycastle, and the beautifully designed Croi (the Gaelic for "the heart") literally became the heart of the Corrymeela Centre in Ballycastle as a much needed focus for worship and social gatherings. The funds for this had been raised largely by the London Corrymeela Link group, which had been formed some three years previously.

While all these and other important facilities were being provided, refurbished or expanded at Ballycastle, the on-going work of the

Community was also focused on Corrymeela House at Upper Crescent in Belfast, near Queen's University. These premises had been rented from Queen's as early as 1971 and later purchased by the Community. They were regarded to be a necessary part of the Community's outreach as an administrative base and meeting centre in the capital city, but also a reminder that Corrymeela was not solely based on the idyllic site in Ballycastle, and far from the centres of conflict that was taking place in many areas of Northern Ireland, as the murder of Sean Armstrong was to demonstrate all too clearly.

His death had a wide impact outside his immediate community. It showed that the violence could touch any individual and strike at the heart of any family, whatever the background. Sean had come from a middle-class background, and he had the privilege of third-level education at a time when it was relatively restricted to a small number of students – certainly compared to the mass education available in universities today.

Sean literally had the world at his feet, but like many of his contemporaries who turned their backs on Northern Ireland and its troubles, he chose to return to try to build a better society, despite the risks. His brutal murder had a particular impact on his colleagues and friends from undergraduate days, and even more than twenty years later a poem written in his honour by Seamus Heaney – another contemporary – was quoted at a major dinner in Queen's University, which was attended by many of those who had remembered Sean in his prime.

Tragically, however, he was not the only undergraduate victim of violence. On 9 February 1975, Gerard Kiely, a first-year student of 19, was shot dead in a random sectarian attack as he emerged from St Brigid's Roman Catholic Church near Queen's. His murder had a devastating effect on his parents, Maura and Edmund, and his sister Mary.

Mrs Kiely, a devout Catholic, almost lost her faith. She said later, "At one point I began to think there was no God. The week after the funeral I remember making a cup of coffee and suddenly throwing it over a picture of our Lord. I was almost at the stage where I was asking God to forgive God. I was so angry. It is so hard to think that you can rear a child to be a good person and to love everything, and for God to allow that child to rise from his bed and let him be shot by someone."[6]

In the early stages of grief she actually felt rebellious. "I suppose I was half crazy. I did not go to Confession for a long time, though I took Communion. But I began to see through the clouds, and there were some bright spots. There was no point in me saying the Lord's Prayer if I was not prepared to forgive. When I decided that the bitterness would have to go, something inside me kept saying, 'Go and meet someone else who has lost a son.' Night and day it kept at me."[7]

A priest suggested that she should do something practical to help others, so she began to compile names of those who had lost loved ones as a result of the Troubles. On the first night thirty people turned up at the meeting, and that was the beginning of the Cross Group which over many years provided help for those suffering bereavement. Maura said, "When I look back, out of evil comes good. Really and truly. I see the hand of God moving from tragedy into something creative – if you have faith that God will work and give you peace of mind after a length of time, and strength to be able to overcome that tragedy."[8]

Maura Kiely was a member of Corrymeela and she carried out the broad objectives of the Community in providing an important service in forming the Cross Group for the benefit of so many other people. It was one of the ways in which the wider community could give structure and support to an individual family, or small group, and was one of the significant means by which Corrymeela played a part to create and to sustain a wider network. In 2004 Maura Kiely was appointed MBE for her contribution to the wider community, and it was a tribute she richly deserved.

The Community, which had been launched publicly through a major political event in 1966 when Terence O'Neill had a given a seminal address at Ballycastle, also retained its links with the political process. This was not directed at any one party, but members and supporters of the Community made their individual contributions, and some did so through the formation of the middle-of-the-road Alliance Party.

This later led to the inevitable jibes that Community was merely "the Alliance Party at prayer". Happily, however, Corrymeela was rather more complex and sophisticated than this tired cliché would suggest, and in 1977, the Community hosted another major conference with the typically tough-minded theme "A Critical Look at Direct Rule".

One of the most significant developments for Corrymeela in the Seventies was the important changes in personnel. In 1978 Billy McAllister died after years of exceptional service as a "general factotum" at Ballycastle, and his death was felt widely both inside and outside the Community. Ray Davey rightly described him as "one of the early miracles of the Corrymeela story". He added, "Billy was there right from the start, as he was the first to live in the vacant building. To us there was something more than chance about that, because he was absolutely right for the situation. In a completely unobtrusive and unconscious way, he created the atmosphere, the ethos, indeed the spirit of the new experiment. Billy was in himself the authentic community man, and in a real sense Corrymeela grew up around him."

As well as his practical skills as a former railway engineer in Dundalk, he had a special way with people.

"He was ready to do any job and relate to any person who crossed the threshold, with incredible patience and goodwill. Sometimes it would be showing some VIP around the site, and then at others, mending a broken 'loo'. He never studied group dynamics, but no one I've ever met could so naturally bring a conference to life and encourage others to participate.

"Everyone somehow felt that Billy had time to listen, and time for them, no matter what their background, age or nationality. We knew how much he meant to a great number of people, but it was when he died in May 1978 that we more fully realised just how many he had not only influenced at Ballycastle, but continued to keep in touch with by letter and the occasional visit... For an untold number, the major memory and experience of Corrymeela had been to meet Billy."[9]

Yet another remarkable stalwart of Corrymeela was Anna Glass, who worked for many years as the cook at Ballycastle, and who dispensed not only good food but also good counsel, as well as friendship and good cheer. She died in May 2007, and Derick Wilson said in his fitting funeral tribute that she had "met all with the same attentive manner. To Anna, all were important, all were potential gifts to one another. The small caterpillar poster that used to be in her kitchen said, 'Be patient, God isn't finished with me yet!' This resonated with Anna. She wished everyone to have the opportunity to fly as gracefully as butterflies."

Another person who made a major contribution was the Reverend Harold Good, the first Centre Director, who moved on in 1978 after some five years in the job. Craig Cameron recalls:

"Harold was able to see what sort of programmes we could run, to lead those programmes and to bring a strong worship element to the community. Because of his background he was able to bring the Methodist thinking into the community very strongly. He had a good way of working with church and social community groups, and he made a major contribution to set the pattern of what a Centre Director should do."

However, the work was extremely demanding and required being on call virtually all the time. Cameron says, "It is a draining position and we felt that the natural cycle for such a post is three or four years." There was also the added complication that Ray Davey was making it known that he would be announcing his retirement in the near future. A committee was asked to consider the matter, and it decided that in the context of a new Leader, it would be desirable to appoint a new Centre Director and to have the person in post before Ray's successor had been chosen.

Harold Good disagreed. He was young, eager and enthusiastic, and felt he needed more time to consolidate the work he had initiated in the physical development of the site as well as the programme, including the innovative "Serve and Learn" programme for volunteers.

"To be the first of anything is never easy, and being the first Centre Director of Corrymeela was to be no exception! When I came to Corrymeela I found an organisation which had grown around a number of diverse people, many of whom had helped it come into being and held strong views on how things should be done. Some of these otherwise well-intentioned people did not appreciate the need for more structure which, as the Centre developed, I and others knew to be very necessary. To be given the title and responsibility of Director by a disparate community which was not agreed about the direction in which it wished to be taken was a far from easy task!

"The means by which the Corrymeela Council and Community sought to resolve all of this is another story, as is the way it handled the appointment of my successor. Suffice to say that, as a community known internationally for its ministry of reconciliation and conflict resolution, these were not Corrymeela's finest hours! Sadly, it seemed to lack either the skill or the will to resolve its own internal tensions.

"For us it was time to move on, in more senses than one. While I had been offered the challenging job of Director of Bryson House, I declined, knowing that my true vocation was to be that of a pastor and preacher. That was a decision I was never to regret. When the Bryson House post was re-advertised, I was very pleased that it was Peter McLachlan, another Corrymeela member, who was appointed to that important position, one which he held with distinction until his untimely death in 1999."

With the perspective of hindsight, it is clear that Harold Good developed his considerable talents throughout his career, and made significant contributions elsewhere. The fact remains, however, that in the complex development of Corrymeela he was the right man in the right place at the right time, and in that context he made an important contribution to the Community and to bridge-building in Northern Ireland and further afield.

"So I hope that I was able to bring the kind of structure which was needed at that time. It was one of the great achievements of Ray and everyone at Corrymeela that it became a sign and a symbol and a beacon through the darkest days and nights. This was symbolised in the saying, 'It is better to light a candle than to curse the darkness.' That has been the importance of Corrymeela for many people, and I continue to be a strong supporter of Corrymeela. I want it to continue to be a sign and a symbol in a wider context, with a larger understanding of the world."

Harold Good was succeeded by a new Centre Director, but the appointment process itself became somewhat complicated, to say the least. An appointment was recommended by a committee set up to consider the matter, and the decision required the ratification of the entire Community. Following a discussion by the Members, including the Leader Ray Davey, the appointment was rescinded and the job was offered to Derick Wilson, a founder-member with a wide experience of the Community, who had also been a candidate for the post. The process showed a basic weakness in Corrymeela's selection procedure, in that the Leader had not been a member of the original appointment committee.

The current Leader, Dr David Stevens says, "It was a difficult time for all concerned. We learned that it would have been better to have had the Leader taking part in important selection groups so that if there was a difference of opinion it could be dealt with inside the group. It also showed that reconciliation communities are no more able to deal with internal disagreements than are other groups of people."

Indeed.

SIX

CORRYMEELA PEOPLE

THE STORY OF THE CORRYMEELA COMMUNITY can be told partly in terms of dates, times, finance, historical progress and in other dimensions. All of these are important, but the essence of Corrymeela also lies in the personal stories of those who have made a contribution to the life and work of the Community.

Of equal significance has been the way in which they have attempted to carry the Corrymeela experience into their entire careers. That, of course, has been one of the primary objectives of Corrymeela in becoming a catalyst to the Church and society at large. Most members of the Community, if not all, have tried to remain aware of the important advice from Tullio Vinay at the official opening of Corrymeela in 1965, when he said, "You – being together – have always open eyes and ears to understand when the Lord is passing nearby, to be able to follow the way He shall indicate to you."

So many people have been involved with the Community that it seems unfair to mention only a few, but the following personal stories give valuable insights into the essence of the Corrymeela experience, particularly in the first half of its history. One of the early work camp volunteers Anne Clark talked about the sense of achievement in changing an old and somewhat run-down building into a symbol of hope and challenge. She said, "It was with apprehension that I arrived there late one evening in July to begin what turned out to be three of the most enjoyable weeks I have ever spent. Work in Corrymeela really was work. I doubt very much if any of us would have undertaken to dig and paint with quite so much enthusiasm and gusto had we been doing it at home. That was the peculiar thing about Corrymeela, the work just seemed to get done without us realising that we were actually doing it.

"Even the thought of a soft bed, a bath and a fire did not stop any of us feeling sorry about leaving. We all felt we had achieved something worthwhile. In several weeks Corrymeela had changed from dull green to brilliant white, and everyone in some measure had helped to bring about this transformation."[1]

Ruth Patterson, who was to become the first female Presbyterian minister in Ireland and eventually the Director of the cross-community Restoration Ministries, was a student at Queen's University from 1962 to '66. She was an assistant Presbyterian chaplain from 1968 to '71, during which time she spent two years working with Ray Davey. She recalls:

"I was very much 'in' on the early discussions and stages of Corrymeela. Those were remarkable years to be a student, or to be working with students. The social awareness, the music, the sense of optimism that we could really do something to contribute to a better Ireland and a better world, and in our particular situation, the leadership, inspiration and integrity of a man like Ray Davey – all of this conspired to give us as young people a sense of vision and hope for the future."

Ruth also remembers the work camps, and the situations and people in the early days which "incarnated the spirit of Corrymeela that would be so stretched and needed in the years to come. While there were many wonderful ideas as to what this new venture would do and become, very quickly its agenda was determined by the onset of the Troubles.

"Through all the chaos, the disorder, the scattering and the anguish of the subsequent years, Corrymeela grew into a safe and trusted place, a place of healing, of hope, of acceptance and also, in some of the darkest times, a place of fun. It developed into a place where dialogue was possible, and where difficult conversations did not end in severance, but rather in a willingness to continue a journey of understanding, however hard that might be at times."[2]

Ruth Patterson's remarks about "difficult conversations not ending in severance" are an accurate portrayal of the then prevailing atmosphere in Northern Ireland where even a conversation with representatives from "the other side" was often taken in some areas as a sign of the betrayal of an individual's church, political or social background. Equally perceptive are her comments about the "journey of understanding, however hard that might be". Her own courageous ministry was not easy at times, but there is no doubt that the Corrymeela experience was a contributory factor to her lifelong mission and outreach.

She recalls conducting worship in a marquee at Corrymeela during the summer of 1972, which was one of the worst years of the Troubles:

"Those times were very special, and the fact that we met in a tent underlined the reality that we were a pilgrim people, always journeying further in our understanding of what it means to be Christian in the Ireland of those days, and in our understanding of reconciliation.... Corrymeela has always been at its most effective when that particular emphasis has been central, namely the fact of being a Christian community of reconciliation. Our recent history, while being very painful, would have been much more impoverished had it not been for the life and witness of Corrymeela, and all the other centres for healing and peacemaking throughout the island."

Another former assistant chaplain at Queen's in the early 1970s, in the Roman Catholic chaplaincy, was Anthony Farquhar, who went on to become an Auxiliary Bishop for the Diocese of Down and Connor. He recalls:

"I had known both Ray Davey and Corrymeela through some mutual friends – all Presbyterians – but by that stage the Community was beginning to extend its influence more widely. I remember attending some 'Corrymeets', particularly at Christmas, and I found that of those who contributed most notably to inter-denominational chaplaincy relations at Queen's, many had Corrymeela connections."[3]

Farquhar still remembers vividly a phone call from Ray Davey and his totally unexpected invitation to join him on a trip to Switzerland to speak at a different venue each night during the Week of Prayer for Christian Unity. He says, "Such joint inter-clergy travels were virtually unheard of in the early 1970s, though subsequently they became more frequent and ecumenically fashionable. I remember speaking at the World Council of Churches, and also saying an 'Our Father' with Ray and Kathleen at Romainmoitier, following in the footsteps of Celtic monasticism."

Tony Farquhar feels that they were all "caught up in the symbol of our visible togetherness against the background of what was happening at home. There is always the risk that the brightness of the symbol can serve as an obscuring escape from brutal reality." That risk was never realised, he believes, because of two main factors.

"I found that it was a week of getting to know Ray and Kathleen in a way that had not been possible in previous one-off encounters. This, together with the realism of Ray, who had already his own wartime memories of what violence can lead to, all combined to exercise a great influence on me."

That influence continued in the following year when Ray Davey invited Tony Farquhar to accompany him to the United States on a fund-raising and publicity campaign on behalf of Corrymeela. "We were accompanied by a Queen's folk group called Scorpio who on occasions provided bright visual relief from the sight of two weary clergymen."

It was a very strenuous trip "particularly over the latter weeks during which I have abiding memories of travelling from one centre to another, through preaching, through journalists, television and radio, and becoming victims of that American characteristic of generous hospitality. Over several weeks one gets to know a travelling companion really well. Moments of tiredness can become moments of exhaustion, perhaps even leading to tetchiness, but Ray's graciousness and kindness never flinched."

Bishop Farquhar believes that during those years he was undergoing an "ecumenical moulding process which continued through the later 70s and the early 80s. Corrymeela, and in particular the witness to reconciliation given by Ray, with the ever gracious support of Kathleen, had become a great influence." There were sad moments too.

"Through those difficult years there were many examples of dignity and adversity in the face of suffering. Sometimes there were cameras and notebooks to record them, but there was always the risk that once, so highlighted, these people of forgiveness would appear to be the exception. I must say, however, that I have had the privileged experience that forgiveness in the face of suffering is nearer to the norm than to the exception, for those who have actually suffered – as opposed to those who claim to represent their views."

Tony Farquhar underlined his great admiration the work put into Corrymeela "by people with that level of forgiveness. I shall not mention them by name, but they have influenced me and so many others inside and outside this country, and I think they know who they are. They are for me exceptional people, because I have had the privilege of crossing their paths."

In 1983, Father Farquhar was appointed as an Auxiliary Bishop. He recalls: "I was told in the strictest of confidence of my appointment by the Papal Nuncio on a day when I was due to spend the same evening at Corrymeela – where, still dazed, I met a group which had been organised by a former student."

When the new Bishop went to his first meeting of the Irish Episcopal Conference, his Corrymeela involvement had gone before him. He was appointed to its Ecumenical Commission, and shortly afterwards, became its Chairman. Farquhar says, "That opened up to me all sorts of ecumenical doors, sometimes accompanied by former Corrymeela contacts. I recall, for example, the eyes of Norman Richardson of Corrymeela lighting up at his first contact with real bass voices in Russian Orthodox churches."

In his ecumenical role, Bishop Farquhar again visited the World Council of Churches, and was also a member of the Anglican-Roman Catholic Commission for Unity and Mission. He was also the Chairman of the official Dialogue between the World Council of

Churches and the Roman Catholic church, a delegation of which met Pope John Paul II. Tony Farquhar says, "I am certain in my own way that Ray Davey's first phone call to me in the early 1970s, inviting me to accompany him to Switzerland, certainly had a knock-on effect. This led to all sorts of inter-denominational commitments, but more importantly for me, it had a knock-on effect in the way in which I view such inter-denominational contacts. As I look back over the last forty years of Corrymeela, I find it difficult to separate the strands where the Community has influenced me, and where Ray Davey himself influenced me."

Appropriately, Bishop Farquhar presented Ray Davey with an historic Honorary Doctorate from Maynooth in 2002. In his citation he talked about the "practical vision" of Corrymeela that touched "real lives", and said, "All of this vision, all of this practical work, was carried out in the spirit of true ecumenism – an awareness of the richness of one's own tradition, and a committed respect for the richness of others."

He added, significantly, "On the day of my consecration as a Bishop, I said of Ray Davey that he was the man 'in whose company I had come to an ever-deepening realisation that respect for another's tradition is in no way dependent on the betrayal of one's own.'" In saying so, Tony Farquhar represented the essence and the practicality of Corrymeela, and he included this fitting tribute to Ray Davey himself. "In spiritual terms you have brought a more enduring hope to what has been at times an embittered world in the North. You have not brought the hope of transient political solutions to transient political problems. Rather, you have reflected that true hope that is based on the resurrection of Jesus Christ."

The experiences of other people at Corrymeela have been as varied as the wide range of those who took part. Rob Wiggs had been a teacher in the east of England before coming to spend a year at Corrymeela in 1977. He recalls:

"From time to time I felt a pull to the Anglican priesthood, but I was deterred by the sense that religion and life were not the same thing. On the whole, I preferred life! But I was restless, and I spoke about this to the chaplain of my old college in Cambridge, Noel Battye, who said, 'You must go to Northern Ireland.' He also introduced my fiancée Lib, a nurse from Southern Ireland, and me, to Norman Richardson, who said, 'You must go to Corrymeela.' So we did."

Rob found at Corrymeela that "religion and life were the same thing. This is what made it possible, at the end of our year, for me to move on to theological college. I remember that Harold Good, the then Centre Director and pastor to the volunteers, did not have a religious 'smell' about him. He did not seem very interested in sin, or in who was and wasn't a 'Christian'. But he did spend hours talking with people made terribly vulnerable by the Troubles, and he was endlessly available to talk to us." They were not treated as juniors, and there were "many Corrymeela people far older and wiser than us who sought and valued our opinions. How unusual this was occurred to me a few years later, when I encountered the hierarchical mindset of the Church."

At Ballycastle, Billy McAllister was, among many other things, the "de facto resident theologian". Rob recalls:

"He introduced me to Simone Weil and Hans Kung. Since Billy was banned from driving because of his poor heart condition, I took him on endless trips to Coleraine and Belfast, allegedly in search of some special nail or screw, but they were really just jaunts, during which he treated me to his passionate take on life, the universe and everything. The faces and names of several grey theological teachers have long faded from my view, while Billy – now dead 28 years – still travels with me on many journeys."

Rob describes Billy, with affection, as "quite a violent pacifist! He didn't have much time for Ray Davey's hero, Dietrich Bonhoeffer, but Ray brought Bonhoeffer's friend and biographer Eberhard Bethge and his wife (Bonhoeffer's niece) for a weekend seminar. Bethge gave us a real felt sense of the agonizing over the assassination attempt on Hitler. Bonhoeffer's starting place was in fact pacifist, but he felt called to pass beyond his own sense of righteousness. Bethge told us that someone once asked Bonhoeffer to interpret the text, 'Those who live by the sword must perish by the sword.' He replied that those are words that in our day we must specially take to ourselves."

William Rutherford, another noted Corrymeela member from the early days, had worked as a consultant doctor in India and brought his colleague Bishop Lesslie Newbigin to Ballycastle for a similar weekend. Rob recalls, "Corrymeela's engagement with its own times and context made it possible to receive the witness of these great Christian leaders with alert attention. And it was theology not in a lecture theatre, but over breakfast."

There were other teachers too. "These were the people who became my teachers because of the generosity with which they shared experiences to which I had not been exposed. Pat Murphy, an 18-year-old volunteer from Ligoniel, told me endless stories of a childhood utterly unlike that of the London suburb where I grew up. Jim and Toddie, who were taking leave of a paramilitary past on the Peace People's 'escape route' out of Northern Ireland were assigned to Lib and me for 'safe-keeping' during the two weeks they were with us. This mostly involved trying to keep them out of bars, or keeping their sojourns there reasonably short."

Rob and his colleagues tried to keep a young man called Sam out of prison by offering him a home at Corrymeela.

"Harold Good was persuaded against his better judgement. Two weeks later while some volunteers were sampling a poteen-like brew with Billy (a necessary inculturation, we were told), Sam 'rediscovered' his vocation as a safe-breaker, and disappeared on one of our bikes. Kathleen Bakewell, the secretary, still wakes up in the night to remember the disappeared Sam and the open safe. On another level people like Martine and Chris, as well as Remo from Switzerland and Okka from Germany, sowed a seed with me that is now a tree – namely that if I spend too much time with people who are just the same as me, the longing for freedom becomes overwhelmingly powerful."

Rob spent many hours with another Corrymeela member Roger Courtney in helping to plan youth conferences, and the "Corrymeet" and "Summerfest" programmes.

"We revelled in disagreement. Roger believed God to be a metaphor, but I believed God to be a reality. So 'Corrymeet' was about God. This, to me, was worth about six month's lectures at theological college. 'Eastermeet' was about lifestyle, accompanied by a completely vegetarian recipe. The youth of Northern Ireland were not impressed by this away back in 1978, and most of the food ended in the bin!"

The volunteers acted as "gofers" for the then resident youth worker Billy Kane. Rob recalls, "We visited youth clubs across the divide in Belfast to help prepare them for the weekend meetings in Belfast. This also gave Billy the chance to share with 'posh lily-livered' volunteers like me from England our lack of readiness for the real world."

The volunteers were kept busy at Corrymeela "but not crushingly so. There was a structure as well as pastoral care, and an interest not just in cheap labour (we were paid £6 a week and full board) but also in our development as people." Rob attended a couple of political conferences, and he was given a week's placement in a Derry hostel for the homeless. He says, "It was only at that stage in my life that I began to think more confidently about the political dimensions of reality, which was essential when I began to be a priest in inner city London, during the early Thatcher years. It is still important for me to return quite often to Ballycastle to pick up that particular blend of political, spiritual and theological insight that is Corrymeela's, and which is expressed by people like David Stevens and John Morrow... It probably sounds as if I am idealising Corrymeela, and maybe I am, but in 1977 to '78 the resident Community of staff, volunteers and people who were often present – like Ray, Gerry McCambridge, Billy Kane, Donald McDonagh and others – really did love one another. We worked and worshipped together, and so many things were funny."

Some people forged lifelong friendships. "For example, Martine Perrochet from Switzerland visits us every year, and sits in our kitchen and laughs and laughs, normally about some memory of our crazy Irish friends."

Rob Wiggs believes that Corrymeela was where he discovered his "charism – not just to be a priest, but to be the type of priest I was going to be – that is, one who had been touched by Corrymeela. Not a very reverent priest, but one who recognised that however much one's own selfishness let one down, the Gospel is founded upon hospitality to the most valuable people. And hospitality to the most vulnerable people, and also hospitality to the most vulnerable parts of all people, those places of darkness in all of us where abundant life is waiting to gush out."

Rob believes that Corrymeela "spoiled" him for theological college which proved to be "two of the unhappiest years of my life. Corrymeela, in a real sense, was my college; but at the 'real' college where, to paraphrase Edwin Muir, the 'Word', which during the previous year I had seen 'become flesh', was now well and truly turned back into a word."

Rob's first experience of a parish was not easy. "At Newham, in the east end of London, there was a group of dwindling but very persistent 'church-minded ' people who wanted to be serviced as the institution died before our very eyes. However, Corrymeela was part of the background, both as action and as an idea, which enabled me not to become completely trapped. I spent months wandering around the estates of our parish, partly a lost soul and partly a pilgrim."

He made friends with a Rastafarian poet "to no purpose but just for friendship" and he also made friends with an elderly West Indian who had lost both his legs "and with many others who did not know what Evensong was. In my next parish, and the one after that, we worshipped and prayed together on the one hand, and on the other we got some quite creative things going with homeless people and asylum seekers."

He adds, "In Gray's, in south Essex, we started a new type of Eucharist (or was it the oldest there is?) with the tramps, many of them Irish, by a bonfire under a railway bridge. These people began to educate the church people in new and rich understandings of discipleship."

When the Kosovans arrived in the mid-90s, Rob recalls that "there were people ready to speak up for them in the supermarkets where they had to take their food vouchers, and to organise the English classes and the clothing stores, and who were ready – if necessary – for the anti-deportation campaigns. Though I had left Corrymeela twenty years earlier, this for me was still quite explicitly about being a Corrymeela person."

Around 1995, Rob felt that he was tired and not as sharp as he had been in recognising the interpretive power of the Gospel. He says, "While on holiday in Switzerland with Martine, I saw various books on her shelves by Roel Kaptein and René Girard. I thus came into contact with a major strand of Corrymeela's thinking over the previous decade. I took a sabbatical to discover these thinkers, and I returned to Northern Ireland to pick various Corrymeela brains."

Over recent years he has led various groups in Essex and East London. "We explore the structuring role that rivalling and scapegoating play in humans being together, and the role that the Gospel – acknowledged or implicit – can play in helping us to find ways out of violence. I am now involved in the theological formation of priests and ministers, and in a number of specific projects which reflect these insights."

Rob has also been involved in preparations for "Safe Spaces". He says, "This is a forum for clergy and church people, who have fallen out over the gay issue, to study together." He has also been involved in a Bible-Koran study group in East London, with the enthusiastic backing of the local priest and Imam, and the aim has been to explore together what the Scriptures of each can teach the other about hospitality and asylum.

Rob sums up his Corrymeela experience thus: "In so far as I am a 'mover and shaker', the day when Norman Richardson said, 'You must go to Corrymeela' continues to be a defining moment. And my continuing involvement in Corrymeela is one of the reasons, that in spite of the religious crisis through which we are all living, certainly in the West, much of the time I have a spring in my step and hope in my heart."

SEVEN

THE END OF AN ERA

WHILE THE CORRYMEELA COMMUNITY maintained its vision and outreach in the late Sixties and throughout the Seventies, the situation in Northern Ireland showed no signs of improving. In some ways it was becoming worse, with a political deadlock in a polarised community which, on all sides, was suffering from widespread violence.

The then Irish Premier Jack Lynch summarised the position well when he declared somewhat despairingly in November 1979 that the situation continued to be "as intractable" as at any stage in the previous ten years. The bombings and killings continued apace, and even today the statistics remain disturbing given the ratio of death and injury they represented in a relatively small-sized population.

In 1979 alone, for example, 113 people died due to the security situation, including 51 civilians. There were 875 recorded injuries, including 557 civilians, as well as 728 shootings, 422 explosions and 142 devices defused. There were 504 armed robberies, many carried out by Republican and Loyalist paramilitaries, and a total of £568,359 was stolen. Over 46,000 rounds of ammunition were recovered by the security forces, as well as 300 firearms and 905 explosives. A total of 6,452 house searches were carried out, and overall 670 people were charged with serious offences including murder, attempted murder, armed robbery, and also with firearms and explosives offences. This was bad indeed, but it was one of the "better" years of that troubled decade.[1]

The political situation remained gloomy, and any attempts at reaching – or much less maintaining – an agreement were constantly jeopardised by the recurring violence and its aftermath. In February 1979, eleven Protestants known as the "Shankill Butchers" were sentenced for horrific crimes, including the torture and murder of Catholics. In March of that year Airey Neave, the former war hero and Tory spokesman on Northern Ireland – and a close confidant of Margaret Thatcher – was murdered when a bomb planted in his car by the Irish National Liberation Army (INLA) exploded in a House of Commons car park.

The next month, four policemen were killed in South Armagh by a Provisional IRA van-bomb, and on 27 August the brutality of the Northern Irish situation hit to the heart of the Royal Family when Lord Mountbatten was killed by an IRA explosion on his small boat off the coast of Sligo. His grandson of 14 and another boy were killed instantly, and the Dowager Lady Brabourne later died of her injuries. On the same day as Mountbatten was killed, the Provisional IRA murdered 18 members of the Parachute Regiment in an explosion at Narrow Water, near Warrenpoint.

In the autumn of that year there was some rare good news for Ireland when a relatively young and certainly energetic Pope John Paul II made a visit to the Republic, but because of the security situation he was unable to travel to Armagh, the ecclesiastical capital of the island. At Drogheda, in a passionate and eloquent speech, the Pope appealed to the Provisional IRA for an end to violence, but it was swiftly rejected by the Republicans with their familiar mantra that only force could persuade the British to leave Northern Ireland.

These were daunting times for peacemakers in general and for Corrymeela in particular, and the Community also faced the considerable challenge of finding a new Leader to replace Ray Davey, who announced his retirement. He had given Corrymeela ample warning of his intentions. He had been Leader since the Community's foundation, when he was fifty years old, and at 55 he assumed the full-time leadership. By the end of 1979 he was approaching his 65th birthday, the normal age of retirement, and although his health was still good, it seemed an opportune time for him to step back and to allow a younger Leader to take over. However, his departure, from every conceivable angle, would be regarded as the end of an era.

Though Davey would have been the last person to claim any personal credit for the establishment of Corrymeela, his name was closely associated with the development and success of the Community. He had been involved with nurturing the idea of "community" since his experiences in prisoner-of-war camps, and also with helping to inspire the small group who made the Corrymeela idea a reality. During the process he demonstrated tough and single-minded leadership skills, though his genial and gentle personality helped to encourage so many others to contribute to ongoing Community work and development.

True leaders, by definition, are not necessarily popular. Indeed a leader who feels the need to be popular, as opposed to being populist, may not necessarily be the right person for the job. It is striking, however, that over forty years after Ray Davey was appointed Leader of the Corrymeela Community there is no one who will say a bad word about him, "on or off" the record. On the contrary, those who talk about him do so with a mixture of continuing affection and respect.

Craig Cameron knew Ray from his early days as the Presbyterian chaplain at Queen's University. He says, "To me, Ray has always been approachable, open and humble, and he has encouraged people to grow. He could delegate naturally, and he had the incredible gift of welcoming the growth of those around him. He was essentially a team-builder, and his relationship with Kathleen was at the very centre of his team-building at Corrymeela."

Cameron believes that one of Ray's gifts was the ability to speak to people in their own language. He says, "One of the lovely things about Corrymeela from the beginning was that most of its thinking was pragmatic, down-to-earth and understandable. Theological language was never a strong point with any of us, and Ray's style of preaching and talking to people was simply a commonsense wisdom."

John Morrow, who was to succeed Ray as Leader, says, "There were so many dimensions to his contribution. He had a sense that the experience of people living and working together could be a theatre in which things could happen. He had seen it in the prisoner-of-war camps, and he had the belief in community and how lives could be changed. He had tried this out also among students to some extent and had seen it 'gel'. So he was able to bring this experience of community in the war during a time of great suffering. It wasn't playing games."

Ray, he believes, was an enabler. "He constantly picked up people who didn't think they had any gifts, and told them what those gifts were. He encouraged them and stayed with them. Ray had an ability to find a place for everybody, and the secret of community is in helping people to feel that they have a place. That was Ray's great skill – working with women whose families had been shattered, and with young lads who had had their brothers shot and were full of vengeance, and wanted to go out and fire a bullet at the first policeman they could get hold of. Ray was able to get alongside those people in a way that was very powerful."

Did Davey have any faults? Morrow says, "We all have our weaknesses, and Ray wasn't easily diverted once he got a thing into his head. If you didn't agree with him, he wouldn't be obstructive, but he would certainly put you on your mettle to dissuade him." In effect he was much tougher than his gentle nature suggested.

"It was kind of deceptive, in a way. Absolutely. When Ray produced the idea for Summerfest, he got it from the German model of the Kirchentag. He said, 'Why don't we do a mini version of that on our site at Ballycastle, and make it a kind of workshop almost of rebuilding society, a place where people can catch a vision, and where they can share their experiences in different ways?' Ray was always wanting to be on the edge, and at the frontier. At times he was vice-like, and he could be very headstrong on some particular ideas, if you didn't agree with him."

Derick Wilson, who took over as Centre Director in 1979, was already a member of the Community and had known Ray for a long time. He also worked with Davey briefly in his latter years as Leader. Derick recalls, "You were always aware that he would support you so long as you didn't do anything crazy. Ray would remind me, he would question me, he would quiz me, but he backed me."

John Morrow was similarly helpful. "You knew that you were with colleagues who supported you absolutely. It didn't mean that they always agreed with you." Wilson confirms that Ray Davey could be tough. "He was tough in that he argued for the things he believed in. He wouldn't let people deviate from the central task. He was tough in that if people wanted to take the soft route, but there was a hard route that really should be taken, Ray would always choose the hard route."

Ray could also be tough with church and religious groups. "If they wanted to ignore issues, he wouldn't let them do that. So if toughness is keeping people to the core vision and task, if it is working with people you don't want to work with, if you have to meet people from a different background and tradition, if you have to cross lines, to build trust, to take risks, then Ray was tough. However, his toughness was not that of a dictator or of someone with a narrow agenda. Ray's toughness lay in the fact that he wanted a certain lines followed across a whole range of subjects."

Wilson tells the story of going to the Northern Ireland Office with Davey and of Ray demanding to see someone in authority because a civil servant had suggested that it was inappropriate for Corrymeela to run a conference on the future of prisons. "There was a feeling of 'Who was Corrymeela to do this?' However, we did it. We brought together civil servants, paramilitary representatives, church people and others, and we talked about the challenges of a post-internment prison population in the sense of people who had experienced internment, and we asked about people being incarcerated for so many years without thinking what they would come out to. So that was toughness again, and Ray just told people that the Government could say what it wished, but Corrymeela was running that conference, and we did."

Ray himself later reflected on some of the tougher challenges. "My most painful times as Leader of Corrymeela was when I had to go against a widespread wish. At times, some people wanted us to move in another direction and I said, 'This is how I see it, this is what I believe is right, and I can't do anything else.'

"That was quite painful because in those moments I was much more vulnerable. However, it was necessary. There has to be a point in the process of changing people's thinking when you have to be able to cross over and to face up to those who are opposed to what you want to do."[2]

One of the problems facing Davey and the others was the lack of a blueprint from the past. They were continually being forced to move into unknown territory. Ray recalls, "We had to make our own decisions, and that could be very demanding. We went through some hard times of friction in the Community among different people, and I used to pray to God and say in effect, 'Over to you, mate, you handle this, because I can't.'

"I must say that when I look back, I am amazed sometimes when I think how it all worked out. Yet even from the earliest days, I never really felt that it wouldn't work out. I felt, without sounding pious, that this was what the good Lord wanted, and that if I carried on there would be a price to pay, but it was the only way we should go."

However, Davey remained critical of those who left it all to Corrymeela and others. "One of the things that annoyed me was when I would speak to a group about Corrymeela to ask for support, and people would say, 'You are doing great work, here's a fiver for your efforts.' They had no idea they, too, had a part to play as peacemakers. A great many just passed the buck.

"There was the attitude of 'Leave it to the police, or the Army or someone else, but it's not our thing. We haven't any role to play.' I spent a lot of my time trying to tell them that they had a role, and that if our society was to change, it would change through the lives of ordinary people who were living with other ordinary people. That's the area we had to work in."

Ray was also critical of the attitudes of some of the Churches. He said, "There was the terrible temptation of merely trying to keep things under control. Some of the attitudes were 'You must be tactful, don't shake up people.' I remember one eminent clergyman whose philosophy was 'Don't rock the boat', and I wondered what the great Biblical prophets would have said to him?

"In contrast, just think of all those ordinary men in religious history who felt that they were under Divine guidance to speak the truth, no matter what the price. The whole Confessing Church of Germany and Dietrich Bonhoeffer made you realise that the age of the martyrs was not finished, and it is something that is very real in many parts of the world today. At Corrymeela we did not have all the answers, but we did what the occasion demanded. What more could we have done than that?"[3]

While he was critical of aspects of Church life, Davey was careful never lose his contacts with individual Christians and Christian institutions. Writing in one of his earlier books *Take Away This Hate*, he said it was clear that there was need for a radical change in the structures and life of the churches, but he was positive as well.

He stated, "Much of what is still customary today was geared to an age that is passed. We should remember that this is also true of all similar time-honoured institutions. The result is that there is a great opportunity for experiment and new thinking in this time of vast social transformation in the world at large." The churches, he argued, should not see this as a threat but as an opportunity.

Davey wrote, "We must always recognise that there is nothing sacred about the particular form of the Church at any particular time. It varies from age to age and from place to place. Indeed 'we have this treasure in earthen vessels' – one remaining constant, while the other changes from one generation to another. It is in this context that the Corrymeela Community should be seen, and we would plead with the churches to understand what we are seeking to do, and to work with us."[4]

Davey was careful to stress that Corrymeela did not see itself as being in confrontation with the churches, or seeking to provide an alternative. He wrote, "We hold a high view of the church, and see it as the People of God coming to us from the past, in which we each have our part to play, and it will go on into the future. Most of us in Corrymeela have come from the Church's life and are still very much a part of it, and I have tried to show how much personally I owe to it."[5]

Davey was also clear what he, and Corrymeela, meant by "community". He stated that "...it tends to be used in a very vague and general way. Corrymeela uses it mainly as applying to those who, while they are unable to live together in the same place, yet are drawn by a common belief, a shared desire to work closely with each other, and to promote certain aims in the wider society to which they belong."

Davey never forgot what Tullio Vinay had said so many years earlier. "He believes that one of the greatest challenges the churches have to meet, in this century, is how modern man, who cannot live the monastic life, can yet experience community life. That is very much how Corrymeela sees it, and it is also the question being addressed by many people and groups of Christians, because as we have seen, it is more and more acknowledged that life together is the very essence of authentic Christian existence."[6]

While the development of Corrymeela owes much to the work and example of Ray Davey, many people have rightly paid tribute to the vision and support of his wife Kathleen, who has also made her own distinctive contribution to the Community. She reflects, "When you think of all the threads that came together and emerged eventually as Corrymeela, it was quite remarkable. There was Ray's wartime experience, and then his post-war appointment as Convenor of the Continental Mission which entailed him travelling to Europe at regular intervals and visiting centres of reconciliation like Taizé and Agape."[7]

Partly due to the commitments to her young family, Kathleen Davey did not become involved directly with Corrymeela until some years after its establishment. She says, "I had no direct role at that point, but I knew what was happening and all the people in it. Eventually, however, I found myself on the Projects Committee, which was extremely interesting. However, when you see all the paper that comes out of Corrymeela now – looking back, we seemed quite amateurish. We prepared papers for big meetings, like AGMs, on a typewriter, but preparations for some other meetings were done in handwriting, with carbon copies. It all seems so unbelievable now!"

There were also tough days, in the midst of violence and mayhem. Kathleen recalls the children of one family whose father had been shot dead. "I remember the face of one young boy who had seen his father shot in front of his very eyes – he had been trying to help a priest caught in crossfire. I became very attached to this particular family. That 'young boy' is now a grown man with a family of his own, and we keep in touch."

It was not easy to define the role of the Leader's wife. "When your husband has a definite place in the scheme of things, he knows what he is doing and what he is supposed to do, but there is a danger that his wife might become something of an appendage. I found my own area was in the garden at Ballycastle."

Children visiting Corrymeela would come round to the garden, and ask Kathleen if they could help her. "Gradually I would find out their names, where they lived and that sort of thing, and they became part of me. I've still got letters from children who wrote to me, after they went home. It was absolutely wonderful, and I loved that side of Corrymeela's work."

In his final report as Leader of Corrymeela, Ray Davey summed up the work and life of the Community from its establishment in 1965. He pointed to the achievements and the challenges of Corrymeela, as well as the limitations. He wrote, "Reconciliation was not only a much-discussed subject, but a very live issue in daily life. We have kept in existence, and we have established our role. Our identity, though we have continually to struggle with it and to clarify it, is a real one. We are an authentic Catholic-Protestant group, and we have become a symbol of hope for multitudes of people in this land and far beyond."[8]

However, there were limitations. Davey wrote, "We have long since realised the limitations of what we can do. It's so easy in this sort of work to create false expectations, and I believe that we are learning to be much more realistic in assessing what we can and cannot do." It was important to work out clearly Corrymeela's aims and objectives, to cherish its independence and to safeguard the voluntary principle.

"We full-time workers are to be enablers, to help members fulfil the aims of Corrymeela. This is difficult, especially for us, as it is so often easier to do the particular job oneself, and very often I've done that. But it is one we have got to work on, otherwise we'll become a group of paid officials who do the work, and the Community concept vanishes." [9]

Davey also laid out clearly the challenges of the future. He wrote that Corrymeela "must be involved in what is happening; supporting the positive and creative attitude; willing to take initiatives and at times risks as we steadfastly witness to the way of compassion and justice; facing challenges and opposition and conflict. We must be willing at times to be a pressure group within the social and political order, and within the structure of the Church. To join Christ today in our world, means – as the Prior of Taizé, Roger Schutz has said – 'struggle and contemplation', and we must always remember the utter necessity of both."

It was a tall order, but not untypical from the man who had done so much to make Corrymeela what it was, and is. People tend to forget that Davey's entire career was lived "on the edge". He volunteered for what turned out to be his seminal war service as a young man, when he could just as easily have opted for the safety of an Ulster parish. When he returned from the war, he broke new ground as the Presbyterian chaplain of Queen's, and he later helped to push forward the frontiers by working to establish Corrymeela.

Throughout those formative years, and during his time as Leader, his clear vision, strong personality and encouraging way with people, all helped to chart the right path for Corrymeela, through all the difficulties. He and the Community made mistakes, and they had to learn as they went along, but he helped to lay the foundation of something very important in the world of peacemaking; and, significantly, he knew when to quietly step aside and let go. On every level, he would be a hard act to follow.

Some of Ray's most enduring qualities were described by Kathleen, who throughout their long and happy marriage, has known him better than anyone. She said, "Ray always stood his own ground, and he was never afraid to go against the stream. If he was convinced of something, there was nothing that could stop him. I wouldn't say that he was stubborn as such, but he certainly was convinced."

He also had a highly-developed sense of fair play, even long before Corrymeela started. "In our student days my brothers and some others were fooling about on a camp site, and they decided to collapse a tent on one of their friends who had gone to bed early.

"They thought that it would be hugely funny to do this and then to flee, so that their friend, emerging from the collapsed tent, would find nobody there. I remember, however, that Ray was the only one out of that mad lot who went back to our friend and helped to put up the tent for him again. That is just a little picture of what I feel came later on.

"Another of Ray's great strengths has been his ability to listen, and to give advice, even if people didn't necessarily have to take it. Also he has had a great sense of humour all his life, and that has taken him a long, long way. In fact I wouldn't have married him if he hadn't. He needed to have a sense of humour, to put up with me!"

Ray Davey was always young at heart, and his guiding philosophy for Corrymeela never wavered. In an interview during his 92nd year he said, "Don't be afraid of change. Life is dynamic, not static. Try to be open to change, because it is important to have flexibility, and life and circumstances are changing all the time. Don't tie your tiller down. If you are not able to change, you may become shipwrecked.

"Also you must try to be open to the acknowledgement of your own mistakes, including the relationships which you felt that you hadn't handled well, or in a positive way. It is important to be able to restore those relationships where you can, even if it is painful to do so. In the end, it is a healing thing. I don't believe that there is any situation that I have not tried to redeem, so to speak. At this late stage of my life, I think I really can say that."

His abiding attitude throughout has been one of thankfulness. He said, "I often switch on my internal video and play back the good bits. My overwhelming emotion is one of gratitude for the immense help I've been given by so many people, and to be able to say that out of all the evil, such as my experience of war and the prison camps, so much good has come as well." [10]

EIGHT

A NEW CHAPTER

THE NEW LEADER OF CORRYMEELA, the Reverend Dr John Morrow, took over from Ray Davey in 1980, and gradually began to establish himself in his new and demanding role. He was well qualified for the job, and he had a solid experience of reconciliation work, both inside and outside Corrymeela. As one of the founder-members of the Community, he had a good sense of what Corrymeela was – or should be – about, and as an ordained minister in the Presbyterian Church he had experience of parish work. Significantly, he also understood the challenge of trying to lead a Community whose members belonged to different churches, but which in itself did not owe allegiance to any one Church.

As has been noted elsewhere, Morrow's early experience as a member of the Iona Community had a profound effect on his concept of establishing Corrymeela. He wrote: "For an Irish Presbyterian like me, this movement awakened a new consciousness on a number of frontiers. Experiencing the searching dialogue across the social and industrial divide in Scotland forced some of us to look at our own situation at home; to recognise many of the same features, such as the complete inadequacy of the privatised Gospel of individual salvation to confront the reality of urbanised culture and its sectarian divides."[1]

Morrow believed that Corrymeela "sought to reflect that Biblical and Iona sense of 'the word made flesh' by rooting its life and work in a shared common life, open to all who were willing to join us on a new ecumenical journey of faith; open also to those who were sceptical, disillusioned with their past experience of the church, and to those who were victims of injustice, discrimination, intimidation and fear in our society."[2]

Another important factor was the idea of establishing a centre where people could exercise their gifts and engage in dialogue with others on the many questions facing them in the modern world. "Many of the lay people and students were frustrated by the narrowness in the range of the Church's agenda. The daily questions facing people in the world's life often seemed to be absent from Christian conversation, and sometimes the impression was given that these 'worldly questions' were not even appropriate. Theology seemed to be concerned with so-called 'spiritual' matters, to the exclusion of the 'material'."[3]

John Morrow's career took him beyond his involvement in the parish ministry and in helping to establish Corrymeela. Some two years after its foundation, he accepted an invitation to become Chaplain to overseas students in Glasgow. Over a period of more than four years he discovered much about the harsh realities of a conflict-ridden world.

He recalled, "I was forced to wrestle with the complex issues of the post-colonial era; to become aware of the unhealed wounds between and within nations, and the legacy of European exploitation of indigenous peoples. Attempts to keep dialogue and conversation going between students whose parents and friends were at war was a sobering experience. It did, however, help me to put some of the issues of conflict in Northern Ireland in perspective."[4]

There was another dimension of which Morrow was also conscious – the Irish Republic. He was being made more aware of "the need to experience life in the larger part of the island of Ireland, if I was to understand more fully the wounds of our history, and the sources from which our enmity rose". Accordingly he accepted the post as Presbyterian Chaplain to colleges and universities in Dublin, and this in turn brought him into contact with a wide network. It included the then newly-formed Irish School of Ecumenics, the Glencree Centre for Reconciliation, and other organisations.

John Morrow returned to Northern Ireland to become Presbyterian Chaplain to Queen's University, where he continued the pioneering work of his predecessors, including Ray Davey. All the while he had remained a member of Corrymeela, and by the time he took over as Leader in 1980, he had a rounded experience both inside and outside the Community which was to prove invaluable.

Inevitably he had a different style from Ray Davey. He was friendly and approachable, and he had his own sense of humour and concern for people. He was a keen debater with a sometimes loquacious style, but always with the sharp mind of a down-to-earth intellectual, and he didn't mind a robust exchange of views. He once admitted, "I would have been perhaps more outspoken than Ray, although he had steel within that gentle exterior. I suppose that I would be known for speaking my mind openly, and sometimes I may have done so wrongly.

"I don't think I'm soft, and I don't mind people disagreeing with me. This doesn't upset me as much as it upsets others, because I can live with a bit of disagreement, on the basis that we have to work things through. We can't pretend that we always have a common mind on everything."[5]

As has been noted earlier, Ray Davey had brought the Community a long way as Leader, and in his final formal assessment of what had been achieved, he also pointed to the challenges which lay ahead. These were both internal and external. Morrow recalls that one of his most difficult challenges was over staffing. "One of my colleagues was being criticised by the Community, and I thought that while it was partially justified, it went too far. To that extent I felt that I had to defend this person against what I thought was an anti-English bias from both Catholics and Protestants. Those were things we had to discover about ourselves, and we did learn, that's the point. In later times people came rightly to respect this person much more than they had done originally."[6]

Sometimes Corrymeela is known as "The Hill of Harmony", which is a translation from the original Gaelic. It can also be translated as "The Hill of Bleating", and there is a certain irony in the juxtaposition of these contrasting symbols. Corrymeela, like any other organisation or family, had had its good and bad times, and some staff appointments could cause particular friction.

Morrow recalls that "Sometimes a person who had worked for a long time as a Corrymeela volunteer felt that, because of the service they had given, they were entitled to a staff job when one came up. However, if someone outstanding appeared in the interviews, we had to take a certain decision, and that wasn't always popular. So we had to deal with considerable unpopularity at times, and to stick with our decisions. Maybe, in other people's eyes, we didn't always do it in the most Christian way, but that is for others to judge."[7]

There was also the inherent tension between permanent staff and members of the Community, because both groups felt sometimes that the Ballycastle Centre belonged to them. Morrow says, "The members believed that they were the founding group who kept it going when there was no staff, and that this was virtually their home. Staff, on the other hand, were working seven days a week at the Centre and they felt that some members believed that they owned the place, and did not respect the staff for who they were."

That, at best, could lead to a creative inter-action. At worst, it could have seriously damaged the Community. "Unless you do a great deal of work on the relationship between staff and members of the Community and encourage them to engage with one another, you could end up with a very difficult situation. The writer Scott Peck talks about a 'false' community and a 'real' community, and claims that until people actually meet and get rid of the 'false' community of everybody being polite, you don't move into real relationships with each other."[8]

Morrow illustrated the point in a different way when describing Bonhoeffer's comments on the growth of Christian Community. "At first, we think everyone is an angel. But soon reality sets in, and we find out each other's faults and inadequacies. At this point we are liable to see only the worst in each other (hypocrites or devils in disguise!). If we are willing to stay on the journey, we may reach the stage where we accept one another 'warts and all'."[9]

Those phases in human relationships were often exhibited in the residential life at Ballycastle, at all levels involving staff, members, volunteers and visitors. Morrow reflects, "It is so easy to love our 'dream' of Community, rather than the real brothers and sisters whom God has given us. To reach the point where we really can give one another their place, when we begin to learn how to call forth each other's gifts rather than crush them, is not without pain. In the process we have to learn to deal with those who reflect back to us those parts of our own being which we cannot face or accept. And because we continue to hurt one another and often fail to listen, our community life is only possible through forgiveness."[10]

Despite the elements of pain on the inside, which was an important but by no means total picture of life in the Community, some outsiders still retained a sentimental view of Corrymeela. They looked on it as an essentially peaceful place which had no tensions of its own, and certainly none resembling life in the outside world. Morrow says, "I've seen that view expressed in plays and in other ways where people were depicted as being nice to each other, pretending to be friends, and not dealing with the real issues. To some extent, I resented that view, because the only answer to that was to become involved and to find out what it was really like inside."

Much of the Corrymeela involvement was, of necessity and also by design, to become manifest in the wider world. "Some of our members are widely known for working with outside groups. Derick Wilson has done incredible work in the wider community, and my son Duncan is also well-known for this. They, and others, are not working for Corrymeela now but for society as a whole.

"Lots of our members have been using the Corrymeela insights, but they have not been running around with a big badge saying 'This is Corrymeela', and we have not been looking for some kind of reputation or praise. Ray Davey once said memorably that 'Corrymeela begins when you leave.' What we were saying during my time as Leader, and what we are still saying is 'Get out there, and what Corrymeela stands for can be discovered where you are, if you engage with it.'"[11]

This presupposes that the Community as such would always be limited in size. Morrow concurs. "That is absolutely true. We had never any intention of growing into a mass movement, and we encouraged people to become involved in the wider world. If they then found that they could not sustain membership of Corrymeela, they were still welcomed as friends. Many of our members have done that, because there needs to be a core group to keep the spirit and the enterprise going, but the constant idea is to flow people into society, and not necessarily wearing the Corrymeela label at all."

Some members and former members, however, found it difficult to work within a wider society and to retain the ethos of Corrymeela. That included working within the Churches. Morrow says, "Some people needed constantly to come back to base, as it were. There were some who found the churches most difficult of all to work in, and they almost gave up their faith. They said to us, 'Maybe there is something to the *Christian* dimension' when they could find it to some extent in Corrymeela, but they couldn't find it where they were. They often told us that they found people in various community groups to be more Christian than some of the people in the Churches."[12]

John Morrow believes that Corrymeela has partly been in conflict with the Church. He claims, "The Church at large does not accept our theology. We are challenging completely the broad centre ground, and indeed more than that. Of course the churches do not have all the same vices. The Catholic Church has a particular set of vices, and it has caused great resentment in subjects like mixed marriages, shared communion, and in a lot of ways to do with education. It is extremely sad, for example, that they have been so negative about integrated education."

What about the "vices" of the Protestant churches? Morrow says, "I believe that there is an absolutely deep-seated anti-Catholicism at the heart of Presbyterianism, and if you scratch the surface it comes out, though perhaps not quite so much in the Church of Ireland. There are justifications for some of this, of course, partly because of the behaviour of the Catholic Church in the past, so it's not all one-sided, but unfortunately the Presbyterian Church did not embrace the changes in Vatican II, and to that extent, it didn't even encourage the development of possibilities that were there. However, it also seems to me sad that the Catholic Church itself has gone back on Vatican II, and hasn't taken it forward in the way that it was meant."[15]

The failures certainly have not been one-sided, and it could be argued that Corrymeela itself tended to recoil from the early lack of appreciation within some of the churches, and did not try hard enough to build bridges with those who chose not to appreciate or to understand them. That is not to say that there was a siege mentality around Corrymeela, but over the years the relationships with the Community and churches might arguably have been closer.

John Morrow says, "In one sense we have all failed, but I feel personally that the churches are not really properly engaged with the task at all. In fact, many have run away from it, but there have been a few outstanding individuals like Gerry Reynolds on the Catholic side, and also the Presbyterian ministers, John Dunlop and Ken Newell. I'm sorry to say, however, that the Protestant community has a lot to answer for in terms of our history here, and it still has not absorbed the message."

He further claims, "The official churches in the main have quietly tolerated us, or in some parts, they have viciously worked against us. I would also say that in some cases they have forbidden their members to set foot in our centre. I am aware of this in parts of the Presbyterian Church, and it has happened to a degree in other churches as well."

Does this mean that Corrymeela's work in Morrow's time as Leader, and since then, has been in vain? He says, "There are faults also on our side which we have to acknowledge. There has been a danger of us saying, 'OK, these people don't acknowledge us, they think we are theologically off the rails, let's just dismiss them and get on with it.' That in itself shows a lack of the spirit of reconciliation. There was the danger that we would simply decide to go our own way, to get stuck in and make our contribution, and I had to make my decision to avoid that.

"I would accept that at times we were not willing to make the effort to build relationships with people with whom we disagreed. Here we were as Corrymeela proclaiming reconciliation for the wider world, but we weren't prepared to do it within our own Community."

On the other hand, Morrow believes strongly that if it hadn't been for Corrymeela, many people would have given up the attempt. "They wouldn't have had the encouragement of Corrymeela itself to work within their own congregations, and I know some who have been very pioneering, including Fitzroy and Clonard. My own Presbyterian congregation at Gilnahirk has a close relationship with St Colmcille's Roman Catholic Church. Some other churches are also being very courageous, because if you set out on this road, you may well have division within your congregation, and it is easier for a minister just to leave it alone. If he or she starts doing this kind of reconciliation work, half the congregation may go along and the other half might not. Therefore the minister ends up in trouble, and may have to leave the country."

Though Morrow did not mention this, one well-known example was that of the Reverend David Armstrong, the former Presbyterian minister in Limavady who left the Church after opposition from some of his congregation when he met the then local parish priest, the Reverend Father Kevin Mullan, in his church to exchange greetings on Christmas morning. Armstrong later joined the Church of England, and then transferred to the Church of Ireland and served as a rector in the Diocese of Cork. His story is a separate issue from the history of Corrymeela as such, but there are still those who believe that if the courageous and enlightened Armstrong had chosen to stay at Limavady and toughed it out in the most trying of times, he would have received even more support locally and from others further afield. He was undoubtedly one of the pioneers at the sharp end of ecumenism in Northern Ireland.

Significantly, there are examples of congregations which have continued bridge-building even in the most difficult of circumstances. One of the best-known is Whitehouse Presbyterian

Church, which is situated in an interface area of North Belfast, where it had been carrying out pioneering work across the religious and community divides. It was almost virtually destroyed by arsonists, but splendidly rebuilt again with the aid of generous funds donated by many people – including local Catholic parishes and a wide range of Protestant churches. Its innovate programme of community and inter-church outreach continues.

All of this is not to deny John Morrow's claims that some of the official churches and its individual members have not embraced the Corrymeela ethos as much as they should. Speaking from the pain of the difficult times through which he worked as Leader of Corrymeela, and since, and given his first-hand experience of the kind of situations which many church members elsewhere would not encounter, Morrow has earned the authority to be taken seriously as an informed participant in ecumenical affairs.

It is difficult, however, to prove, or to disprove, his claims without the kind of detailed examination of church life across a wide spectrum which is impossible in this particular exercise. However, his assertions and observations have a strong ring of truth, and they should act as a renewed challenge for Corrymeela and the Churches to continue trying to improve their dialogue. Morrow believes, however, that the reconciliation work of Corrymeela and others has not been entirely in vain.

He says, "In the early days there was a deep-seated anti-Catholicism because of the Troubles, but there has been a coming back from that somewhat extreme position in the Seventies. Many people have come to realise that the Churches could not any longer put reconciliation down their list of priorities, but I believe that they have not embraced reconciliation with the kind of priority that it really ought to have."

He warns, however, of the danger of all forms of "feeling superior". He says, "We learned to be flexible and to recognise that priorities did change, and we had to respond to that. New volunteers constantly provided us with an on-going critique. They would ask, 'Why are we doing this programme? Is it still relevant?' On the other hand we had to remember that people came from different places in their journey towards reconciliation, so what seemed elementary to one was still new to others."

One of the perceived failings of Corrymeela in the early days was its lack of awareness of the needs of certain groups. Morrow recalls, "At one point we failed the middle-classes by becoming so preoccupied with the needs of working-class people who, admittedly, were suffering. I think that sometimes the middle-class people did not feel that they were really welcome. In some of the early youth programmes, we bent over so much in dealing with grassroots groups that people from more sheltered backgrounds might have felt to some extent not recognised and given their place."

This was partly due to the origin of Corrymeela as a middle-class student movement. "We decided early on that during the Troubles we had to become much more involved in working-class communities, and we appointed some staff who were oriented in that way. Billy Kane, for example, brought an avalanche of working-class youth into the Centre, and in a sense this was a tremendously good thing to happen. The Community needed this, but at times, we were almost brutally unfair to young people from middle-class backgrounds."

Morrow admits, "We sometimes forgot that we had been guilty of some of the prejudices that we ourselves were impatient in coping with. Corrymeela always was, and hopefully always will be, a learning experience."

NINE

DOWN TO EARTH

DURING THE FIRST PART of John Morrow's term of office as Leader, the Centre Director at Ballycastle was Derick Wilson, who also made a significant contribution to the development of Corrymeela in a number of different areas.

He first experienced Corrymeela at the age of 17, shortly before he went to Queen's University to study maths and physics. He recalls, "My early experience was one of 'liberation', although I wouldn't have used that term at the time. I was exhilarated, and I found Corrymeela a warm, friendly and outward-looking place. I didn't know it then, but it was a gateway to a wider world that lay beyond my working-class Presbyterian tradition in North Belfast."[1]

Though he had trained as a scientist, Wilson found himself drawn to community work, and particularly to Corrymeela. "I became steeped in it, partly through the issues raised by the civil rights movement in Northern Ireland at that time, and also working with Ray Davey and organising summer programmes and work camps. My mother always said that she knew where to find me. I was never at home, but always either working with Corrymeela projects, or at Ballycastle. It was wonderful in the Sixties to be part of that experience."

Later he applied for the job of Centre Director at Ballycastle. He says, "As everybody in the Community probably knows, I was not nominated first time round by the appointment committee, but that was in the days when the post had to be ratified by the whole Community." In the event, they chose Wilson and not the candidate nominated by the committee – as has been noted earlier.

Derick recalls, "When I first heard I hadn't got the job, I was in bits, but when the Community appointed me, I had to do two things: I had to prove to those who thought I wasn't good enough that I *was* good, and that it was a demanding job. I also had to prove to everybody that I was doubly good anyway!"

Certainly, he did not feel like walking away. "This was partly because I wanted to do the job so much, and stupidly because, I suppose, I was maybe a bit 'thran'. But I have no regrets. The people who were on the appointments panel and I have had very open relationships ever since, and those days have long passed. At the time that was the employment process at Corrymeela, and I went along with that because I was in a strong position with the backing of people. And I threw myself into it."

The challenges were clear. "Harold Good, my predecessor, had helped to make it a relevant Community, and I had used the Centre for family groups and young people all my working life. I had also trained youth workers and had brought them to Corrymeela, so I knew what it was like. Harold had opened up the notion of developing an open centre all the year round, whereas when we were students it was really a weekend and seasonal centre, and a full-week summer place."

Wilson worked initially with Ray Davey, and later with his successor, John Morrow. His good working relationship with Davey has been noted earlier, and this continued under Morrow. He recollects, "John brought to the role of Leader his strong sense of values and ethics, and also his intellect. He never really allowed anything to 'motor' unless he felt that a project had a shape and an integrity. Then it was fine. He forced as all to be clear about what we wanted to do, why we wanted to do it, and then led us along the road of 'how' to do it. That was the challenge which John brought – the project had to be clear, well thought out, and relevant to the work of reconciliation."[2]

One of Wilson's major objectives was to try to make Corrymeela become a centre of learning. "It wasn't just a place of refuge, sanctuary and rest. It was also a place that had something to teach people, and I recognised this because I had been a Senior Lecturer in Community Work before I went to Corrymeela. I knew that the residential experience was potentially one of the most enriching that people could have. It was the experience of living in community with a diversity of people you might never meet in the rest of your life. That crossed the lines in our society, and it was also about a wider world. That, to me, was the educational and learning kernel of Corrymeela."

The objective was trying to live with difference, against a background of enmity and distrust, and finding ways in which to move beyond fear. To many outsiders, this might have seemed naive. Wilson agrees. "It was gloriously naive in the sense that it was mad enough to work, and I believe that in conflict resolution we need a lot more 'zanyness' and unexpectedness to happen. Conflict is not rational, and it is not going to be changed only by rational means. We need the unexpected."

Part of that "unexpectedness" for Wilson was in meeting people like Frank Cahill, a community worker from Ballymurphy, a Nationalist area. "Frank knew and trusted Ray, and he had been interned twice. He was the number one community worker in Ballymurphy, and a wonderful man. To a Presbyterian like me from Duncairn Gardens, it was like encountering someone from another world. It was very exciting to meet people from other traditions, and at the height of the Troubles to have discussions with those who were victims, and others who probably had victimised, though not those who were necessarily victims in the same place."

This helped to pave the way forward for new projects, and Corrymeela developed a youth programme about working with vulnerable young people in association with Billy Kane, the Youth Worker, and Rosie Walsh as Volunteer Co-ordinator. "Out of that came the Rathcoole-Twinbrook connections, the links to New Barnsley, Moyard, Ballymurphy, Turf Lodge, Shankill, Short Strand, and other places across the religious divide. All of those areas were feeling the heat of the conflict."

This included a number of radical programmes. "We were working with difficult guys and girls who in many cases turned themselves round because the workers in those areas and at Corrymeela trusted one another. They spent hours and hours within programmes at Corrymeela and with programmes at their home base, as well as north-south and international projects. Some people who came to Corrymeela had no qualifications, but now have Masters degrees, and hold significant positions in youth work themselves."[3]

The early projects had a ripple effect. "We developed a Seed Group which involved some twenty or thirty young people meeting for six weekends. They came from different backgrounds – north and south, well-off and less well-off, medical consultants' daughters, and single parent mums, and many others. Every year some of the people on the programme would travel together for a week or two. There were some drop-outs, but most stayed on course. They learned to talk together about all sorts of things, including their views on religion, sex, politics, conflict, trust, love and hope. They shared those experiences, and the programme had a tremendous ripple effect."

Some critics would claim that there was a danger of Corrymeela over-estimating its success. Wilson says, "I don't think that Corrymeela has estimated enough what it has achieved, but at the same time, it is not about success. It's about working as if change is possible. We know from a Christian Gospel understanding that lives can be changed in new relationships of love and acceptance, and that this needs to be made real in people's lives – whether they are victims, or rich and well-to-do, or crusty and closed, or whether they are poor and vulnerable. Ray and Kathleen Davey always seemed to place hope in people, and that, I believe, is part of the secret. Corrymeela did work as if change was possible, and in my own work nowadays, I find that a lot of people don't believe that any more."[4]

After roughly seven years, Derick Wilson gave in his notice to quit. He says, "It was a question of 'time up'. I had spent seven years of being down at the Centre at 7.30am, and crawling into bed at 3am. That was the reality. In those days we formally closed the door of the centre at 1am, but informally at 2am. You had to be present, you had to be with the groups and you had to support the volunteers. To be honest, you probably had to lose part of your own family life because of the needs of the Centre."

The demands of the job were considerable, not only on a Director but also on the wider family. Derick was totally supported by his wife Dot, whom he had met initially at the Ballycastle Centre and who was also a member of the Community. He says, "We talked about it, and we knew it was time to go, even though I didn't leave with the promise of anything. I gave notice that I was going the following year, and left Corrymeela plenty of time to find a successor. It just felt right. Looking back, I don't think I'd have changed anything. Dot would say that although our relationship didn't go asunder, she became more locked in with the family, as I became more locked in with the work at the Centre, even though she was a Community member.

"It wasn't that the relationship was being hollowed out, it was just that one person was getting wedded to the job, and the other person compensated and got wedded to the family. And I think that it was the same with the others in the same position."

There were tangible successes during Wilson's period as Director, as there were for others at different times. He says, "We developed family work, schools work and youth work. We developed new patterns of operation with church groups, and we put Corrymeela back on the political map that Des Rea and Harold Good had got it to by 1973. It was a place where political people met, and where they came to discuss politics. So I think we expanded the canvas, as far as we were able, in terms of what reconciliation in our society should be."

The initiatives included a major political conference in March 1981 on "Models of Political Co-operation". This was held at Queen's University in partnership with the Glencree Community in Dublin. Some three months later, Corrymeela launched the ambitious and successful Summerfest series at Ballycastle, which was intended to be an all-age Christian Education Festival examining current issues in the light of faith.[5]

Other initiatives undertaken during the tenure of Derick Wilson and John Morrow was the participation from 1983 of Community members in the then newly-formed "Inter-Church Group on Faith and Politics". In 1983 the Community appointed a Roman Catholic priest, the Redemptorist, Father Gerry Cassidy, as a member of staff, and they also held the first joint conference for Catholic and Protestant clergy, which was in itself an important initiative. A year later the first full-time Schools Worker, Carmel Heaney, was appointed.

There were also failures. Wilson says, "We failed to challenge in an invitational way those from more evangelical and fundamentalist viewpoints. I think we just pushed them away, and that was our failing. Maybe they didn't them want to come, but they should not have been condemned. I have since had to revisit a lot of assumptions I made in those years. People who didn't agree with us didn't simply walk through our door, but we have lots of evidence to show that they walked past and wouldn't come in. I still think that Corrymeela probably should have done what ECONI later did – to try to make the bridge between the evangelicals of different traditions and the reconciliation agenda."[6]

Arguably, there were other failures too. Wilson admits, "We failed in terms of some work with young people. We failed in terms of some work with the Orange Order. We failed with some of the work we wanted to do with the Republican prisoners' movements in the late Seventies and early Eighties. We failed in the sense that we got them there, we got them into discussions, but then they went off and were able to create their own strong identities without necessarily the cross-community identity."

Despite the failures, there were also notable successes, and during those years Corrymeela was systematically reaching out at all levels. One important development was the establishment of the Understanding Conflict Project in 1985. This was a joint venture between Corrymeela and the University of Ulster, and the intention was to bring the Community's practical experience of working for reconciliation within an academic framework. The idea was also to provide training for staff from public and other bodies, including the police, trade unions and local government.

Derick Wilson was closely involved. "The original title was 'Understanding Conflict and Finding Ways Out', but some people thought it was a terrible title, so the working title for six years or so was 'Understanding Conflict'. The same project has gone on since 1985, and has survived even today. It is now called 'Future Ways' and it is concentrating on ways and paths, and also about the future."

A number of people had a significant input into the programme, including the Queen's University academic Frank Wright, who died tragically young, and also the Dutch facilitator Roel Kaptein, who also had much still to contribute before his own untimely death. Derick Wilson explains some of the thinking behind the project.

"Frank Wright gave us the theoretical underpinning of divided societies and ethnic frontiers. The central issues are agreed law and order, equality and freedom of employment, identity and culture, securing education, providing access to education, and also education as a possible site for conflict. That was the agenda, and with a few glitches, that was the Corrymeela agenda as well."

It was important to explore things. "Always talk about politics, always explore religion as an instrument of healing or as an instrument of revenge and retaliation. Always explore education, and its use for reconstructing a society, or reproducing old tribalisms. Explore identity, explore the world of work with trade unions, and the whole issue of poverty and justice. Roel gave us that in theological terms, and John Morrow, Ray Davey and Frank Wright gave us the political agenda."

This sounded grandly ambitious, but did Northern Ireland society remain in an impasse for far too long? Wilson says bluntly, "We are still at an impasse, but at least we are not shooting one another to the same extent. We are talking about difficult issues, including some of the issues we found how to talk about at Corrymeela. It has been an open place, so there were unexpected meetings and heavy discussions, and people making links across lines. We used to say that it was like a train station, except people also met as they passed each other."

It seemed as if the world and his wife, or partner, went through Corrymeela. Wilson says, "They met people like me and Duncan Morrow, and we would talk and argue. When I look around me now, and see the projects and the knowledge and the narrative of peace-building, I believe that the narrative that has relationship-making in it has lasted. Those who are different to us have to always be part of our consciousness in a society where the other, at best, has often been seen as the other who is out to 'threaten' me in Northern Ireland terms, or the other is the one out to kill me. As a world we need places that remind us of that 'otherness', that someone has to be included in my world and I have to take account of him or her all the time. That is a big statement."

Is it so big that part of the message of Corrymeela may have been, and still is, misunderstood? Wilson replies, "I think that Corrymeela hasn't often communicated what it really is about. It hasn't needed to be judged about being a 'success' or not. It was a voice about acknowledging others in a society that never did. This was a society where, if we had aligned ourselves with any of the Churches, they might have wanted to tell us even what to sell on our bookstall. We said, 'No thanks.' We needed our independence. Corrymeela probably needed the cover of being thought of as being people who walked about in open-toed sandals so that it could do lots of other things that it did.

"Throughout the days of the worst of the conflict, it was a group that came together, stayed together, worked together and took risks together in a society that was otherwise flying off in polar opposite positions. Perhaps not so much now, but at the time, that was a success in a society that did not want to meet. We had a place of meeting and our Community met together."

On those terms, and during those most difficult days in a society which was bitterly – and in many cases murderously – divided against itself, that was indeed a success worth remembering.

TEN

MORE TROUBLE

DURING THE YEARS of John Morrow's leadership at Corrymeela, the violence in Northern Ireland continued, as it has done for most of the Community's history. The statistics of such violence are a grim reminder of the backdrop against which Corrymeela had to operate, and which continually shaped attitudes to peacemaking and reconciliation.

In the period from 1980-1993, a total of 1,121 died in Northern Ireland, and there were more than 12,400 recorded injuries. There were over 3,200 explosions and more than 7,500 reported shootings. A total of over 3,200 firearms were recovered, as well as some 42,000 kg of explosives and 471,500 rounds of ammunition.[1]

These statistics, grim as they were, gave only part of the picture in those difficult days. Leading businessmen were kidnapped and murdered, including the Belfast antiques dealer Leonard Kaitcher who died on 8 February 1980, and the German industrialist Thomas Niedermayer whose body was found in West Belfast on 11 March. He had been kidnapped and had died some seven years previously. On the religious front, there was distrust and disillusion too. The Presbyterian Church in Ireland voted to leave the World Council of Churches because of its alleged support for terrorist groups. It was not an easy time for peacemakers anywhere.

The Troubles continued throughout 1981, and they set the tone for the rest of the decade. On 16 January the civil rights activist Bernadette McAliskey and her husband survived a murder attempt by gunmen at their home near Coalisland, and only five days later two leading Unionists – the elderly Sir Norman Stronge and his son James – were murdered by Republicans at their home in Tynan, which was also set on fire. There was continued political stalemate, sporadic rioting and general unrest.

One of the most serious and divisive issues of the entire Troubles took place in the early Eighties when Republican prisoners went on hunger-strike for the right to obtain 'political status'. This was a fierce battle of wills between the Republican movement and the British Government led by Margaret Thatcher, and the argument centred on the question as to whether or not paramilitaries convicted of serious crimes could enjoy a special status in gaol, or should be treated as 'ordinary' criminals.

The first hunger-strike began on 27 October 1980, when seven Republicans demanded the right to political status. This ended in confusion several weeks later when the Government made an offer of new conditions. However, on 25 January 1981, Bobby Sands, the 26-year-old leader of the Provisional IRA in the Maze Prison, claimed that moves towards a settlement had broken down. On 1 March the struggle entered its literally deadly phase when Sands embarked on his hunger-strike, to be followed progressively by others in a sustained campaign aiming for sustained world-wide publicity. A number of hunger-strikers dying over a planned period would keep the story in the headlines for a correspondingly longer period.

The hunger-strikes led to the deaths of ten men, including Sands, who was the first to pass away on 5 May 1981 after sixty-six days without food. By 20 August, the tenth Republican prisoner had fasted to death, but in mid-September the campaign had lost momentum, particularly after the relatives of four of the hunger-strikers intervened to ensure that they would be fed under proper supervision. Six others were made aware that their relatives would do likewise, and by early October the hunger-strike came to an end.

The Government announced shortly afterwards that prisoners would be allowed to wear their own clothing, and that fifty per cent of their lost remission would be restored. The reactions in a polarised community were predictable. Unionists protested at the "concessions" made by the British Government, and the cynicism in Loyalist circles was illustrated by the derision of their much-publicised graffiti, "We'll never forget you, Jimmy Sands". The Republicans, on the other hand, could claim the development of an historic new dimension in their struggle, and immense global publicity for their cause.

Not everyone, however, saw the issue in the same way as the Republicans. When Mother Teresa came to the Corrymeela Summerfest at the height of the campaign in 1981, a reporter looking for a particular angle to the story thrust a microphone in her face and asked what she thought of the hunger-strikers. After a short pause she remarked that in her country people died from hunger because of the lack of resources, but she found it difficult to understand why people would choose deliberately to starve themselves to death.

There is no doubt that the hunger-strikes further polarised an already divided community in Northern Ireland, and caused immense political and other problems between London, Dublin and Belfast. In May 1981, an estimated 70,000 people attended Bobby Sands' funeral, but the 25th anniversary commemorations in 2006 were comparatively low-key, and were hardly noticed outside Republican strongholds. In fact the main headlines were generated by the Republicans' holding their key anniversary event in Casement Park, Belfast despite the wishes of the controlling body of the Gaelic Athletic Association, who managed the grounds.

Despite the 25th anniversary commemorations, there was a continued division of opinion among those who felt that the hunger-strikes had not achieved any major political victory against the British, and particularly the redoubtable Mrs Thatcher, and those who still believed that the hunger-strikers had achieved much of the same Republican status as the original Irish Republican revolutionaries of 1916.

IN THE EARLY EIGHTIES, however, there was no opportunity for anyone to form an historical perspective and judgement on those difficult and dangerous days in the history of Northern Ireland. Certainly the Leader of Corrymeela, John Morrow, had no illusions about the difficulties posed by the Troubles in general and by the hunger strikes in particular, which he described later as "One of the tensest periods in the life of the Community."

Writing in his book *On the Road of Reconciliation*, which was published more than two years after the hunger-strikes had ended, he claimed that both the events themselves, and the way they were handled, led to wide differences of view within Corrymeela's membership.

He stated, "At the same time, there was the need to respond to families caught up in the tension, who needed to get away for periods of stress relief. We learnt a lot about the limits of rational debate in a situation where our gut reactions were very different – depending on our cultural and religious background. We had to learn, in sometimes painful ways, to hear each other without trying to convince each other that 'we were right'. We learnt that part of reconciliation involves living and accepting unresolved issues at times, as well as honesty and openness."[2]

Despite the tensions and challenges of particularly serious developments outside Corrymeela, such as the hunger-strikes, Morrow had to continue with the important daily work of the Community. He stated, "As Leader… my responsibility was not only to support and guide the work of our Centres, but also to guide the ordinary members in their own local situations or special callings. Over the years the Community was to become more and more diverse, changing from the very student-centred group of the 60s, to one that included people from every walk of life."

The work with families under stress had thrown Corrymeela into contact with people who were giving leadership at the heart of grass-roots communities. "Some of these, like Margaret and Gerry Mulvenna, had become full members. A number of couples from inter-church marriages had also found Corrymeela geared to their needs, as well as offering them a chance to share the richness of their experience of life."[3] Corrymeela also worked closely with those who had lost family members as a result of the violence. Morrow stated, "The tragedies of bereavement had linked us with many of those who had suffered deeply and those, like Maura and Edmund Kiely, who became full members, found support and opportunity to move beyond victimhood and to become key agents in the work of reconciliation through their outreach to others."[4]

Several years into John Morrow's period as Leader, he was joined as Centre Director by Michael Earle, who had succeeded Derick Wilson in 1985. Michael had originally come from London and had studied at Queen's University, where he was involved with the Church of Ireland Centre. During this period he also attended Corrymeela work camps in 1969, and also Corrymeet. He says, "I have memories of mixing with a lot of young people who had great energy and idealism. It was the start of my own ecumenical journey."[5]

At Corrymeela he met his future wife Anne, a Northern Ireland girl, and after their marriage they lived in New Zealand, where Michael worked with Presbyterian Social Services. "We both wanted to spend some time in a Christian community, and at the start of each year we used to ask ourselves, 'Where is it going to be?' The vision started clouding a bit, and then I heard that there was a vacancy for a Centre Director in Corrymeela."

At that stage they had been in New Zealand for ten years, but despite the vast distance from Ballycastle, Earle readily accepted an invitation to travel to Northern Ireland for an interview. He says, "I remember that it was an amazing experience, just coming to the Centre for a members' weekend, and being exposed to the Community and being part of the rhythm of their life. There was a lot of excitement involved, whether or not I was offered the job, and there was something inspiring about it."

He remembers going back to Christchurch and telling Anne, "I've seen a sort of a vision of the Church in the 21st century. What I saw from that weekend was a Christian Community which was bridging the divides not only in terms of Catholic-Protestant, but also working class-middle class, people in all sorts of work and career paths, with different political and cultural perspectives. I saw something that not only inspired me in terms of Christian community, but also something about reconciliation that was much broader than the Catholic-Protestant divide."

In the event, Michael was offered the job and the family had only a few weeks to pack up and travel to the other side of the world. It was no easy task. "We had three young children, aged seven, five and two, and for six weeks, all five of us were living in two rooms of the Corrymeela annexe, with all our hand-baggage from New Zealand. And it rained every single day! It was a huge transition not just personally but emotionally, culturally and in every single way. People used to ask us, 'Are you settled in yet?' but without any understanding of what we were actually going through."

The Earle family, and the Community itself, were on a steep learning curve. Michael says, "The bottom line was that I had been at Corrymeela as a student, but I had been out of the country for fifteen years, and a huge amount had happened during that time. I knew a few members of the Community, but most of it was an unknown.

"I didn't know the staff, or what programmes were being run, and I had no relationship with the user-groups coming in. So I was very much on the starting blocks. Somewhere, in there, was some thinking to do with the appointment of an outsider with fresh eyes, but I don't believe there was any real understanding of where we actually were at, and what we were expected to do."

The motives on both sides, however, were genuine in trying to further the aims of Corrymeela. Earle reflects, "Probably I was extraordinarily naive in accepting the job, but there was a strong sense of being guided, that this was the *right* job. On the way across on the plane from New Zealand for the selection weekend, I talked to the person next to me about what I was hoping to do. Within half an hour I noticed that he had turned over a page in a magazine he was reading, and there was a recent article on Corrymeela. To me it was one of those coincidences that affirmed you in saying, 'Let's give it a go!' From our point of view it certainly was a step of faith."

Neither Michael nor Anne had been involved in residential work before coming to Corrymeela. "It was again a huge transition just understanding what it was like to be available for virtually 24 hours a day, and for the first few years our energy was used up in just keeping things going, and keeping the Centre moving. There was a lot of 'winging it' but there was nothing like jumping in at the deep end, and understanding what it was. I sort of came in and found a sense of 'love and chaos', and I remember making comments about that at the time."

Earle felt that "there were a lot of areas of the administration which I could give some attention to, and I was very aware of the radical edge of some of the programmes, including the 'Seed Group' and Summerfest. There were also a lot of sharp encounters, and I remember a particular weekend with teenagers from Glasgow, the East End of London, and Derry. It was the group from Derry who bridged the differences between them."

He was also impressed by the volunteer selection process. "Whereas I would normally have selected the teams in terms of people being similar and having a lot in common, Corrymeela chose the model of Jesus' 'Upside Down Kingdom' and chose people who were extraordinarily diverse and different to each other. I was challenged by that, and struggled with it at times, but I also realised the benefits of being able to get such diversity."

Like others, Earle was aware of the relationship between the Centre that was owned by "a sort of invisible Community, and actually being run by staff and volunteers who were very visible, and the sense of tension about the use of the place. Another tension I sensed in those early days was a distance with the local Ballycastle community. There were various incidents, and at times a sense of 'us and them', and these were some of the things that I wanted to address."

When Michael Earle was leaving some five years later, however, he was invited to a reception by the local Council. "They were thanking Corrymeela for being part of their community, and I thought, 'Maybe I've had some small role in that', but it was part of a thirty year relationship. To be acknowledged by the local Council at a time when we had maybe 10,000 people coming through a year was a significant point in that relationship."

Earle was keen to encourage Community members to bring groups to the Centre. "I felt that this was one way in which we could support our members in the outreach to their own community. A classic example would be one member working in a primary school and another working in a school from a different tradition, and being able to spend time together in residence at Ballycastle. That was quite a conscious thing to further."

However, things did not always go smoothly. Earle says, "Certainly there were difficulties. I don't want to make excuses, but Corrymeela had unwritten rules and you had to understand what some of those were about. I'm sure that I learned from my mistakes, from that point of view." He gives, as one example, the process of imparting information to the Community. "I put it on a notice in the kitchen where I thought that everyone would come through and see it, but I discovered that the Corrymeela way of doing it was to get all the people together and to pass on the information face to face."

John Morrow, as Leader, was aware of the situation. He noted later, "Following Derick Wilson was not an easy path to walk in, and the contrast in style of leadership and management was a difficult adjustment for all concerned. It was another painful process of learning on the road of reconciliation that revealed to us all some of our deep-seated prejudices."[6]

Michael Earle comments, "After reading John Morrow's book about those times, there was obviously a reaction to me as being English with a public school background, but nobody talked to me openly about that at the time. So there were different levels of communication, and I found that hurtful. I think, however, that I was big enough to be able to say that I went through a huge learning curve myself."

It wasn't easy, however. "It was like being at the mountain top and in the valley on the same day, or even the same moment. But that was part of the reality of living in a Christian community of reconciliation, so there was all that stuff I was working through. It was a hard road, but looking back I have a sense that it is in the hardest periods that you learn far more about yourself and the Christian journey. It may have been a struggle at the time, but the person you don't get on with can in fact offer you the treasures that one of your best mates could never do."

Part of that is the whole question of vulnerability. "Rather than being defensive about that, I would still say that Corrymeela was the best time of my life, even though it was the hardest time of my career. It's about being vulnerable, and I don't think our male make-up is necessarily to go to the vulnerable place. But if you are willing to go to the vulnerable place, there's a huge amount to learn."

The centrality of The Croi at Ballycastle was important to Michael. "It was significant for me in terms of keeping my vision, keeping that sense of calling, and being there both on the mountain top and in the valley. I will never forget the story, which again challenged me, and the thinking that I got from Roel Kaptein. A volunteer was leading worship at Ballycastle one evening, and as we had invited different groups, there were some skin-heads and also elderly people present."

The skinheads seemed uncomfortable with the worship, and there was back-chat. Earle reflects, "In my heart I wanted those people to leave, but in my head I heard this message from Roel, 'If you scapegoat them and ask them to leave, the Christ will go with them.' So we got through that worship in spite of the tensions and everything else, and the Christ stayed with us, in the midst of it all. That was a huge learning for me."

A number of significant developments took place during Michael Earle's time as Centre Director. "I remember working with Louis Boyle in some of the political groups and discussions we were having with Sinn Fein and others, at the time of the Anglo-Irish Agreement. Because we were in Ballycastle we were obviously steps removed from what was happening politically in Belfast, but we had encounters at the Centre between politicians from the different parties, and we were encouraging dialogue and debate at that time. It was a very useful function, just getting people talking."

Earle tells the story of one dish-washing session at Ballycastle. "During one weekend lunchtime there were five of us washing the dishes, and having great 'craic'. I remembered afterwards that it was most unusual, because if you had put on labels, there was an Army chaplain, an IRA man and a UDA man who both had served time, a guy from the House of Lords and myself. Where on earth would you have found a group like that, washing the dishes together and getting beyond the labels? That to me was part of the vision."

Michael Earle also placed great emphasis on other kinds of inclusiveness. "I think that we were able to make space for some of the evangelicals to come into the Community. I remember that that was an issue with some of the staff. There was a sense that they were different, and I strongly wanted to make space for those differences. We had a few gay Christian groups as well, and I made space for a speaker from Republican Sinn Fein to come and speak to one of our groups. I may have been a bit naive and idealistic at the time, but when I look back, it was all part of the inclusiveness."

After his five years at Ballycastle, Michael Earle and his family returned to New Zealand, but they came back to Northern Ireland later, when Michael was appointed General-Secretary of the Irish Council of Churches, in succession to David Stevens, who became Leader of Corrymeela. In one sense, Michael could look at Corrymeela from afar, having been away and returned, while at the same time still being physically near in Belfast, though he was not a member of the Community.

In the summer of 2006, he took part in a weekend reunion of his first-year volunteers who had worked at Ballycastle from 1985-86. He recalls, "They couldn't believe that when they had met me first I was around 35 or 36 years of age, as they had seen me as being much older at that stage! We heard a lot of the stories and the laughs, as well as some of the painful stuff, but we found that the experience for that particular group had been life-changing and transforming in so many different ways. They also had experience of travelling, and their eyes had been opened in so many different ways."

Many in that group "were later in the people-caring business, whether as psychologists, social workers or whatever. One of the signs of hope for me is how many of the young people who had attended the work camps during my time at Ballycastle are now in key positions in Northern Ireland. That gives me huge hope and confidence in terms of policy-making."

He believes that Corrymeela's "original vision as a Christian community of reconciliation, a place of dialogue and of telling stories is there, no matter what. We are in a post-conflict society in Northern Ireland, but I have no problem with Corrymeela's role in remaining a place where people can talk. When you think of the changes in society and the hard-edged issues like policing, housing, education and racism, those are the issues which we as a community – let alone the Corrymeela Community – should be wrestling with. And the churches too, which is part of my responsibility. There is no shortage of hard issues dividing people that a Christian community of reconciliation could be, and is, a venue for addressing."

Earle believes that Ray Davey's original concept is still extremely important. He says, "Ray's vision for Corrymeela has to remain the foundation for its work, and if it compromises on that, we will miss a huge opportunity for the Churches. The Churches in Northern Ireland are still a major part of our community way of life. One of Corrymeela's roles is to be a question mark to the Churches, and maybe that is something which they can develop a bit more."

He also believes that Corrymeela is much more than the Ballycastle Centre. "I've always felt that Corrymeela is really expressed through its Community members, and I think that there should be much greater emphasis on supporting them where they are. From where I stood in New Zealand, it was amazing to see a place like Corrymeela active in a divided community, and I still think there a is a place for a Corrymeela in New Zealand, because we have differences just as crucial. There is a need for Corrymeela and its approach of bringing people together."

One of Michael Earle's abiding memories was of running a marathon in Belfast to help raise funds for Corrymeela. He says, "I will never forget the experience of preparing and training amidst all the heavy demands of those times, and then actually doing the running, and being amazed by the numbers of people along the route who recognised my Corrymeela vest. It was easy to forget that a lot of people had been through that Centre and had some relationship with it, and that it was such a precious gift."

ELEVEN

CHALLENGE AND CHALLENGE

THE NEW CENTRE DIRECTOR at Ballycastle was Colin Craig who had
a long experience of Corrymeela. He had applied for the post in
1985, when Michael Earle was appointed, so there was a reverse
continuity between the two appointments.

Craig said, "When the post re-emerged in 1990 I was encouraged
by Community members to apply, and I was pleased to be offered the
job, after we had gone through the appointments process. I simply
wanted to develop the work from its foundations and to keep a
'cutting-edge', whatever that would entail. However, I knew that
circumstances would determine that, to some degree."[1]

Colin adopted a hands-on approach. He said, "I wanted to keep it
financially viable, to keep the ship fuelled, and to find out where my
experience from my earlier work and career could be fed into the
process."

His first experience of Corrymeela was when he attended St
Augustine's School in Belfast in the early Seventies. "My headmaster
needed 'volunteers' for a community relations conference with
Strathearn School. He walked into our classroom and said, 'I want
four volunteers – you, you, you, and you', including my twin brother
Peter and me."

One of the speakers was Derick Wilson, who was then a young
schoolteacher in Belfast and was running community relations
projects. He impressed Colin as "the most inspiring guy at the

conference by far" and he readily accepted an invitation to visit Corrymeela at Ballycastle. "I was a Catholic and aged about 16 or 17, and I had the impression that Corrymeela was quite a Protestant place. Actually it was, in its own way, at that stage. I had this idea that somebody might ask me, 'Are you saved?' but I was immediately struck by the spirit of the place.

"There was something that I could not quite put my finger on logically, but I felt that I had found a home. It spoke to all parts of me. It didn't preach Christianity, but it actually *did* it, not in a pious way, but in an activist, radical sense. It walked the walk, and it was prepared to go where others were fearful to tread."

Craig went to a Corrymeela work camp in 1971, which was a year of particular upheaval in Northern Ireland, including the furore over internment without trial. He left school after passing his O-levels, and he took a job as a trainee manager with a manufacturing company in the troubled area of North Belfast. He spent many weekends and evenings at Corrymeela in a period of continued violence throughout the wider community, and although he was carving out a successful business career, he was attracted to the work of the Community.

He also went to college, and worked in a number of jobs, in Northern Ireland and elsewhere, and he developed skills in project and organisational management and consultancy. When he was appointed as Centre Director at Ballycastle he decided to try to apply the management skills he had acquired.

He recalls, "I had expected Corrymeela to be a bit more organised, and I was looking forward to help putting things on a more coherent management footing. Much of this was to do with administration. The programme team was working in what I called 'silos', and there was very little crossover. Schools did schools stuff, youth did youth work, and so on. I was interested in developing what I called 'joined-up' work."

Early on in Colin Craig's period as Centre Director, John Morrow indicated that, in his own words, "My energy was fading a bit, so I decided to take a Sabbatical break, but with the additional request that the Community begin the process of looking for a future leader. Colin brought some new energy to the task of Centre Director, and together with Rachel, his wife, they were soon taking hold of the direction and development of work at the Centre."[2]

John Morrow was given a Sabbatical break in 1992, which he and his wife Shirley spent in New Zealand and Australia, and shortly after his return, he retired from his role as Leader. He later took up the post of Northern Ireland lecturer and co-ordinator of the Irish School of Ecumenics.

John had made an enormous contribution to Corrymeela, not only as a founder-member but also as Leader. He had a different style to Ray Davey, but he had the capacity to retain and protect the vision of the early Community and to help it remain relevant to the turbulent times in which it found itself. On every level, Corrymeela owed him a massive debt.

John said later, "To be honest, only God and others can judge what I achieved. I survived for thirteen years as Leader, and for more than forty as a member of the Community. If I were to assess what I did in any detail, I would say that I was strong on vision and on building a Community, but probably weak on administration. In spite of all the difficulties, and all that I've had to face, it was a great privilege to be part of the Corrymeela venture. In my family life, the loss of my wife Shirley was a terrible blow because she meant so much to me. That's also a measure of the joy we had together. She was heart and soul in everything that we did, and her contribution was second to none."

As a Centre Director, Colin Craig was only able to work for a short period with John Morrow as Leader, but their relationship went back a long way. He recalls, "John was academic, and a theologian, and he conceptualised in a certain way. He framed the world in a particular format, and he was always thinking about the big picture. John and I were only really working up our partnership at Ballycastle when he began to think of moving. When he came back from his Sabbatical he had already decided that the move was going to take place."

As noted elsewhere, Morrow was succeeded by Trevor Williams. Colin Craig says, "I'd had a long-standing relationship with John but I didn't know Trevor all that well. He was a 'people person', and he was deeply concerned about the pastoral aspect of the Community. He had come out of the environment of a parish minister, and here was this organisation which was deeply involved in other 'big-thinking' stuff, so he needed to learn something about that as well."

Colin worked constructively with both men. "I had a huge regard and fondness for both of them. I would debate and argue my case, and they both respected me and gave me the space to say what I needed to say. If they said, 'No', for whatever reason, I felt that this was their decision and it was their right to make that call. So I always had a deep partnership with them."

Colin was always conscious also of the inspiration of Ray Davey. "He was the leader who stepped down. He was the guy who called the vision forward, and entrusted people to live with it. By doing that, he created a precedent which allowed Corrymeela to adjust itself. It wasn't constrained or locked in, and Ray would have been the first person to defend that passionately."

Even in his early 90s, Ray remained a radical. Craig observes, "His memory was not as great as it had been, but when he locked on to the fundamentals of Corrymeela, he could led an army over the hill. He still had the power to inspire people and to get them up and to go. I've seen him listen quietly for hours, and then say two sentences and convince everybody to go in a certain direction because he had given them permission to do so.

"Ray stood up at one very important meeting about rebuilding the old house at Corrymeela and he gave permission for people to let go of the old building and to find a way forward. He told them, 'It's only a building. This is not about bricks and mortar, it's about what we are doing.'"

Colin further recalls that "Ray was truly amazing. He was the guy who called me forward, and he helped me so much. In the early days when I had some ideas to develop youth programmes, Ray was the Leader and I would go to him in some trepidation, worrying that a project might not work. He would ask me, 'What's the worst thing can happen?' and I would say, 'It mightn't work, and we'll make mistakes.' He would reply, 'You learn from your mistakes, and that's the greatest experience you can get.' He gave us permission to make the mistakes, but also to acknowledge them, to learn from them, to translate that experience, and to move on."

During his first few years as Centre Director, Craig learned a great deal. "I found out where I was, what I was doing, and what the problems were. By 1994, however, we had the first ceasefires, and people – including journalists – were asking me, 'Will Corrymeela close now, as its job has been done?'" That, to me, was a completely ridiculous question, because it showed the naivety about what was going to be involved in the so-called 'Peace Process'.

"It wasn't like using an on/off switch, or saying, 'We are at war/now we are not at war.' There was always going to be the legacy of history: distrust, anger, hurt, victimhood, and all the complications of that nature. We were only at the ending of one thing, and the beginning of something else.

"As others have pointed out, the ceasefires – paradoxically – made things more difficult. Prior to that, people knew who the enemy was. Now they were going to have to find a new pattern, and that in itself was creating fear and anxiety. People began to have really hard conversations about how they invent a Northern Ireland that they could live in together."

Another major issue was funding. "This was also going to be harder, because what we had done was to tick the right box, and the money train kept moving. Corrymeela at that stage had become complacent, and it had developed its own eco-system. We had around forty to fifty staff, including volunteer staff, and we were by far the biggest core-funded group."

It was not easy, however, to make changes. "Corrymeela had to be reshaped to move into the new world we were encountering. First of all we had to deal with the legacy of the conflict, in the sense that we may not be killing as many people as before, but we were going to have to make a huge journey out of that. That's self-evidently true, even today."

There was yet another dimension which Ray Davey had outlined long ago. "Corrymeela was called forth in the aftermath of the Second World War, and its vision was never just about Northern Ireland. I was very impressed by that. We also had learned a methodology and a way of working which had huge validity, exceptionally and practically throughout Corrymeela's history."

Lessons were learned the hard way. "We learned by screwing it up, by getting it wrong, by telling ourselves, 'Oh, the problem is that people are prejudiced because they don't meet each other and they live in different worlds. Let's get them together and they'll discover each other. Happy days, they'll all go back and re-invent the world they are in!' That was nonsense. Of course you had to engage with each other, but that was just the start. It certainly wasn't the end point. We at Corrymeela had become brilliant in creating the contacts, but who was going to do the follow-up?"

Was Corrymeela ever in danger of speaking mostly to itself? "There were edges of that, but I don't think that it ever went all the way. The trouble was that Corrymeela got complacent because they knew that they did very good work and some people believed that the money would continue to flow in. It is important to stress, however, that at the core of the Community were people like Derick Wilson and John Morrow and others who were deeply in tune with what was happening on the ground, and they were speaking coherently about it. In fact there were lots of people inside the Community who knew better than that, because they were leading in lots of other places."

The "Peace Process", including the ceasefires, had created new funding sources. Colin Craig believes that Corrymeela moved forward by confronting the realities. "We were able to generate real opportunities by emphasising that we were going to do a specific piece of work over a specific period of time to achieve certain key objectives. That was a new way of generating time-limited and high-impact work."

This included interface work and the training of young adults in a number of different ways. Corrymeela already had a Family and Community programme, which was mostly about respite work with families coming to the Ballycastle Centre. Craig says, "My colleague, Mary Montague, who was then the Family and Community Worker, had developed important conduits across the paramilitary organisations in the interface areas. My problem as Director was the fact that, strictly speaking, this was not the work of her post, which was to bring families away from the troubled areas to get some respite. However, she was doing critical and really hard-edged work on the ground, which was high-risk as well. In discussion with Mary, I was able to translate that into a project supported by the International Fund for Ireland, and I got Mary working full-time on that. This made a major contribution, and it helped to bring Corrymeela outside the Centre in Ballycastle."

Another success was the development of the QUEST programme. Colin Craig says, "It was self-evident to me that Corrymeela needed to re-engage young adults actively in the same way that I had been engaged, and I felt that we were no longer doing that. It wasn't just a matter of asking people to come to Ballycastle and to wash dishes together. I wanted them trained and engaged in the projects alongside the programme staff. I wanted them to gain direct line experience, and we developed the idea of inviting young adults back again."

The programme was meant to have an edge. "In a way it was really what Ray Davey used to do – to invite people into service, then into leadership, and the idea was that as they engaged in leadership training they would start their own programmes. In theory that would start the engine again, and some of those people would spin off into the community. I think it worked, and over a three-year period we had more than a dozen young people involved."

Colin believes that Corrymeela hit a "purple patch" between 1996 and 1999. However, times were changing, and it was a question of adapting sufficiently to meet the challenges of the future. He says bluntly, "My single biggest failure was that I was unable to get the message across because they blocked the messenger."

He suggested that Corrymeela should set up an organisation called TIDES, with the purpose of training the trainers. "To be candid,

TIDES is probably the most spectacular concept on which I failed with them. I was clear that a huge niche existed in the community relations market for using the knowledge we had gained and translating that into programmes for people delivering the work. Corrymeela recognised that this was an interesting idea and was supportive that I should set it up, but not inside Corrymeela. They just didn't get it."

Craig eventually left the post of Centre Director, partly because his contract was expiring after three extensions – which had not happened before – and he established TIDES outside the Community. He says, "There was a certain irony involved. I think that TIDES could have been a real income-earner for Corrymeela, but they did not take it on. A short time later, a prominent member of the finance department said that if Corrymeela was really a business venture, he would buy us out and take over TIDES. In other words he was saying, 'I would like to bring you in again!'"

However, Colin Craig believes that if TIDES had been accepted as a project within Corrymeela, it might not have been able to develop in the same way. He says, "Because we were small we were able to move fast and to retain a hard cutting-edge. I don't think Corrymeela can do this, as it struggles with trying to take the staff and 200-plus Community members with it, in making operational decisions – though I do think it has come long way in that respect."

He says that when he arrived as Centre Director in 1990, "I could not buy a washing machine for the laundry without getting permission from Council to buy it. By the time I had left we had budgets, and a lot more organisation was there. Nowadays the audit controls for funding are such that you virtually have to count the paperclips. Money comes with the high price-tag of accountability, openness, goals, aims, strategic plans, operational plans and all kinds of things."

Yet within the constraints of such increasing bureaucracy, hard decisions had to be made. Craig says, "Some people thought that the accounts were fine, but I said, 'It's not now that you should be looking at! Here's where this ship is sailing, and those are the waters it is sailing into.' They just either didn't believe me, or didn't get it. I told them, 'You are not going into a crisis, you are now *in* one!' That was certainly true by the late Nineties."

Apart from project funding and tailoring its product to fit into the prevailing community relations market, Corrymeela also had to find money for significant rebuilding and refurbishment during those years. Colin Craig recalls, "That took a huge amount of time and energy. We renovated the Village, we rebuilt the House and also the Cottages. We delivered all of that during this period, and raised over £2.5 million. That didn't happen easily!"

This was an understatement but, fortunately, this essential work was completed, and there was the added bonus of a "surprise" visit from Prince Charles for the opening ceremony of the new House on 2 June 1998. This was performed, appropriately, by Ray Davey himself, with the ever-present support from Kathleen.

Nevertheless, the underlying and inevitable tension remained between the concept of Corrymeela as a business and also as a Christian community. Craig says, "I think there was a sense of fear among some people that professionalism was taking over and that the staff were becoming more powerful than the Community. I remember one member at a Council meeting who burst into tears when we were discussing the funding to rebuild the main house. She was a victim of the Troubles and was rearing her family as a single parent, and the idea of raising £1.5 million to rebuild the main house was just so much beyond her experience that she burst into tears. I understood why that happened."

Given the financial pressures of recent years, does Corrymeela need to re-invent itself? Craig says, "It may have to do this if it doesn't deal properly with structural questions, and this is because of the way money is assessed these days. People will not continue giving resources to do what seem to be the same old things, even if they are still the right things to do. Funders do not think in that way, and Corrymeela has to work on that."

Colin Craig believes that Corrymeela will also continue to rely strongly on its volunteer supporters. "It developed a large professional base, but I am sure that it will go back to its volunteer roots, because that speaks directly to people, and that's how it will survive. Its spirit will always come through. Young adults and others will find a space which will speak about healing the divisions, and the hurt and the anger which we all feel in our lives.

"It may not be about sectarianism in the future, and the environment may be a major factor. The world is becoming an increasingly unsafe place at a lot of levels. Corrymeela knows about safe spaces, and about holding that space for people to engage in and to imagine different possibilities. Why is that the case? It's not because we have all been brilliant managers or because of what we do well or not so well. Corrymeela works despite the screw-ups that a lot of us have been involved in. Let's say that this is due to the Spirit, which is still very strong at work in Corrymeela."

Despite the setbacks, the Community has never appeared to be in danger of losing its Christian vision and commitment. Colin Craig says, "Even though I have been trying to analyse and to provide a critique of the Community, there is always a mystery to Corrymeela which you can describe as magical or spiritual. When you stay on that site at Ballycastle, something happens, and people engage with one another in a new way. There is still a sense of mystery and of possibility that was there when I first went to Corrymeela in 1970.

"We've changed the buildings, we've changed the staff, we've developed professional programmes, we've done this and that, but there is still something deeply 'right' about that place. If I knew how to bottle it, I would do that, and sell it! I've seen people, thousands of times, turn round to me and literally they get a shiver, and they say, 'There is something very real about this place.' It could be a woman from the Shankill Road, or somebody from a different part of the world, or a child. It touches something about the prayer, the stories that have been shared, the tears, the laughter, the madness, whatever has soaked into the fabric of the place."

Many leading figures at Corrymeela have pointed out that, although many members belong to one or other of the Christian denominations, it is not in itself a "Church". Colin Craig, like others, was aware of the challenges. "We were living in a society that was secularising fast and we were in a Christian Community that, for example, worshipped twice daily in The Croi. Those of us who grew up in the earlier period were comfortable with the language of worship, but I was increasingly aware of young volunteers who wanted to be engaged with Corrymeela, but they had not come out of a Church environment."

The vision of Corrymeela was still very alive, but there was a need to think about the language of worship. "If you go to worship and people talk about 'God of all the Heavens, Saviour of all, blood of Christ' – this is not language which sits easily with those who have not gone to church. People might be asking themselves, 'What am I required to buy in to here?'"

Perhaps the Christian Churches will need to invent themselves to meet new challenges, as the major institutional structures crumble. Craig says, "The spirit is deep inside Corrymeela, the Holy Spirit if you like. I think that Corrymeela tried with the Churches but the Community became marginalised as 'the folks on the hill' or 'the Alliance Party at prayer'. I think, however, that the Churches will come looking at those places like Corrymeela which have held on to something and which still speak to the young. I don't mean that in a fundamentalist sense. If you give black and white answers to people in a time of chaos it is great, but the world isn't like that. I think that the sustaining peace of Christianity is that it can reflect upon the world in which it finds itself, and Corrymeela does that."

There is also the important question of inter-faith relationships. "When I was the Centre Director at Corrymeela we were saying, 'How do we work with these people, how do we speak together?' So we had to deal with inter-faith matters. We asked ourselves, 'Can we offer a space in a Christian Centre for, say, Muslims to pray?' We did that, but for some in the Community it was a troubling issue because we may have been seen to be supporting Islam. But that was the way ahead for us."

Colin Craig, who was a member of the Corrymeela Council until late in 2006, believes that there are new "fault lines" emerging in society. "This is due to the rapid change that is occurring in Northern Ireland and elsewhere, through migrant labour and the sheer diversity that is emerging. Corrymeela is beginning to put its head up and to look at these issues, and I am concerned that we are going to see conflict occurring at a variety of levels. This will not be the old Protestant-Catholic stuff, though sectarianism is still the big elephant in the room. However there is also a baby elephant in the room, which will be about racism and inter-ethnic activities. If we get a downturn in the economy, watch the heat go up. We are facing real problems, but I think that Corrymeela will be up to handling them."

Corrymeela, however, needs to restructure. "That is painful, and will continue to be painful, and the Community is by no means out of the woods yet. We need to create a balance between the money we can generate and what we are going to spend, and right now – in 2006 – we are in a declining income situation, which will compel us to look at re-structuring."

Colin believes that Corrymeela was "hi-jacked" by the Troubles. "In 1965 they weren't planning for this, like having three residential units with 120 beds. Why do we need so many beds? Running a residential centre is a high-cost business, and if there are few people staying at Ballycastle it costs a fortune, because you need to keep the infrastructure for when everybody is there – the kitchens, administration, housekeeping and maintenance. There is a danger that you end up by being driven by the buildings, and not by what you do."

Colin Craig favours a scaling-down. "We should strip back to the minimum required, so that we run only two units, and let the need for buildings to re-emerge according to use. We should also increase our numbers of volunteers, and not just the 18-25 year-olds, but all the people into early retirement with all that wisdom and energy available. In short, we need to advance voluntarism, to reduce staffing and to start applying ourselves to a post-sectarian world where we are not just driven by a concept of the history of our troubles, but that we remain relevant to the pain and the fault lines that are coming, all over the world."

The original building (c. 1950s) on the Corrymeela site

Corrymeela chalets

A Corrymeela work team in June 19

Summerfest, c. 1981

Archbishop Desmond Tutu at a Peace Conference in Queen's University, Belfast

Mother Teresa visits Corrymeela's Summerfest in July 1981
*The Reverend Dr Ray Davey, Kathleen Davey and the Dalai Lama
in the Croí, 2005*

George Mitchell, the former United States Senator, visits Corrymeela

Reverend Dr Ray Davey receives an Honorary Degree at the Pontifical University, St Patrick's College, Maynooth in 2002

Author Alf McCreary and Ray Davey, July 2006

The Reverend Harold Good, former Centre Director, at Ballycastle

Current Corrymeela Leader, Dr David Stevens

Canon Trevor Williams, Corrymeela Leader 1993-2004

Ray and Kathleen Davey take in the scenic view of Corrymeela

Whatever the future holds, Colin Craig is certain that one of the Community's major virtues will remain. "It is able to enter into the pain of the world without being frightened of that pain, or falling into the temptation of going for easy answers. Spiritually it is still the beacon in the hill, which inspires so many people, but Corrymeela does not get pious about itself. If you cut me in half, you are going to find Corrymeela written through me, just like a stick of rock. Corrymeela has woven me, framed me and shaped me. You just can't take it out of me."

TWELVE

RELATIVE VALUES

TREVOR WILLIAMS HAD A CONNECTION with Corrymeela long before he became Leader in 1993. He had grown up in Dublin, and had trained for the Anglican ministry at St John's College in Nottingham. He recalls, "I never had any wish to go to Northern Ireland, but I was given an offer which I felt that I couldn't refuse. I accepted a post as assistant Church of Ireland chaplain at Queen's University, instead of continuing with what I regarded as another boring curacy in another parish in England."

During William's time at Queen's, the Presbyterian chaplain was John Morrow, and they both were part of an inter-chaplaincy group, which led to his involvement with Corrymeela. "I felt that this was a hugely important and necessary complement to church life in Northern Ireland, and I quickly became a member."

Later in his career, Williams became well known as the presenter of *Sunday Sequence*, BBC Northern Ireland's flagship programme on religion and ethics. He says, "I was there for some eight years, dealing with religion and other current affairs issues. It was all about the problems which we have with one another, and the greater the violence, the bigger the story. I was still a member of Corrymeela at this time, and it was an important antidote to the hype of media 'fame'. It kept my feet on the ground, in terms of 'What are we going to do about this stuff?', rather than just reporting the bad news."

He had a possibility of staying with the BBC, but after eight years, he felt it was time to move on. "When I left, I realised not that I was near burn-out, but that the regular broadcasting had taken its toll."

His next move was to a Church of Ireland parish at Newcastle in County Down. He recalls, "That was a good experience, and I kept involved with Corrymeela, although it was difficult being a minister, with the time constraints."

After five years at Newcastle he was approached by Corrymeela to see if he would allow his name to go forward as a candidate for the post of Leader. After the due appointment process, he was offered the job, and his first reaction was one of delight. He says, "I felt that Corrymeela was trying to address the issues that other people were skirting around. I liked the way that Corrymeela was trying to face the realities."[1]

Williams believes that when people fall out, many of them "scurry into different corners. From my own experience, when I fall out with someone, the last thing I want to do is to see them. In Northern Ireland it seems that every time there is a difficulty, people don't meet to try to resolve it. They start shouting at each other from a great height."

Some of the weaknesses of Corrymeela, he believes, are also its strengths. "It seeks to do things in a very human way, in a frail way. Corrymeela tries to offer each individual certain opportunities and choices, but it also realises that if there is to be real growth and progress, the people involved have to make the choices themselves. Corrymeela could never pre-determine the outcome. You tried to provide a fertile soil for growth, but you knew that you could never force-feed the seed."

One of the realities has been that Corrymeela has always worked with a relatively small community, in a relatively small part of the world. Williams says, "We don't have a grand vision that we are saviours of the world. It is not about that. It's about living in a way that represents the freedom of the Gospel, and part of that is sharing with other people."

Williams quickly learned that the job as Leader "was totally impossible". He recalls, "You had a dispersed community of, say, 150 to 200 people, many of whom met in cell groups. How could you keep in touch and make them feel part of the whole? How could you successfully engage all their talents, aspirations and activities?"

There were also some thirty staff, and an annual budget, in those days, of more than one million pounds. There was also the added dimension of an organisational structure that intentionally involved people in decision making. "That's partly what I mean when I say that some of the strengths of Corrymeela are also its weaknesses. In terms of achieving goals, it would be easier to do that in the managerial, focused way of industry which is concerned with the bottom line and profit margins – and everything is sacrificed to that. If you are involved in a Community like Corrymeela and doing it together, it's a totally different way of working."

In other words, people cannot be pushed. "You may try, but people can also say, 'No thanks', maybe because they do not have the energy and the commitment that you said were the priorities. The point is that the Leader of Corrymeela is not 'the Boss'. It's more like being a facilitator. Since I left the Leadership I tell people that I have been 'promoted' to being a member, because as Leader you are really the servant of the Community."

The expectation of leadership, he feels, is much clearer in a church parish. "In a parish, the people expect you to be on the pedestal of decision-making. I don't like that approach, because I think it tends to let some people off the hook, and Corrymeela in a sense is quite the reverse of that."

During Trevor William's time as Leader, there was still a disturbing level of violence, and on 23 October 1993, a particularly horrific incident took place on the Shankill Road in Belfast when a Provisional IRA bomb tore apart a fishmonger's shop on a busy Saturday afternoon. Nine (and eventually ten) people were killed, and 58 others were injured. One of the bombers died, and another was also injured.

The pattern of violence had continued throughout that year, with the Provisional IRA exploding large bombs in London and Oxford, and at various centres in Northern Ireland, including Bangor, Newtownards, Portadown and Magherafelt, and also near the Unionist Party's headquarters in Belfast, where a 1,000lb bomb extensively damaged the area around Glengall Street. The Loyalist paramilitaries also persisted with their deadly campaign. During the same period, the UDA planted incendiary devices outside the homes of two SDLP councillors, and the UFF killed four Catholic workmen at Castlerock, while the UVF threatened to kill politicians in the Irish Republic if Republican violence increased.[2]

However, while individual acts of horrific violence made all too many headlines, there was stuttering political progress. Cardinal Cahal Daly, the then Catholic Primate who kept a close touch with all developments, predicted as early as January of 1993 that there could be peace "by the end of the year". Behind the scenes, important cross-border initiatives were taking place, and these culminated in the Downing Street Declaration of 15 December 1993.

Many people on all sides were closely involved with the evolution of this historic agreement, and not least the British Prime Minister John Major and Taioseach Albert Reynolds, whose close friendship and constructive (if at times blunt) working relationship, ensured that the best intentions of the bridge-builders survived all the tortuous machinations of politics to emerge as the Downing Street Declaration.

In effect it guaranteed to Nationalists that their aspirations and traditions would be respected, while it tried to re-assure Unionists that they would not be rail-roaded into a United Ireland. It also assured paramilitaries on both sides that they could enter the political process if they fully embraced, and acted upon, the concept of non-violence.

Archbishop Robin Eames, who had played an important role as one of the "honest brokers" behind the scenes, said later, "The Downing Street Declaration was an historic document whose time had come, and was seen as part of a greater and a developing understanding between the two sovereign governments. I had lived through years of megaphone diplomacy across the Irish Sea, and I had witnessed at a high level the events which were bringing the two governments together. Without the Downing Street Declaration, there could have been no Good Friday Agreement."[3] Equally,

without the political agreements, there could have been no
paramilitary ceasefires, however imperfect they turned out to be,
especially in the early stages.

Paradoxically, the gradual emergence of the ill-tempered but
gradually improving "peace process" proved difficult for Corrymeela.
Trevor Williams says, "While the violence had been the main factor,
as in the past, everyone knew where they were in relation to that.
Corrymeela also knew where it was, and what it had to do. It was
really quite a shock for us to realise how much we had been
dominated by violence, as people committed to reconciliation."

Williams recalls one joint meeting which took place shortly after
the Provisional IRA ceasefire had been declared on 31 August 1994.
He says, "The Catholics in the group were euphoric, but the
Protestants seemed depressed. We asked ourselves, 'What's this all
about?' There was a clear sense that the ceasefires and what lay ahead
was redefining who we really were, but this was not articulated. A
whole new order was going to emerge about who were the 'good'
guys and the 'bad' guys."

This was an emotional, rather than a rational, process. "I think
that the Protestants seemed 'depressed ' because the 'bad guys', in
their case the Provisional IRA, had gained the high moral ground in
that they had declared a ceasefire. The Catholics were elated because
in a sense the Provisionals had done the 'right' thing and had shown
up the others.

"At Corrymeela we had talked a great deal about not defining
ourselves against our enemy, and yet when the ceasefires happened,
we felt it emotionally ourselves. We realised that we were as much
caught up in the mess of Northern Ireland as everybody else. We
began to learn the hard way that the whole process of emerging out
of violence was going to be another large and important part of our
agenda."[4]

From the onset of the important new developments in the peace
process, Corrymeela entered a period of reflection and discussion,
and asked itself whether the Community needed to deconstruct its
existing programmes and do something different. Williams says, "We

realised very quickly that what we were doing was precisely what was necessary in an emerging peace. Looking back, that could sound like an easy way out for Corrymeela, but it was not an 'unthought out' position, and we did consider it quite carefully."

In fact, the Community had already been looking hard at some of its existing programmes. Williams recalls, "We already had a well established list of projects at Corrymeela, and one of the difficulties was the very success of our programmes. We established successful streams with schools, families and all the rest, and because of their effectiveness they 'became' the work. While there was still imagination and initiative within those schemes, it all became a bit too solidified, and other initiatives were proving to be slow."

There was also the important factor of Corrymeela's size. "We always had a fear of expanding too much, and we never wanted to build an empire. We also realised that the larger we were, the bigger the need for infrastructure, and the more bureaucratic you became, and in the end you also became an institution. Corrymeela does not work that way. In one sense its size means that it should be an institution, and its inspiration means that it should be a Community. There is always a tension between the two."

Williams believes that one of his greatest challenges as Leader was finance. "In fact, it became the greatest worry of my ten years of tenure, to the point of being overwhelming. I would put it as strongly as that, and I don't think that Corrymeela is out of it yet. During my time as Leader we found that, for a number of reasons, a major restructuring was needed in our finances. We were hugely stretched just to keep going, and at the same time the demands suddenly increased about our accountability in financial matters."

Trevor Williams recalls the early days of his Leadership when it was all so different. "I remember our then financial director Angus Macpherson coming in to me waving a big cheque and saying, 'I've just received this from a charity which has heard of our work and they have asked us to report back to them in a year's time as to how we spent the money!'"

However, in a very short time, a whole new system of accounting had to be set up. "This was about outputs and systems, of breakdowns of bed nights, food and so on. So we had this huge task just to keep everything running at the same time, and to do an amazing amount of extra administrative work as well."

Williams says, "Our expenditure increased, but so did our grants – partly because of the 'peace money' that was coming in. Our problem was that we did not have in place the financial systems to track our money, and that brought us into a huge sort of crisis. By the end of my time as Leader, however, we were addressing that problem, but if I had known in advance that finance was going to be a major part of my role as Leader, I wouldn't have taken the job in the first place, because finance is not my strength.

"I never wanted to be a businessman or a financial wizard. I believe that I had been elected as Leader because they recognised me as a member of the Community, and as a person who could work with people. So as Leader I was extremely worried about the financial situation because it was a serious time, and I knew that I was having to deal with areas that were a weakness in terms of my interests and my abilities rather than playing to my strengths."

Williams, on reflection, believes that he should have left after seven years, when his contract was about to end. "People asked me to stay because we were going through this crisis, but I regret that I did not bite the bullet and say, 'No.' It was a critical time then, but it was actually easier to leave three years later, after a decade doing the job."

As Leader, Trevor Williams would have liked to have spent more time directly in programme work, rather than in administration. "I found constantly that I wanted to be involved in programming, but rarely in any day was there five minutes when I could do that."

Despite his misgivings, Williams sells himself somewhat short. During his Leadership there were important developments in programming and other matters, and he is right to conclude that he presided over a period of radical change. There were important initiatives in interface areas and in spreading the knowledge and expertise that Corrymeela had developed. There was also continued international and local recognition. In 1997, for example, the

Community was awarded the prestigious (and financially valuable) Peace Prize of £100,000 by the Japanese Niwano Peace Foundation.[5]

Williams says "In those difficult times we held together what Corrymeela was about, namely that Northern Ireland's 'intractable' problems are actually very simple, but they are the 'simple' things that people refuse to do – namely to find a safe place where they can talk openly and honestly about their differences. That is what we refuse to do in Northern Ireland, and we hear about it on the news every day."

Corrymeela's relationship with the Churches was always important, though not easy to describe. "Churches acknowledge that they wish to influence and to serve society and the Gospel, but institutionally they are designed to preserve their own. I say that as a member of the Church of Ireland. That's what institutions do, that's what they are for – survival. It is difficult to have a partnership with the Churches because they essentially don't want to have partners. They want to control, and Corrymeela is the reverse of that. Our aspiration is to form networks of partnerships, rather than to control empires."

Williams feels that "a lot of people hang on to the Churches because they are still members of Corrymeela. I think that the Churches themselves would be missing some of their more uncomfortable members if Corrymeela wasn't around. Unfortunately there is always a tension that Corrymeela becomes a substitute church, and we want to avoid that."

One of the "miracles" of his time as Leader was the continued relationship with his two distinguished predecessors, Ray Davey and John Morrow. Williams says, "I can't think of any other job where it would be a joy and a privilege to have your predecessors working with you. I never felt threatened, and if Ray or John made a suggestion I knew it was coming from a position of respect for me, and for what I was carrying as Leader. They were totally supportive and helpful, but that does not mean that things weren't said when they needed to be said, but it was never a threat. I seriously welcomed every suggestion. I am sure, however, that they must have restrained themselves a lot!"

Both former Leaders helped him in their different ways. "Ray was an amazingly courageous person. He would give huge responsibility to inexperienced young people, which others might think was being reckless, but he did it. That is one of the inspirations Corrymeela still leans on. Ray demonstrated that within every person there is locked-up potential, and all that has to be done is to let it go, and be developed. Sometimes it has blown up in our faces, and some of the people we've accepted as volunteers have caused mayhem. But in the end they have grown tremendously. It is important to be willing to take risks, and also to live with the consequences of that."

John Morrow, for Williams, was like a "steady rock during a turbulent period. He had a wonderful mind and he was politically astute, and he was also a theologian of some depth. The combination of all that was an inspiration to me." Both Ray and John could be tough when required, but Williams saw himself as slightly different in approach. "I'm more of a softie, but what I am attracted to and hold onto tenaciously is unquenchable hope. That's what makes me dogged, if you like."

Some people might find that also bit naive. "I'm sure I do sound naive, except that when I share with other people the stories that touch me deeply, they are moved too. It is about our vulnerability as human beings and how, at the point of vulnerability, the greatest connections can be made. The very thing that we hide from each other is the thing that has the most hope. That is, in effect, turning the world upside down, and to live with that kind of approach requires a toughness of a different kind."

Williams tells the story of a Corrymeela volunteer who led a small group of Catholics and Protestants at Ballycastle. "They were asked to share their experiences of the Troubles and they told their stories of bereavement and of grief. In the end they fell into each other's arms and wept. Something was happening there, which was just amazing, and wasn't happening on our streets. That story still inspires me, because it shows that there is another way, that it is a human way, and it is about facing our realities and the underbelly of our vulnerability. That stories tells us that it is alright to be weak – in fact when you are weak with one another, all sorts of strengths can grow from this."

In his final Leader's Report on 2 April 2003, Trevor Williams outlined the main themes of his term of office. He stated, "This has been by far the best job I have ever had. It has allowed me to discover and to pay attention to what I have come to learn are the most fundamental truths about life. Our life is a search for community. Relationships are what matter most, not only those between like-minded people, but also the relationships with those who are different. Meeting these differences in trust helps to open us up, to grow, to move on, and it also enables us to create for others much more than we could do on our own."

Corrymeela, he claimed, had learned from the beginning that it was important to hold together the questions of Faith and Life. "We must not settle for a fuzzy faith that produces warm feelings, but refuses to embrace the hard realities of life. So, with faith comes doubt, exploration and movement, living in a dialogue between the realities of our life and the Judeo-Christian story. We also seek to live by the truth that when we accept one another as we are, when we release one another from the fear of being judged or cast out, we are providing the space for growth and change."

Despite the achievements, there were also problems – some of which Williams summarised later, in November 2005.[5] He noted that during his time as Leader "there was little time to dream dreams, when experiencing the nightmare of financial crisis. The restructuring of the Community which has followed will be healthy, but it has had a cost."

He added, "The organisation and management of the Centre has become more and more demanding. The commitment of members as lived out in their home, at work and in church settings has not received the focus and attention it should have done. As a result, the potential of Corrymeela has been curtailed."

The employment of professional staff working to high standards has meant that some members feel that they have little to contribute to the Centre. Williams says, "The members programme, where the values of Corrymeela are worked out in the life, work and church context through discussion, reflection, study and sharing, remains largely underdeveloped. Maybe we are not the kind of people who do that. Corrymeela membership is a 'voluntary' activity, and time for volunteering is becoming increasingly scarce in the frenetic lifestyles which most of us follow."

Despite all of this, Williams still feels hopeful about the future of Corrymeela. "I'm hopeful in the sense that Corrymeela is essentially about people who are on a journey together, and if the whole institution collapsed, we could create something else. For me, Corrymeela is still the centre of who I am. It is still what gives me meaning in terms of what I do, and what I believe. Corrymeela is a sense of how to be a church in a different way, and what the Gospel means. That is the core of my identity and my commitment, and Corrymeela shows me more clearly than anything else what that is actually about."

Corrymeela, he believes, cannot measure "success" in traditional terms. Williams says, "We have been written off by lots of people all the time. They say, 'Here you are, committed to reconciliation, but there's still no peace, so you've failed. Why do you continue?' That is nothing to do with Corrymeela. We are not something that is there to stop conflict. That is undeliverable, and we are not about that. We are about finding a way to live together with difference."

Is it worthwhile, therefore, that Corrymeela even exists? Williams says, "Of course it is, because what alternative is there to conflict? Corrymeela is making a valuable contribution, but don't hang round our neck the task of bringing peace to Northern Ireland. We are just a small candle, but is it worth having even a candle? In the context of the darkness, it certainly is."

THIRTEEN

SUMMERFEST
– AND GOING DUTCH

WHEN CORRYMEELA WAS ESTABLISHED in 1965, it was meant to become much more than a Christian reconciliation centre based in Northern Ireland. This was clear from the challenge issued by Pastor Tullio Vinay at the official opening ceremony when he said that Corrymeela had to be "a question mark to the Church everywhere in Europe so that it may review its structures and task and may be free from this instinct of preservation to hear the time of God for its mission in the world."

One of the tragedies of the violence in Northern Ireland was the way in which it virtually overwhelmed local society, including Corrymeela, in the early stages, but even in the worst of times the vision of the Community, and the international aspect of its work and outreach, was never lost.

Over many years, Corrymeela continued to attract volunteers and visitors from all parts of the world. They learned much from the Community and they also gave much to Corrymeela in return, as will be outlined later. Despite the constant demands arising from the violence and disruption within Northern Ireland, the Community and its members remained open to new ideas.

One of the most exciting and challenging developments arose following a visit by Ray Davey to the German Kirchentag. This is a major event which is held every two years by the German Protestant Churches and which inspires tens of thousands of young people from all over Germany, as well as other parts of the world. The idea was to stage the Kirchentag in a major German city, and to create a focus "for an interface between faith and current affairs, between the church as an institution and emerging models of Christian service and witness, and as a place of celebration."[1]

Davey was so impressed by the Kirchentag that, on his return, he asked John Morrow and a few others, "Why can't we do something like this in Northern Ireland?" Doug Baker, a young American Presbyterian who had come to Northern Ireland as a volunteer in 1970, was to play a major role within the Community, not least as the main organiser of what came to be known as the Corrymeela "Summerfest" events at Ballycastle.

Baker was part of a US Summer Mission Service project team which had been arranged in conjunction with the Presbyterian Church in Ireland. On arrival, three of his companions were despatched to Corrymeela at Ballycastle, and he was assigned to Belfast for a week to help with preparations for an international work camp later on. He stayed at the Presbyterian Centre at Queen's University, where he met Ray and Kathleen Davey, and several other members of the Corrymeela Community.

A few weeks later, Baker found himself as part of the international work camp in Belfast, which was led by Peter Moss and supported by Diana Carson, who were both Corrymeela members. It was only towards the end of that summer that he actually went up to Ballycastle to help with running a Family Week for young people from several children's homes.

His early experience in Northern Ireland provided him with valuable insights. He recalls, "Unlike many others, my encounter with Corrymeela began with the dispersed Community, and only then proceeded to the Centre. As a result, I have always understood Corrymeela first and foremost as a community of individuals with a shared vision and commitment, and the Centre as a resource for the wider work of the Community. Years later, when I joined the staff of the Centre in Ballycastle, I became very conscious of the temptation of reversing this, and seeing the Community as a support structure for the running of the Centre."

Such early insights were invaluable to a young outsider, who soon became an insider, and who ended up with a major responsibility for running one of the more important of the Community's initiatives. Baker recalls some of the discussions which led to Summerfest.

"Ray had a vision of Corrymeela of taking over the Balmoral Showgrounds in Belfast to run a major event. He and John Morrow thought that I might be able to co-ordinate this, but by this time John was thinking of something more manageable – such as an event to be held on the University of Ulster campus in Coleraine.

"We then brought together some members of staff, Community members and contacts from the Churches to start to explore the idea. Interestingly, it was some of the non-members who emphasised to us that the Centre at Ballycastle would be the best venue. The idea of a shared 'celebration', in a land where there were many 'celebrations', was strong in their thinking. So we began to pursue certain concepts of making it more of a festival than a conference, and we came up with the name 'Summerfest'."

All that remained was for a group to organise it. Baker says, "At that point in Corrymeela's programming, it was difficult for some people to find a way in. The emphasis was on lower income groups, on youth and on people outside the churches, and above all on those who were already part of specific groups, rather than individuals being able to come to the Centre as individuals, and to slot into some programme."

Accordingly, the concept of Summerfest had to be challenging. "We wanted to find a way to help to provide access for new people, and also to make it attractive to those in Churches, but not to create a 'churchy' event. It was also important to connect religious faith and life in terms of politics, social concerns, international affairs, family life and other dimensions."[2]

Another objective was to make Summerfest all-age and ecumenical. "We aimed to lift up the issues and messages as high and as wide as possible, and certainly beyond the constituency which Corrymeela was normally reaching. The idea was to advertise it widely, and to allow anyone who showed up 'on the day' to be welcomed in as much of the programme as possible."

The project had to be financed, but this was not the prior consideration. Doug Baker recalls, "The budget was never even discussed, but the unstated understanding seemed to be that we would do it with our own resources, and as economically as possible." All of which sounded visionary, yet sensibly earthed, and very "Corrymeela".

Doug Baker admits it was "with more naiveté than know-how" that they began to plan the first Summerfest for July 1981, which was a particularly difficult year. "The IRA hunger-strikes had a polarising effect, even within the Community. With so much bad news on the streets, Summerfest truly was good news, and with political issues, which had the potential to drive a wedge between Corrymeela members, it was helpful to have a common task towards which we could all work."

Baker and his colleagues realised that they had to organise an event which would really put Summerfest on the map, and so they invited Mother Teresa to take part. The story of her eventual involvement is a good example of divine inspiration which defied normal logic, communication and organisation. Doug recalls, "We realised that it was very important to get her to agree to come to Corrymeela, so we worked as many channels as we could to try to persuade her to do so, or at least to clear the way for her to accept."

Baker, for example, contacted the then Apostolic Nuncio in Dublin, and he also wrote to Mother Teresa herself. After waiting in vain for a written response, he decided to phone her office in Calcutta. He says, "Amazingly, she was there, rather than travelling somewhere in the world, and I was put through to her. I reminded her of my letter, stated again why we felt she could make such a difference to Summerfest, and urged her to come, if at all possible."

During the telephone conversation Mother Teresa agreed to Corrymeela's request. Baker recalls, "I was stunned, but also delighted. However, a few days later I received a letter which she had written to me when travelling in New York, and explained why she would *not* be able to accept our invitation. The letter was post-marked with a date *before* we made contact by phone."

Thus Doug Baker, and Corrymeela, were left in a delicate situation. He says, "I had heard her say 'Yes' on the phone, but I also had a letter from her saying 'No'. We never did receive the letter from her saying that she *would* come, but we checked with members of her Order in London, and they assured us that she would indeed be at Corrymeela."

Formal arrangements were confirmed on both sides, and details of Mother Teresa's scheduled visit were released to the media, which suddenly had a good news story to report, in the midst of the ongoing dark saga of the Republican hunger-strikes. Then, unexpectedly, Mother Teresa's brother died in Italy and there was speculation that she might not be able to visit Corrymeela, after all. However, members of her Order in London assured the anxious Corrymeela Summerfest planners that the visit was still on.

Doug Baker takes up the story. "On the night she was due to arrive from London on the last plane, two people from Corrymeela went to meet her at the airport. On the same evening, an Ulster Television crew was filming evening worship at the Ballycastle centre. I was on the podium beside Robin Boyd, who was speaking, when suddenly a voice whispered, 'Psst...' Then someone handed me a note which read 'She wasn't on the plane.'"

Baker, in full view of the television cameras, tried to remain calm while Robin Boyd was speaking, but he was churning inside. After evening worship ended he bolted straight for his office. He says, "We phoned her Sisters' house in London and they told us that Mother Teresa had missed a plane connection in Madrid on her journey back from Venezuela. Then she came onto the phone herself, apologised, and said that she would be on the first flight from London to Belfast the next morning."

Mother Teresa arrived in Belfast early. Baker says, "We arranged a police escort to bring her up from the airport to Ballycastle, and she arrived only half an hour late. She started speaking to a huge crowd which had gathered to hear her. A few minutes later, the heavens opened, and it poured for hours – leaving everyone and everything soaked." It rained so hard that many people could not hear clearly what she had to say, but it did not dampen the occasion. Baker emphasises, "All that mattered was the fact that she had come, and that people had been there at Corrymeela to share with her."

For those who actually could hear Mother Teresa, her message was challenging. "Her message was 'Love Till It Hurts', but her subtext, both in public and in private meetings, about Corrymeela was deeply encouraging. She told us, in effect, 'This is good. What you are doing here is important. God is using you, if you let Him do so.' Getting *her* to Corrymeela had been so important for us, but she had turned around the message to be all about *us* and God!"

It had been a memorable occasion for everyone, including this writer, who had been invited to meet her, and the media reported the visit widely. Mother Teresa's presence had made an impact in so many different ways. Indeed, one man in the line of people positioned to greet her seemed so nervous that he sang a hymn when she met him face to face, but Mother Teresa smiled gently, and literally took this in her stride. Her brief visit to Corrymeela had brought the Community, and Northern Ireland, some welcome good publicity and it literally had put the initial Summerfest on the map.

The theme for that first year was the Lord's Prayer, also known as the "Our Father". Baker says, "This was something we all shared in common, and which embraced so many spheres of life as our theme. The phrases lent themselves to be shared in many different ways." The over-arching theme was "Your Kingdom Come", and there was an opportunity to hear a wide range of challenging speakers. These included Bishop Lesslie Newbigin, and such influential local luminaries as Bishop Edward Daly of Derry and the Reverend Dr Eric Gallagher, the prominent Methodist and peacemaker.

In all, there were thirty-eight workshops on topics as diverse as "Models of Local Ecumenical Witness", "What Hope for the Unemployed?", "Life-Style", "Food and Cooking" and "Irish History" – and all of which gave much food for thought. An attractive cartoon in the *Corrymeela News* of July 1981 neatly encapsulated the essence of the ambitious event. Above the drawing of a fairground merry-go-round were the words "Food-Concerts-Speakers-Children's Activities-Marketplace and Workshops".

The well-attended first Summerfest was a great success. Baker says, "While thankfully it was much smaller than we had imagined in our wilder visions, Summerfest had made a big impact. People were soon asking, 'Will there be another?' Part of me was aghast at the prospect. We had been fortunate to survive the first Summerfest with no greater hassles than we had experienced, but part of me was excited at the prospect of staging *another* Summerfest; could we be actually greedy enough to have so much fun a second time?"

There was, of course, a second time, and in 1983 the theme was "A People at a Crossroads". Again there was a list of challenging topics, workshops and speakers. They included Bishop (later Cardinal) Cahal Daly, and from Liverpool, the Roman Catholic Archbishop, Dr Derek Worlock, and his Anglican counterpart, Bishop David Sheppard, who had built up their ecumenical partnership in a city which had known its own religious and social divisions. Another noted speaker was the South African, Dr Allan Boesak, who at that time was the President of the World Alliance of Reformed Churches.

In 1985, the theme was "The Upside-Down Kingdom", and Summerfest examined the Beatitudes. It was neatly summarised thus in a Special Edition of *Corrymeela News*: "Getting a vision of his exciting, upside-down world which Jesus proclaimed, and beginning to understand the changes which could us lead into it, is what we hope this year's Summerfest will be all about."

The series of Summerfests, at roughly two-yearly intervals, continued for some thirteen years, until 1996. Baker says, "There were many highlights, including the magical evening when the American singer and songwriter Tom Paxton came to Corrymeela and gave a concert, at a time when Northern Ireland was pretty much starved of first-class entertainment due to the Troubles." Other noted contributors the ever-popular Sands brothers from Northern Ireland.

Although there were many distinguished outside contributors, including the American, Senator George Mitchell, who had done so much to broker the Good Friday Agreement, others who had experience of the sharp end of the Troubles in Northern Ireland also made valuable contributions. They included the Very Reverend Dr John Dunlop, who became a Presbyterian Moderator, the Reverend Ruth Patterson, a former Corrymeela volunteer and also the first woman to be ordained by the Presbyterian Church in Ireland, and also Mary McAleese, who went on to become the second female President of Ireland.

Dr John Morrow, who paid tribute to the work of Doug Baker and the Community's members and friends in organising successive Summerfests, also summarises some of the atmosphere of the event. He wrote, "In addition to providing a wider vehicle for participation, this festival acted as a support for many people struggling to keep the flame of reconciliation alive, often against great odds, in their local situation. It gave those who felt isolated a sense that they were not alone, and it challenged others who were still only putting their toe in the water."

There was also a lighter side to Summerfest "in the clowning, drama and concerts. When the weather was fine, the scene on our glorious cliff-top site was truly magic. However, the Irish weather and the North Atlantic winds kept a note of reality alive, and on many days we struggled to keep our marquees upright, and to prevent all and sundry from being washed away. The efforts of young volunteers and the maintenance staff at our Centre, together with the miraculous work of our catering team, was truly praiseworthy. It was indeed a team effort that tested us all to the full."[3]

Doug Baker, who did so much for Summerfest, believes that the real importance of this series of events was not in the speakers or the themes, but in the diversity of people assembled together, and the atmosphere which led to so much sharing. "Each time, it was Summerfest itself which became the draw, and the fame of the speakers, while always important, became less and less. People came to renew friendships, to experience a broader vision of the church, to be filled up, and to go back to a setting where they struggled to keep working on tough issues."

Many became involved as participants or as leaders in Summerfest, and then moved on to become members of the Community, for varying periods. Doug Baker says, "I believe that Corrymeela, and some of the themes and issues important to it, became more widely known as a result of Summerfest, and that other organisations and initiatives working for reconciliation in our society also benefited by being given a profile through our programme."

The continued success of Summerfest over the years also symbolised the local and international dimension to the Community's life, and the synergy created by this interaction. Long before Summerfest had been invented, people like Jean Vanier – founder of L'Arche communities – had made their own valuable contribution to help shape the ethos of Corrymeela. Reference has been made to this in an earlier chapter of the book, and John Morrow neatly summarised Vanier's influence thus: "Having faced up to the experience of living together with mentally handicapped adults, Jean had realised some of the profound truths about Christian community which applied to us all."[4]

Sometimes the other insights from outsiders were difficult – even painful – for some members of the Community to accept, and a classic example of this was the Dutch connection. This arose from relationships which developed between John Morrow and Derick Wilson and the Dutch Northern Ireland Committee, whose then secretary David Stevens was also Chairman of the Corrymeela Council.

The Committee, to which reference has been made elsewhere, helped to stage seminars in Holland for various key groups in Northern Ireland, including clergy, police, journalists, community workers and many others. In the Netherlands, the Committee was able to offer a safe and neutral space where hard-pressed individuals and organisations caught up in the Northern Irish situation had time to reflect and to meet one another – and sometimes to confront themselves.

The Committee had its own tensions, but it did some good work – even if, on occasions, the Dutch sense of thoroughness clashed with

the Irish way of doing things. For example, this writer recalls a visit
to a Centre near Amsterdam with a group of Northern Irish
Protestant clergy, and the outbreak of a polite "mutiny" when the
Ulstermen demanded that their Dutch hosts allow them at least one
afternoon off for sightseeing and buying presents. The Dutch agreed
to do so – but reluctantly!

As these visits to Holland continued, it became clear that the
Dutch might share their experience more economically and more
effectively if they held their seminars in Northern Ireland, and this
included the possibility of greater co-operation with Corrymeela.
One of the most forceful, insightful, maddening, eccentric and
basically likeable of the Dutch facilitators was Roel Kaptein, to
whom reference has been made several times in this book.

Kaptein, a trained psychotherapist who had held a senior position
in the Dutch Reformed Church, looked like a slightly deranged
professor with a winning smile, a huge heart and a vice-like grip,
which was often not just a hand-shake but also an enthusiastic and a
suffocating bear-hug. He was predictably unpredictable, and while he
loved people, he was no respecter of persons. David Stevens recalls,
"He was one of the bluntest men I have ever met. 'Tell me, what is
your interest in this?' or 'Tell me, Mr Bishop,' he said to an actual
Bishop. He was one of the brightest men I have ever met, and his
capacity to think on his feet was astonishing.

"He had a profound influence on a lot of us, but obviously there
were people who could not abide him. I recall someone from the
Glencree Community in the Irish Republic saying to me, ruefully,
'That guy really scares the stuffing out of me.' You could see a
particularly southern Irish way of evasion. Roel would just cut
through all of that."

David Stevens describes well Kaptein's working methods. "He
changed our style of work. He combined 'head' work and 'heart'
work in a unique way. We worked on our questions; we told our
stories, and he would stand no evasion or messing around. He would
ask, 'Why does this matter to you?' He worked with a flip-chart, he
drew diagrams; we worked for a week at a time, morning and

evening. At the end of fifteen years I had learnt a little about relationships, peace and reconciliation – and about my evasions, denials and hypocrises."[5]

Roel Kaptein, along with his engaging colleague, Father Andre Lascaris, a Dominican priest, introduced Corrymeela to the work of Rene Girard, who was among other things, a distinguished French literary critic and an exceptional commentator on Biblical texts. Girard's philosophy was complex, and beyond the scope of this publication, though it is well summarised by John Morrow elsewhere.[6]

The essence of Girard's approach was summed up by David Stevens, who referred to his ability to bring forth ideas "about rivalry, scapegoating, conflict, violence and the birth of culture, which have profound implications for peace and reconciliation work. Girard also provides important insights into how to understand the Biblical message, and the uniqueness of Jesus. He opened up a view of the world which I find enormously exciting. I have not been the same since."[7]

The work of Girard made sense to many people in an academic, literary, and peace and reconciliation context. Whether or not it would have appealed directly to the men and women of power in London and Belfast during the worst of the Troubles is another matter. This writer recalls one occasion when he was persuaded by the other members of the Dutch-Irish Committee to use his journalistic contacts to arrange a meeting between the then Northern Ireland Secretary, James Prior, and members of the Committee, including Roel Kaptein. The meeting was called off at the last minute, following a phone call from an urbane and worldly Stormont Press Secretary, but only God knows what Prior and Kaptein would have made of one another. This may have been one of the minor missed opportunities of Anglo-Dutch history!

Despite the many attributes of Roel Kaptein and his colleagues, a number of Corrymeela members and friends felt bruised by the working methods of the Dutch, a development which was well observed by John Morrow. He wrote, "The first experience of this was far from painless for many of us. This was partly the result of a culture clash, as we experienced his [Kaptein's] approach to be so direct and abrasive that some of us were in danger of 'retiring hurt' and licking our wounds.

"However, as Roel himself mellowed, and adapted a little to our Irish ways, some of us began to learn some important new insights about human relations and the dynamics of conflict. We began to understand and acknowledge the degree of manipulation that was often occurring in our relationships, and the subtle ways in which we could often scapegoat each other."[8]

Much of Corrymeela's peacemaking work and initiatives cannot be measured precisely, despite the attempts of some Government bodies and other funding agencies to do so in statistical and in other ways. Throughout its history, however, it has been awarded a number of prestigious prizes, which have been a reflection of outside independent opinion on the value of its work. These have included the Peace Pole Award in 1988 from the Society for World Peace, and a year later Norman Richardson and Carmel Heaney, both Corrymeela members, were awarded the Kohl International Peace Prize for their peace education work.

One of the biggest awards for Corrymeela was the Niwano Peace Prize in 1997, when Trevor Williams was Leader. The Niwano Peace Foundation of Japan announced in February that year that Corrymeela was to be the recipient of its 14th Annual Peace Prize, which was awarded to individuals and organisations "which have contributed significantly to inter-religious co-operation, thereby furthering the cause of world peace".

The Foundation had asked around 1,000 individuals in 125 countries to propose suitable candidates for the Prize, and the nominations were screened by a seven-member committee, including representatives of Christianity, Buddhism and Islam. The citation for Corrymeela noted the Community's role in helping to dispel fear and distrust, and its work in establishing reconciliation among the grass roots.

It underlined how Corrymeela had provided "a place for

Protestant and Catholic leaders to meet and talk, has offered care for families who have lost loved ones in the conflict, and is deeply involved in education for mutual understanding among youths, so they can transcend differences in faith and take part together in volunteer activities." Trevor Williams, accompanied by his wife Joyce and Carmel Heaney, attended the formal award ceremony in Tokyo.

It was interesting to note how Corrymeela decided to respond to the invitation, because according to Japanese custom, it was the Leader who would have been guest of honour, but the Community decided to send three people – two women and a man, representing both the Catholic and Protestant communities. In his acceptance speech, Trevor Williams said, "What keeps us going is that in our experience as a Community we have glimpsed the possibility of another Northern Ireland, where the differences between us are no longer a source of threat, but a cause for celebration."

The Niwano Peace Prize carried a welcome financial award of some 170,000 US dollars, but even more important was its further recognition of the world's network of peacemaking and reconciliation centres.

Without doubt the international dimension to the work and witness of Corrymeela has been a central part of its vision and evolution, right to the present day. That international dimension is likely to increase as the pressures of reacting to the daily trauma of life in Northern Ireland have decreased progressively over the past few years.

John Morrow sums up: "Anyone who knows anything about Corrymeela would very quickly realise that we are about much more than Catholics and Protestants in Ireland. Politically speaking, there are few examples in the world where people of two national identities have to learn to live within one nation, and if we were able to work out a political model here, it would have significance for many other places. We have always had a global outreach in our volunteers, and many of our programmes have people coming in. We are not exclusively focused on the Northern Ireland problem.

"Out of our suffering, many creative things have happened, even though there is still an awful long way to go. That suffering has given us authenticity. We have been in the mud, and to some extent, we have served our time. However, my happiest memory of Corrymeela is the tremendous sense of joy which I have seen on the faces of people who have shared in various aspects of our work. That has been such a positive experience, and nothing can ever take that away."9

FOURTEEN

CORRYMEELA LINK

WHEN THE CORRYMEELA COMMUNITY was established in 1965, one of its objectives was to be "A question mark to the Churches", not just in Ireland, north and south, but to Churches and Christian communities everywhere. This was particularly appropriate because Corrymeela itself had drawn inspiration from many sources, including Agape, Taizé, Iona and others.

Although the spiritual and moral support of groups inside and outside Northern Ireland has been of immense value to Corrymeela, there was also a necessary and reassuring hard-headedness about the Community which had the knack of turning some of its support into bricks and mortar. Another good example of this was the construction of "The Croi" worship centre, with the help of funding from a group called the London Corrymeela Venture.

This support began around 1971 when Christians from Christ Church, Lancaster Gate and Holy Rosary, Marylebone Road in London "borrowed" an RAF plane and took Protestant and Roman Catholic children from Northern Ireland for a holiday to London. This was a success, and it led to later visits, and the cementing of relationships with Corrymeela and those who had gone to London.

The initiative continued for a couple of years, but in 1973, a group from London came to Belfast and Ballycastle to ask how they could help the work of Corrymeela more directly. The delegation included the Reverend Reggie Askew, the then vicar of Christ Church, Father Seamus McGrogan, the assistant priest at Holy Rosary, and Ian McDonald, an Anglican.

The meeting between the Londoners and Ray Davey was described by Askew in his own inimitable way. He wrote later, "We met Ray Davey for the first time on 14 June 1973. He turned on us a bright eye and said grimly that we should give him between forty and fifty thousand pounds, so that he could build The Croi at Ballycastle. We flew breathlessly home."[1]

The Londoners gamely accepted the challenge, and began an extensive fund-raising programme, which they named "The London Corrymeela Venture". They staged a wide range of events, including "the rattling of tins in the street, and a grand auction at Bonhams". Reggie Askew left to become Principal of Salisbury and Wells Theological College, but his successor, the Reverend Roger Symon, continued the work, together with his church and cross-community colleagues.

The money was eventually raised, and the splendid Croi Centre was built and opened, much to the enrichment of the Corrymeela Community. By a gentle irony, one of the main sponsors, Christ Church, Lancaster Gate was itself demolished in the meantime, and with more than a touch of thoughtful symbolism, a stone from the London building was built into The Croi. As Reggie Askew noted, "This was to remind everyone that the spirit of co-operation is not easily destroyed."[2]

In Biblical terms it was also the working out of the message from Ephesians that "All things work together for good to those who love the Lord and are called according to His purpose"; and at a time when the London Corrymeela Venture began to wind down, the link with Greater London and eventually all of England and Wales was maintained by the new Corrymeela Link, based at Reading.

This arose out of a visit from a group of young Corrymeela people to the Reading YMCA in 1975. Again Ray Davey played a leading role in this important outreach. He attended a meeting between the London Corrymeela Venture and church leaders, and the Link was formed in 1976. Many people contributed significantly to the success of this support group, and not least its' long-time co-ordinator John Martin.

He outlined its main objectives, which were "to encourage spiritual support for the Community, and to provide an educational programme. In addition, and as a result of these two, the Link is able to raise financial resources for Corrymeela."[3] At its height, the Link created a significant network, and established some thirty local Corrymeela Support Groups. The Link also distributed a twice-yearly newsletter to each of its registered 7,500 supporters.

A key focus in its outreach was to hold a Corrymeela Sunday each year, shortly before St Patrick's Day, 17 March, and some 25,000 information packs, including suggested forms of service, were distributed to a wide range of churches and other institutions. Significantly a national ecumenical Service was also held biennially on Corrymeela Sunday. The Link also maintained and supported a speakers' list of around 135 people throughout the country, and provided a Prayer Partnership. It also organised a range of events which attempted to communicate the vision of reconciliation which Corrymeela sought to express.

This was achieved by largely voluntary support, and at a time when Irishmen and women were carrying out a campaign of violence against British troops in Northern Ireland, it was salutary to remember that an undaunted group of Christians on the mainland, including the Churches and other organisations like Corrymeela Link, were strongly supporting peace-building and reconciliation initiatives.

One typical, or perhaps atypical, volunteer with the Corrymeela Link was Ray Netherclift, who eventually became Chairman. He recalls, "I first discovered Corrymeela from a tea-towel which I picked up at a village fete run by my friend Sally Stuckey, who was a great supporter of Corrymeela. I also had a connection with Northern Ireland because of my business career. So I had heard of Corrymeela, but I wasn't able to go there until 1992, when I retired."

The Ballycastle Centre had everything which he had expected. "Its situation was astounding, and the whole ethos of the place just hit me. I found The Croi most striking, and I've often told people that I've never been to anywhere else in the United Kingdom which crackled of spirituality so much as that place."

Ray had been a regular church-goer since the later stages of the Second World War. He had originally joined the Church of England, and then the Congregational Church, but he returned to the Church of England worship in a parish which was near his home. He says, "I did so mainly because it was there, but I consider myself a 'non-conformist Anglican', more than anything else!"[4]

Ray Netherclift made an important contribution to Corrymeela Link. He says, "At one stage Corrymeela was well known and well respected in the area. Consequently when local churches were staging a 'Week For Peace', the theme would often be Corrymeela. It was taken very much at face value as one of the great spiritual and physical organisations for promoting harmony."

There was also an increased perception in local schools about the work of Corrymeela. "This was part of the sixth form syllabus of religious studies, so that in itself spread the knowledge of Corrymeela quite substantially. However, I think we failed to capitalise on that, and to get an organisation established within the university network. However, I am sure that there is still much goodwill there."

Ray summarises Corrymeela as a contrast between darkness and light. "Someone told me that if you visit the British Museum and walk through the halls devoted to the history of Babylon, Nineveh and other empires, there are statues of all these ugly guys with great beards, but when you move out of this, you come to a section displaying the Elgin Marbles. In effect, it's a journey from darkness to light, and Corrymeela is like that." He contrasts the troubled areas of Belfast with the beauty of Corrymeela at Ballycastle. "A couple of years ago I toured the 'Peace Lines' in Belfast. I had no idea how vast they were. They were like a big ugly scar, and they made an appalling impression on me. That was one side of the picture in Northern Ireland, but there is such a contrast at Ballycastle. You walk into Corrymeela and it has that air of practical holiness. They don't spend their time preaching, but they just roll up their sleeves and get on with it. I wish to God someone over here would do it to quite the same degree. It's just the general atmosphere, rather than one particular thing, which I love about Corrymeela."

Nevertheless, he believes, the magnificent setting on the North Antrim cliff-top can also be a practical drawback. "It's just a pity that it's that more difficult to get to Ballycastle. If more people went there they would be able to imbibe the atmosphere of the place, and it is something quite different. It isn't Taizé, it isn't Lourdes. It *is* Corrymeela and that's unique, but it's a shame that it's not more approachable, physically.

"By contrast, if you want to go to Taizé, you can step on a bus at Victoria Station and be driven there. If you want to visit Lourdes, you can fly there – it's just like going to Blackpool, but it takes such an effort to get to Ballycastle! However, when you eventually get there it is very uplifting to share with the other groups, and to find out what is going on."

One of the problems of recent years, as mentioned elsewhere, has been the impression outside Northern Ireland that the conflict is over. Netherclift says, "While Northern Ireland was in the headlines, people were interested, but now that it is so rarely in the news, there is an impression over here that all is well over there. People don't really understand how many problems still remain, but I think the practical work of Corrymeela will always be in demand.

"They have a hands-on approach which is still very much needed. It's not just sitting and talking, it is also saying this is *how* you do it, this is *how* you break the ice, *these* are the themes you should be following. The work of Corrymeela is valuable, and the requirements are not going to go away, and it is not hard to make the connection between its work and the challenges which face so many people elsewhere today."

Inevitably, there has been a degree of English exasperation with the Irish situation. "People have said, 'That's the Irish, and that's how it is going to be for ever more.' Now, however, there's a feeling that the Muslim situation is on our own doorsteps, and that something has to be done about it. The business of reconciliation is worked out by sitting and listening to what the other guy is telling you, and trying to put yourself in his shoes. That's the whole work of Corrymeela, and the practical example they have given will always be in demand."

Despite the good work that was being done by and through the Corrymeela Link, the wind of change was continually presenting it with new and difficult challenges. This was two-fold, both in the nature of the Link itself, between Corrymeela in Northern Ireland and the Reading-based group, and also within the ranks of the volunteers themselves. One man who had a foot in both camps is Ian Gilchrist, an Ulsterman who settled in the south of England, and who also made an important contribution to the Corrymeela Link.

An Anglican, and an engineer by profession, Gilchrist was educated at Methodist College in Belfast, and later at Queen's University. From his student days, he involved himself closely with the work of reconciliation, and as early as 1969 – when the Troubles accelerated in intensity – he presented a report to the chaplains at Queen's about the establishment of a Community Relations Group. He also created a working group to further the proposals in the report, and this led to the establishment of "The Cam Forest Project".

This involved the conversion of a forester's cottage near Limavady into a centre for Protestants and Roman Catholics from East Belfast, but by the time the project was firmly established, Gilchrist had taken a job in England. However, he continued to support the project which came to the end of its natural life, but provided an important prototype for the eventual establishment of the Christian Renewal Centre at Rostrevor.

When he came to England, therefore, Ian Gilchrist already had invaluable practical experience of reconciliation work, and he became involved in the London Corrymeela Venture. When it, too, had completed its task and had begun to wind down, Gilchrist was asked by Ray Davey to act as a guardian for the Corrymeela Community's interests, and in essence he later became the founding chairman of the Corrymeela Link.

Significantly, however, the Link was established as a separate entity from the Corrymeela Community, and this would have an important bearing on developments later on. In 1977 Gilchrist became a full member of the Corrymeela Community, and the next year he set out a Constitution for the Link. For much of its twenty-five year existence, Ian Gilchrist was an office-bearer, but he had a clear idea of his own position.

"My concept of the Link from the outset was that it should be seen as a group of people from England who felt drawn to support the work of Corrymeela, rather than an outreach of the Community itself." Although he was Chairman for a period, he says, "I was a 'reluctant' Chairman, and with my direct involvement in the Community – and also my Ulster accent – I preferred to work behind the scenes, as much as possible. I felt that the Corrymeela Link should be represented by an 'English' voice."

The early arrangements between the Community, based in Northern Ireland, and the Link, based in Reading, were judged to be appropriate at the time, but circumstances changed. In 1995 Ian Gilchrist called for a major review of the role and function of the Link. In his Chairman's Report in June of that year he noted, *inter alia*, the changing situation in Northern Ireland, partly as a result of the ceasefires and the Downing Street Declaration.

He stated, "As violence ceases, the bridges kept open by Corrymeela can now be crossed by people too afraid to stir outside the barriers of their minds to meet their enemy, and find the friend inside." He also noted, like others, that the decrease in violence would almost certainly remove Northern Ireland from the headlines with important consequences for development and fund-raising.

There were other reasons for change. The administrative arrangements were proving somewhat unwieldy between the Community and the Link, which were legally separate bodies. There was also the reality of the limited support possible in the Reading area, despite the national network profile. As well, the Corrymeela Community was in the process of changing its fund-raising procedures. It was decided, therefore, to work out a strategic plan for the future of the Link, and also to proceed to Limited Liability Status.

A review was duly carried out, and the long-term result was the formal closure of the Link on 31 March 2001. The decision was also taken to appoint a Development Officer for England and Wales. An Office was maintained at Reading, and the intention was that the work on the mainland – or more accurately the larger island to the east of Ireland – would continue under the auspices of the Community in Northern Ireland. This new arrangement, it was hoped, would provide new potential and scope for future development.

The new Development Co-ordinator appointed for England and Wales was Honor Alleyne, a modern languages graduate from Queen's University, who had spent part of her early life in Belfast. However, she lived most of her adult life in England and later on she became principal of a girls' school in Guildford, Surrey. She had known about the work of Corrymeela, partly as a result of meeting Ray Davey in Belfast during her student days, and as headmistress of her school, she made her pupils aware of the work of the Community, among others.

She says, "I saw to it that the school supported Corrymeela financially, and I made a point of having speakers in from the Community, because it was important that the girls would be confronted with a variety of life situations. I also became aware of a document inviting applications for the post of Development Co-Ordinator, and I applied, partly because I knew that I was nearing the end of my career in school-teaching, and also because I was interested in the work of Corrymeela. To some extent also, I was paying back my dues. I had spent all my professional life in England, and I hadn't gone back to Northern Ireland."[5]

Honor worked with some twenty-three Corrymeela groups in England and Wales, with the emphasis on development, education and support. It became clear, however, that the priorities were changing, and over the next few years the Community decided that fund-raising would become a priority, rather than development. Accordingly the post of Development Co-ordinator was wound up in mid-2006, with a view to appointing a full-time fundraiser for the rest of the United Kingdom. It was not a decision with which Honor Alleyne and others agreed.

She says, "When the question of a full-time fundraiser was raised, I suggested that from my experience of employing people, if you appoint committed part-timers, you get more out of them. Corrymeela did suggest that having a team of people regionally-based would have been more effective than just one person working on his or her own. My point of view was not accepted in the end, and the Community were perfectly within their rights to disregard what I said."

The point at issue was not a personal one, but rather the uncertain challenge which faces many other organisations and charities. This is whether to prioritise fund-raising while continuing with the education and development work, however imperfectly, or to try to win and maintain new supporters as a priority, in the hope that they would continue to provide financial support. It is difficult to achieve a balance between the two, and there was no easy answer to this question, despite the integrity of the views held by people on both sides.

Honor Alleyne looks back on her experiences of Corrymeela with candour, and also with appreciation. "I discovered that the Community had significant insights into the nature of, and the need for, reconciliation. I also learned that, like all communities, it was full of stresses and strains, and that there were tensions between members of the staff and the Community, who did not always see eye to eye.

"I also came to believe that the Community ultimately had relatively little knowledge of what happened on the larger island, and that sometimes people were not very interested in knowing, anyway. That, however, may be a very harsh judgement on my part."

Honor emphasises, however, what she learned from working with Corrymeela. She says, "I gained a huge amount, including my reconnection with Northern Ireland, which I valued. I also gained an insight into an organisation I greatly value, whatever else I am saying about the Community. I speak partly in sadness, and not in anger, because I think that Corrymeela has important things to give, and I greatly value the staff in Northern Ireland who do a fantastic job in a very difficult situation.

"I also gained contact with lots of wonderful people in the United Kingdom, as well as members of Corrymeela and those who became associated with the Community. I also learned a great deal about reconciliation, in a way which I had not taken on board before. I learned the need to accept that people who are different are not a threat, but that they can offer opportunities. Through that can come a closeness, and a working together, and some sort of reconciliation of ideas and people."

She is aware, like others, of the challenges facing Corrymeela in an era of decreased funding. "Initially I discovered over here that some people felt it was an 'Irish problem', but I made it my job to say, 'This is only a microcosm of how we all live, we are all caught up in these tensions.' The people who were most deeply committed to Corrymeela did realise that there was a deeper resonance than simply looking at it as an Irish problem."

However, Corrymeela's role is more difficult to define now, because the nature of peace and of the Troubles in Northern Ireland has changed. Honor says, "I believe that Corrymeela is already trying to re-invent itself, and that is usually a painful procedure for any group or organisation. However, I also believe that Corrymeela needs to remain rooted in practical work. It's all very well having ideas about reconciliation, but you need to work it out in human terms."

Honor Alleyne feels that Corrymeela should commit further resources towards the educational outreach, and to "make common cause with those who think similarly. This may be happening, and I may be speaking out of profound ignorance, but Corrymeela needs to talk more regularly about a common cause with these people." She also believes that the Community should publish its findings more widely. "Educationally speaking, there is a great perceived commitment by the Government to social, moral, religious and spiritual education. I believe that Corrymeela feeds immediately into this. It has things to say in this area of the curriculum, but I don't think that Corrymeela has properly accepted the opportunities which arise through publishing to dive into that area."

Overall, she says, Corrymeela has been an enriching experience. "I have found Ballycastle a warm and welcoming place, and the people as well. There is an attitude which is not rushed or hurried, though the downside is that sometimes things don't get done! However, there is also an up side – it's a wonderful site in geographical terms, and its a lovely place to be. It is a great haven of welcome and of peace. Of course I will miss it, though I hope not entirely, and I shall continue as a Friend to be a part of the group of people who support the Community. I hope that through this, I may continue to hear something of its triumphs."

The experience of the Corrymeela Link, and the ongoing structure of the arrangements for the Community as a whole and for its work generally, is very much rooted in the financial and other changes which have faced Corrymeela in the past twenty-five years. Craig Cameron, who chaired the group which produced the new plans for England and other parts of the UK, believes that in recent years the Community and its Council have not maintained enough enthusiasm for the link with Britain, and if steps are not taken to maintain this, the support may dwindle away.

He also believes, however, that there is great potential. He says, "The lessons which Corrymeela has learned after forty years at the coal face are directly applicable to the challenges that are now being faced in England, in terms of the growing fear between Muslim and Christian communities, and equally the growing insecurity and cultural divisions. We've got to find a way of sharing that with the people in England and elsewhere, who are facing the challenge of dealing with the tensions between the different communities.

"Corrymeela came into existence because some people in Northern Ireland learned from the experience of Iona, and Agape and Taizé. Ray Davey learned from his tough experience in the Second World War, and that experience was brought back to Northern Ireland, mulled over, distilled, and looked at in the context of Ireland, and put into practice. Corrymeela was never an 'Irish solution for an Irish problem'. What we need to do now is to find a way of sharing our experience with others who are facing parallel but slightly different challenges elsewhere."

This overall challenge, and also the strains created by a increasingly difficult financial climate, were very much part of the thinking of the Community and its successive Leaders in recent years, and not least that of David Stevens, who took over from Trevor Williams in 2004. There was some comfort, however, from the continuity between the past and the present, and the hopes for the future so well expressed by the Corrymeela's evolution of its distinctive forms of worship, which lay at the heart of the Community's existence.

FIFTEEN

WORSHIP – AND FACING THE MUSIC

ONE OF THE MOST DISTINCTIVE characteristics of the Corrymeela Community is its worship. This is most usually associated with gatherings in The Croi, which many people believe is the heartbeat at Ballycastle. In fact, *croi* is a Gaelic term for "the heart", and the building resembles the shape of a human heart, with different chambers flowing into one another. It also resembles an ear, and it is meant to be a place of listening – to God and to one another.

The theme of the building is peace, and the word is etched on the door handle as a greeting to all who enter. The Prayer of St Francis is engraved on the glass entrance screen as a reminder of Corrymeela's mission. So much about The Croi is symbolic of so much else. The Bell, which calls people to worship at the Ballycastle Centre each morning and evening, was formerly installed in the parish church of St Patrick, Kilcock, near Maynooth.

It had been cast in 1869 in Dublin by the firm of Curtis and Sons, but had been off its mountings for some fifty years. Following an appeal by Corrymeela, this Dublin-Kildare bell was located by the then Church of Ireland Primate Dr George Simms. A working party from Corrymeela removed it and transported it to Ballycastle.

Inside The Croi is an Irish turf model of an ancient High Cross, which was used within Celtic Christianity to instruct people in the stories and doctrines of the faith. It is modelled on the early 10th century High Cross of Muiredach, which is situated at

Monasterboice in County Louth, and it was a gift from a group in Omagh, following a Summer Family Week in 1980.

The Candlestick most often used at The Croi was presented by the representatives of the Oekumenischer Jugenddienst (Ecumenical Youth Service) in Magdeburg to a group of young Corrymeela adults who visited East Germany in 1981. It is made of iron ore from local mines. The Corrymeela group presented their hosts with a replica High Cross made from turf, and in this way both groups possessed something reminiscent of the earth of their respective homelands. The gifts were also reminders of their common allegiance to Christ, and their sharing in a one world which transcended nationality or politics.

The Candle at the heart of The Croi is symbolic of the Corrymeela motto, "It's better to light a candle than to curse the darkness", and the open Bible is a constant reminder of the work of reconciliation through healing and forgiveness. One of the most striking features of The Croi is the magnificent Tree of Life Mural. This is based on the text from The Book of Revelation: "and the leaves of the tree are for the healing of the nations".

The Mural, which was designed by Elizabeth Andrewes – a Friend of Corrymeela from England – contains some five hundred embroidered leaves and twelve fruits. Each was created by people from all over the world, many of whom had known of Corrymeela only through various international peace and reconciliation networks. Each leaf was sewn on to the Mural under the supervision of Liz Perera (née Howard), who was a volunteer at the Centre. It remains as striking today as when it was first created.[1]

The Croi structure was designed by the Belfast architects, Norman Hawthorne and Gordon McKnight, and built under the supervision of Alex Sharpe and Mick McCarthy from the nearby Glens of Antrim area. The stained-glass window was designed by the artist Neil Shawcross, and the rugged stones of the building came from a quarry near Cushendall. The Croi was opened on 16 June 1979, and Canon Reginald Askew, who had been part of the London Corrymeela Group raising money for The Croi, offered a poem on entering the building. It captured in words the atmosphere of this unique place. Part of the poem reads:

> It is a quiet place
> For the bones of saints to lie in
> A good Irish king would wish
> To be buried here. Simple and white as Easter
> It describes the tomb of Christ
> From whence our resurrection springs,
> The place is set for Easter morning.
> It has the dimensions of an egg
> The possibilities of new life.
> And I know that people will come
> At once, and use it in different ways...

The unique Croi and its contents are strong visible reminders that Corrymeela is primarily a Christian community, and that worship lies at the heart of its activities. Like much else about Corrymeela, however, this worship and liturgy have been evolving over the years.

John Morrow outlines the philosophy behind this development. He says, "We experimented quite a bit in trying to introduce drama and aiming to relate the worship as much as possible to the groups who were coming in on a regular basis. We had to be adaptable, and what worked with one group might not have gone down so well with another. We also encouraged them to make a contribution to the worship themselves, and some were more able to do that than others."

Gradually the Community realised that it had developed material with a lasting value, and it produced its first worship book, with the help of people like Roger Courtney, Norman Richardson and Doug Baker. It was called *Celebrating Together – Prayers, Liturgies and Songs from Corrymeela*, and it became extremely popular. John Morrow recalls, "Basically we were 'low church', except in the sense that we tried to introduce more responses, and this developed some elements of 'high church' worship. In the main, however, we were always flexible, and we were trying not to use the Iona pattern of worship because it was a quite a high church liturgy itself. At Corrymeela we tried to adapt and to use the language that related to the realities which people were living with."

One of the difficulties of conducting worship at Corrymeela was the sensitive issue of Roman Catholics and Protestants and Communion. According to the rules of the Roman Catholic Church, Protestants and Catholics cannot share Communion, except in extreme circumstances, including "danger of death". This vexed a number of Community members and others who felt that people who shared so much practical Christianity in carrying out the work of Corrymeela should also be able to partake jointly in one of the most intimate aspects of the Christian faith. Morrow and his colleagues were well aware of the difficulties. He says, "It was a sensitive issue, and we tried to deal with it in various ways." Despite the varied and sometimes apparently spontaneous nature of the worship at Corrymeela, it always needed supervision. Morrow recalls, "We were taking risks in allowing a lot of different people to contribute, but without working behind the scenes and making sure that those taking part had some guidance, the whole thing could easily deteriorate, and you could find things happening which you were not prepared to stand over.

"Sometimes it was a case of people ending up by singing their favourite pop songs, and they imagined that in some way they had conducted worship, when in fact there had not been the slightest connection with worship! Some people, of course, don't require supervision, but at times the Community has thrown too much weight on to young volunteers who knew very little about the Community when they arrived, and were expected to carry the load for a year. Even though you provide them with a worship book as an aid, some are not really confident enough to carry it off. So we have been working on that, in terms of how more members of the Community can be present at the Centre to contribute at that level."

One of the most distinctive features of the worship and liturgy at Corrymeela has been the Community's use of music, and a major contribution in this area was made by the Corrymeela Singers.

Norman Richardson, one of their former Directors, recalls his early association with the Community:

"My first impression of Corrymeela – still probably the strongest – goes back to a clear late June evening in 1967. I was sitting on a bench outside the old Work Camp at Ballycastle, and looking beyond the cliff-top Corrymeela Cross towards Rathlin Island. Someone was reading 'The Sea' from *Prayers of Life* by Michel Quoist, and from that point, everything changed for me."

It was Richardson's first day in Northern Ireland. He recalls, "Apart from a few hours in Belfast, Corrymeela was the first and only place I had visited. Conditions in the Work Camp were primitive – toilets only in the house across the field, no kitchen, a stand-pipe for water outside the main chalet, and a cooker in the corner. I was a twenty-year-old student teacher from England, trying to make sense of several years of fairly narrow conservative evangelical influences and experiences. I knew nothing of Northern Ireland and its troubled history, but a chance encounter with a Queen's University student had brought me to this previously unknown spot for a week-long work camp. Yet that simple but stunning meditation on a cliff-top challenged my narrow confusions, and began to point out new possibilities, and new relationships."[2]

Richardson returned to Corrymeela, and kept returning. He says, "I led many work camps myself, and spent many weeks each summer – often leading worship, and frequently returning to the beautiful and challenging meditations of Michel Quoist. Northern Ireland later became my home, and Corrymeela remains my spiritual home, mentor and motivator. Cliff-top meditations graduated to the summer workshop tent, and later to The Croi, though there were many returns to the view over Rathlin as a backdrop to worship. I think that the inspiration of that first Corrymeela worship echoed on into later years when, as members of the Corrymeela Singers, some of us travelled to more distant places with the words and music of peace, justice and hope."

The origins of the Corrymeela Singers arose from a number of "ad hoc" gatherings in 1973 and 1974 to provide music for radio broadcasts from the Ballycastle Centre. According to Norman Richardson, "It was agreed to meet regularly to present music and words around the issues and concerns of Corrymeela – peace, justice, reconciliation, hope."[3] In the next few years, the group made four recordings, and sang widely all over Ireland and the UK, and in parts of Europe.

Richardson recalls, "There were Catholic and Protestant church services, peace rallies, open-air events (often disastrous in terms of rain, wind, cold and an inability to be heard!), radio and television programmes, and many more occasions." The group shared platforms with a wide range of performers, including choirs from Austria and Poland, and also with rock bands and folk musicians. They even performed with Tibetan Buddhist monks in St Anne's Cathedral in Belfast.

One of the most memorable evenings was in September 1983. Richardson recalls, "We stood on a large floodlit stage in Vienna football stadium, and I conducted the singers and instrumentalists in Janet Shepperson's song 'One Small Candle'. Just a few yards to my right sat Pope John Paul II, holding a candle that was being lit by young persons, while – all around – the stadium became filled with pinpricks of light as many thousands of young people shared the light."

John Morrow, who was a member of the Corrymeela Singers, also remembers the event vividly. He says, "We were actually one of two choirs. The other one was a choir from Warsaw, which had been to Ireland several times, and we sang a couple of pieces with them. It was amazing to see the whole stadium being lit from one candle and then throughout the whole audience of some 60,000 people. What a thrill it must have been for Janet, who was with us, to hear and see her song being sung in that situation."

There were many other memorable events. Morrow says, "It was amazing fun. We went to a festival in Graz, Austria, and this was partly through contacts made by the late Peter McLachlan. We sang for the Conference of European Churches, and in Cathedrals all over England. Every time there was a Corrymeela Sunday in England, run by our support groups, the Singers were invited to take part." In Liverpool they performed at an ecumenical service in the Roman Catholic Cathedral, but not without incident.

John Morrow explains, "We had young people doing mime as part of the drama of the service, and they were carrying placards with typically Belfast graffiti such as 'No Pope Here' and 'Prods Out', you name it! A local MEP spotted them going in to the Cathedral, and she thought that they were going to disrupt the service. So she rang the police and they were all arrested. We had the greatest job getting them released in time for the rehearsal!"

Morrow enjoyed his time with the Corrymeela Singers. "They were good ambassadors for the Community, over a number of years. Many of the things they did were 'out and about' rather than at the centre, and they operated much more as part of the dispersed Community. Their centre of gravity was more in Belfast than in Ballycastle, but they did contribute to the general patterns of worship that were used at the Centre. For quite a while they were doing things that were widely appreciated, and they sang a number of songs which they had written themselves."

One of the best-known of these was "The Pollen of Peace", which was written by Roger Courtney, a member of the Community. The background is outlined by Norman Richardson: "For many years Roger's song has been associated with Corrymeela as a kind of unofficial theme song, which seems to capture the essence of the Community's ideals and its commitment to peacemaking."[4]

The "Pollen" was written in 1974 when Courtney, then a social science student at Queen's University, spotted a number of children's peace posters which were on display at Corrymeela House in Belfast. One of them had the message "Spread the Pollen of Peace", and it portrayed a flower and a butterfly. The song quickly became a favourite at the Ballycastle Centre, and a choral arrangement was quickly taken up by the then newly-formed Corrymeela Singers, whose guitarist was none other than the songwriter himself.

Richardson notes, "Over the next few years, the song was performed – often with audience participation – wherever the

Singers went in Ireland, Britain and even further afield. It has been translated into several languages, including German, Polish, French and Irish. In 1980 it provided the title track for the Corrymeela Singers' first recording, and it has been recorded and broadcast many times since, again by the Corrymeela Singers, as well as by church and school choirs and others."

Ray Davey used "The Pollen of Peace" as the title of one of his books, published in 1981. Norman Richardson points out, "The words and music have appeared in published forms in various hymnbooks, songbooks and School Assembly Collections, as well as by the Corrymeela Press in sheet form. In one version, the Christian-based words were adapted, with permission, for use in inter-faith contexts. Significantly, when the Corrymeela Singers gave their farewell concert in the autumn of 1994, 'The Pollen of Peace' was the last song they sang together."

Nevertheless, Norman Richardson believes that "there were times when some Corrymeela members felt that it was over-used, even over-simplistic, but nonetheless the song has never failed to appeal, and more than thirty years on, it remains popular and widely-known beyond Corrymeela". In October 2005, there was a fascinating new dimension to the "Pollen" story, when it was broadcast on BBC Radio Ulster from Newtownbreda Presbyterian Church during the Community's 40th anniversary celebrations.

The church choir was joined by a group called Ceol le Ceile, the Irish for "Together in Music", which includes several former members of the Corrymeela Singers, including Roger Courtney. Norman Richardson takes up the story. "Rachel and Helen Bergin, two new members of the group, later told their mother Elish about the pieces they had been practising. They were surprised when she said that she had been responsible for the song as the young teenage pupil at St Brigid's High School (now Drumcree High) who had made the original poster."

Elish met Roger Courtney later on, and they talked about the origins of "Pollen". She told him, "My father kept bees, so it really began as 'the pollen of bees'!" Talk about bees and pollen was a common experience in the orchard county of Armagh where Elish grew up, so when the art teacher was seeking entries for the poster competition, the image of "pollen" seemed entirely appropriate.

Roger and Elish had met earlier in the 1970s and he acquired her original poster which, incidentally, did not win the competition. Sadly, the original was lost or mislaid within a local television station after a broadcast, and it would be fitting if it was ever to re-emerge. However, the tune and the lyrics live on as one of the most memorable songs in the history of Corrymeela. The first verse reflects the spirit of the whole, though the words alone do not do justice to the song:

> O let us spread the pollen of peace throughout our land;
> Let us spread the pollen of peace throughout our land;
> Let us spread the pollen of peace,
> And make all conflict cease,
> Let us spread the pollen of peace throughout our land.

During the thirty year history of the Corrymeela Singers, there were several musical directors. Norman Richardson left in 1985 to be followed by Jill McLachlan (now Kershaw). Some three years later, she was succeeded by Barbara Jennings (1988-90), John Chilvers (1990-1995), Rowena Eames (1996-2001), and Mary Braithwaite (2001-4). Roger Courtney, a founder-member, survived longer than most, and brought to the group his many talents as a songwriter, guitarist and singer.

Norman Richardson looks back with affection. "It was a thirty year period of highs and lows – musically, symbolically, and in terms of hopes, ambitions and achievements. I'm tempted to quote the children's song, 'When they were good, they were very, very good ' but it would be unkind to complete the line! One of the greatest difficulties was ensuring the continuity of personnel, and therefore of performance standards. But the good performances were very special!"

Richardson also lists a number of performances which were particularly special for him They included not only the evening with

Pope John Paul II in Austria, but also performances in Coventry Cathedral, a reflection in St Martin-in-the-Fields in London, and a joint concert in Belfast with the late Sydney Carter, who wrote, among much else, the celebrated "Lord of the Dance". Norman says, "At a different level, however, there were few occasions more moving for me than when a deaf dancer performed on the chancel steps of Coventry Cathedral as the Singers sang the Easter carol 'Now the Green Blade Riseth'."

Norman Richardson also wonders to what extent the Singers were able to influence the liturgical and musical life of Corrymeela. He says, "At that level they never had the impact of, for example, the Jacques Berthier music at Taizé, or of the Wild Goose Music Group at Iona. So far, Corrymeela has not achieved its own distinctive musical style, and this may be the single most disappointing aspect of our thirty years as a group."

Richardson believes that a Community with the inspiration and influence of Corrymeela deserved a more prominent and distinct musical-liturgical role. He says, "Some might regard this as a very peripheral element in relation to Corrymeela's greater task, but in my view we are the poorer without such things in the overall life and work of the Community. Nevertheless, I believe that one of the most important contributions of the Singers has been to take the concerns and ideals of Corrymeela out to places where music most definitely speaks to people at a level that mere words cannot achieve."[5]

The Corrymeela Singers formally disbanded in October 2004, after a celebratory concert in Dunmurry, but the fond memory of their historic and distinctive achievements lives on. So too does the modern worship at Corrymeela and in 2001 a new book titled *Travelling The Road of Faith* was launched by the Community. The editor Jacynth Hamill says, "The title and the content reflect the change and movement in the Community's life. There was a need to change the language used in the worship, and a desire to make more permanent the best of the ephemeral liturgies around the Community."

The book was produced by a group of around ten members.

Individuals worked on liturgies concerning particular themes, and the first drafts were shared and defined. Everyone contributed ideas for the Prayer and Song sections, and Jacynth worked particularly on the theme pages, worship calendar and song section. She says, "It was not possible to have a liturgy for every theme, so these pages provide references for Bible readings, songs, prayers, dramas, symbols and activities for twenty-six themes such as 'remembering – the painful and the joyful' and 'mutuality/learning from others'. The book has proved to be a great resource for the Community and for people in other places."[6]

Another noteworthy publication was *Make Your Kingdom Come*, a collection of songs from the Corrymeela Summerfest between 1981 and 1984. This was edited by Roger Courtney and Norman Richardson, with notes by Doug Baker. In a foreword to the worship book, he underlined why so much of the material at Summerfest was fresh and original: "We extended an open invitation for songs related to the theme. For the most part the response was in the form of original songs, and it is these contributions which form the heart of this book."

Throughout the decades, the evolving forms of worship at Corrymeela were always at the heart of the Community. Norman Richardson sums up: "Corrymeela is not only about cliff-top insights and visions, but alongside all the other challenging, hard-edged and mundane moments that we have to deal with, we have been absolutely right to stay with those times of reflection and worship, providing not just physical space, but inner, spiritual space for people of all faiths and 'isms', and those of none. Since that first moment of the cliff-top, almost forty years ago, nothing for me has been the same."

SIXTEEN

VOLUNTEERING

A PART OF THE LIFE-BLOOD of Corrymeela has been the role played by volunteers. Indeed, Corrymeela was so short of resources at the beginning that it would not have survived without voluntary help. Dr John Morrow recalls the challenges, and the sense of adventure of those early days. He says, "Ray Davey's whole concept from the start was that we had a site which needed to be totally rehabilitated. In the beginning there literally wasn't any other programme apart from volunteer work camps. The place was not fit for anyone to stay, except those working on-site, and only gradually was it sufficiently habitable for groups of people."

He remembers helping to build huts which were blown down in a storm. "They just went down like matchwood. It was a warning about the amateurish nature of our work!" Some of the later creations were more substantial, however, and Morrow remembers volunteers making tables from doors and putting the legs on. According to a Corrymeela report, the volunteering during the early years was informal and "ad hoc".

There was no formal process of recruitment. People would just turn up to see how they could help, whether in housekeeping, the kitchen, gardening or maintenance. Most volunteers were locals and short-term, and they usually came at weekends, or in the summer. Morrow says, "If someone turned up out of the blue and was willing to work, he or she would be found a place somewhere."

As well as the locals, however, there were international volunteers, who came mostly in the summertime. John Morrow says, "The tradition of having external volunteers goes back right to the beginning. We had people from Czechoslovakia in 1968, when there was turmoil in their own country, and I remember them telling me that they didn't know whether to go back home or not."

The international volunteers had an important effect on the Community as a whole. "They lifted the whole perspective of Corrymeela out of a purely 'Northern Ireland' kind of world, and the international perspective of bringing reconciliation into a wider sphere was very important."

Detailed information about volunteering was compiled by Corrymeela members and friends, and published in October 2002. It arose from a project originally conceived by Neil Bole as part of a thesis at Queen's University. Information from 305 volunteers before the year 2001 was compiled. Each was asked to complete an extensive questionnaire dealing with the background and family, the experience of Corrymeela, the volunteer's most significant influences in Northern Ireland, and the effect of the volunteering experience on later life.

However, Neil's illness and tragic death in July 2002 profoundly affected the project. The data remained unanalysed at the time of his death, but later Thomas Stevens took over and, with Stephen Roper, he helped to produce a lengthy report titled *The Corrymeela Community Longterm Volunteering Programme – Personal and Social Development Effects*. Much of this chapter has been distilled from the comments and statements contained in that report.

In the mid-1960s, the difference between the staff and volunteers was somewhat blurred, and some of the early "staff" were actually volunteers. Apart from doing the physical work of clearing the site, which was crucial in itself, those early encounters played an important role in developing the ethos and culture of the Community. For example, a hut on the Ballycastle site became a focal point for group events.

John Morrow says, "An incredible number of activities took part in that hut – including meals, dances, social celebrations, discussions with the army and police, and parents who were up at the Centre. In a strange way, the hut became almost a kind of heart of the Community. People saw it as the place where the early work was done, and it had a strange sort of psychological identification on the site."

As the Ballycastle Centre developed gradually, so too did the nature of volunteering. This was stimulated in part by the political and social developments in Northern Ireland, which in turn were being worked out against a background of violence and political turmoil. It is important to remember also that, each year, Corrymeela continued to recruit both long-term and short-term volunteers to perform a wide range of tasks.

The report indicated that the age of volunteers varied from 18 to 65, and that most came to Corrymeela in their late teens or early twenties, usually after they had finished their secondary or tertiary education. A smaller number left their jobs and volunteered in their late twenties and early thirties. Just over 50 per cent came from the British Isles, with a strong representation from Northern Ireland. Others came from overseas, and particularly from Germany, Switzerland, Scandinavia and the USA. A large majority of the long-term volunteers were women.

Many had a religious background, with 53 per cent indicating that they were Protestants. The majority of the remainder (40 per cent) were Roman Catholics, with 3 per cent from other faiths, and 5 per cent having no religious identity. The overwhelming feeling from the survey was an appreciation of Corrymeela. Different volunteers stressed different aspects of their experience, and negative comments were less common. Some of these, however, provided valuable insights for the Community at large.

As the work of Corrymeela increased, so did the resources for the management of the volunteers. After the Reverend Harold Good took over as Centre Director in 1973, a more formal structure was developed. Duncan Morrow, a long-term Corrymeela member and later Chief Executive of the Community Relations Council, recalls that the increasing workload led to the establishment of residential volunteers. He says, "They needed people who were able to stay for longer periods. Students weren't able to do that."

The number of residential volunteers was also increasing, and by the late Seventies the new Centre Director, Derick Wilson, developed the programme "Serve and Learn", which provided the framework for volunteering for the next decade or so. The basic idea was to create a volunteer group of ten people who would serve for a year, with the emphasis on a good balance between gender, religion and nationality.

The volunteers were given considerable responsibility and freedom of decision and action, within the overall Corrymeela strategy and ethos. They learned communication, youth and community skills, but the benefits were not just practical – they were also personal and spiritual. Duncan Morrow says, "Corrymeela's ultimate purpose is the exploration of what it means to be a Christian community, and I think that the voluntary experience provided a foundation for many young people at a point of departure in their adult lives where they learned what it was to be a human being."

As the volunteering programme developed, it was necessary to appoint a co-ordinator, and the first person to hold this key post was Rosie Walsh. Part of the role was to be responsible for the training and management of volunteers, and also to develop a sense of community among them as well. Significantly, as time went on, there was a noticeable difference in the type of people who volunteered to work and live at Corrymeela.

The main source of volunteers originally had been among middle-class students, but increasingly they came from working-class and inner-city backgrounds. This was partly due to changing social trends which meant that fewer students were volunteering, and also to the significant influence of Corrymeela's dynamic youth worker, Billy Kane. John Morrow says, "Billy was producing people whom he believed could contribute, and who could be realistically part of his scheme, provided it did not become too unbalanced. We could use a number of volunteers who came from fairly tough backgrounds, and it was important to try to extend this opportunity."

By the late Eighties and early Nineties, the volunteers' programme was shifted away from the concept of "Serve and Learn", and more towards personal development. Trevor Williams, a former Leader of Corrymeela, recalls, "The aim was to invite people into a programme where they would learn skills, find their potential and have the opportunity to explore themselves. So the programme became very much centred on the benefits to the volunteers."

This reflected a general trend in the wider community, particularly at a time when successive governments were attempting to promote volunteering as a means of creating full employment. However, this created potential problems for Corrymeela, as Trevor Williams points out: "If you are doing accreditation only to a pre-set model… then you are going to be getting people jumping through hoops, as if the volunteering experience is the same anywhere, and teaches the same skills. So there was a danger in taking accreditation 'off the shelf' and trying to apply it to Corrymeela."

However, the Community discovered that an informal accreditation for short-term volunteers worked well. Williams says, "Our scheme documented for them what they had done and the progress they made during the year, and it was worth doing. In effect, we were saying to them, 'You have given something to us, we have noticed that, and we feel that you should have this back.'"

The volunteering programme itself was continually developing. In the mid-Nineties, for example, older volunteers were welcomed, partly because of their availability and also the mature dimension that they could offer. Trevor Williams says, "It was very helpful to have someone related to the same volunteering group, but at a different place in their life. They added a richness and a roundness, and they brought different skills and experience, and a bit more maturity."

The job of the residential co-ordinator was particularly demanding, and at one point, the decision was taken that the co-ordinator would no longer be based within the Centre at Coventry House. This, however, was not an unqualified success. Williams says, "The resident co-ordinator had no space or privacy, and it was unsustainable to expect people to live like that. Yet by moving the co-ordinator out of Coventry House we lost something, and it proved not to be a particularly fruitful decision. We realised what we had lost and we needed to get it back."

In the Nineties there was a significant increase in the number of international volunteers, particularly from Eastern Europe, Asia and Africa. However, this raised a number of important issues for Corrymeela, particularly as to how some people from different cultures could fit into the Community. Williams says, "There were some people from a quite different context, and the cultural difference meant that their integration into the team was much more difficult. I am not convinced that it ever happened completely.

"Maybe we did not tackle that challenge proactively enough in terms of our supervision and our facilitation of a particular group, but the truth is that you can have a certain level of diversity, yet beyond that it becomes counter-productive." There was also the challenge of keeping in contact with former volunteers. Duncan Morrow reflects, "This was a big issue. People were coming to Corrymeela from the Balkans, Azerbaijan, Kurdistan and all sorts of places, and that was fine. However, when they returned home we couldn't keep any connection. For example, there is no ongoing community in a place like Kurdistan."

Significantly, the decline in funding for Corrymeela raised the question of appointing specialist volunteers, and people who had particular skills to offer. Trevor Williams says, "We had developed a system which was very generalist. In other words, people did a whole range of tasks, including housekeeping, kitchen work and reception, but a generalist in certain situations is not always that helpful, whereas a person who is going to be trained in a particular area, like administration, would make the system more efficient."

Without doubt, the vast majority of volunteers benefited from the Corrymeela experience. This gave most people their first opportunity to work with groups, including former prisoners, the victims of domestic violence, cross-community school groups, and those who were physically or mentally handicapped. A Swiss volunteers recalls, "I worked with a group of former prisoners and paramilitaries, and their lives were so different to mine. I learned a lot from them in a very short time."

A European volunteer found that "a 'nightmare' family group showed me what family love is". For Northern Ireland volunteers it could also be an awakening experience. One 1990 volunteer recalled, "The international groups opened my eyes to the world outside Northern Ireland. Working with Protestant groups, I had previously had very limited and destructive experience of the Protestant community, and this offered a period of transition for me."

The demands on the volunteers were considerable. Another Swiss visitor noted that volunteers were expected "to be always cheerful, energetic, enthusiastic, giving, superhumans who could survive on two hours' sleep, and serve toast for breakfast with a big smile and a song". There were also mixed views from volunteers about how they were managed by the community. A local volunteer from 1999 claimed that the management was not efficient enough: "There was a lack of feedback and training, especially in the Northern Ireland situation – not for me but for others."

An American volunteer felt that the management at times had been "fairly loose. More training skills are needed at the beginning of the volunteer term, other than the fire system and how to turn off the furnace." In contrast, another local volunteer felt that the management had been caring: "Our strengths were identified and best used and our weaknesses were recognised and worked on." A Finnish volunteer had only positive recollections: "The staff gave us the frame. They taught us what was expected of us, and put us with a warm hand on to the job and made us part of Corrymeela."

There were contrasting views about the volunteers' inter-action with members of the wider Corrymeela Community. One Northern Ireland participant said that volunteers played an essential role, and that Corrymeela wouldn't exist without them. However, an English volunteer made an important distinction by stating that long-term volunteers "played an important role in the life of the Centre. Not so much in the Community."

An American noted pointedly, "It depends on what you mean by the 'Corrymeela Community'. To me that meant the staff and volunteers, and the Ballycastle Centre. In that case we played a crucial role, as we made the residentials happen each week and weekend. To others, the 'Corrymeela Community' primarily meant the dispersed community of members, and we didn't have much interaction with them."

At times there were tensions. One Northern Ireland volunteer said, "There was a sense that some members would waltz in once a year, make a series of demands of volunteers and claim the kudos for the important work done at the Centre, without being part of it all."

Another volunteer said that many members were "warm and supportive, but a significant minority treated the volunteers as slaves and were not pleasant to have at the Centre. Some of this minority thought they owned the place, and treated volunteers with a certain amount of contempt." On the other hand, yet another volunteer found Community members "very friendly and welcoming, especially for me as a foreigner. I was glad to stay with Community members in Belfast."

There were also mixed views from volunteers about how their Corrymeela experience affected their attachment to the Church or other faith communities. A majority of 38 per cent said that Corrymeela had not changed their attachment, some 29 per cent felt that it had been strengthened, while 17 per cent felt that it had been weakened. One Irish volunteer, when asked how Corrymeela had affected his attachment to the Church, replied, "It didn't influence me hugely."

However, a New Zealand woman recalled, "I now have a different view on church-going, and value it for our family. Without Corrymeela, I probably would not have had my children baptised, or been baptised myself with them." Yet another volunteer said that her experience at Corrymeela had weakened her links with organised religion. She said, "I felt disheartened with the divisions it can cause. I felt that I needed some time out to work out what I actually believe when no one or no creed is telling me, 'You must believe this.'"

Many volunteers had warm recollections about their time at

Corrymeela, though some had less happy memories. One Israeli wrote: "I am very thankful for everything Corrymeela gave to me, though I am very sorry that such a committed Centre does not exist here in Israel." Another volunteer wrote: "My year at Corrymeela was the single experience that has had the biggest impact on me. There I did a lot of my growing up. I am eternally grateful for that opportunity."

In contrast, another volunteer wrote that "inadequate management and being over-worked has contributed to current mental health problems." Another volunteer said that Corrymeela had been a very positive experience but that "my year would have benefited greatly from better management and decisive organisation. My general opinion is still that a shake-up is necessary to improve relations between programme staff, volunteers, kitchen, housekeeping, etc."

Another volunteer found that the programme "was totally inspirational and gave me a great opportunity to learn new skills and to change my career path completely. I decided not to keep in touch with Corrymeela at all, as I did not want to become one of these people who never leave the place and who never moves on. However, I have nothing but extremely positive memories from the year, which was the best I have ever had." The Corrymeela experience lingered on in the lives of the volunteers. One, aged 40, wrote to say, "I've had a great and exciting life so far, but that one year at Corrymeela always stands out as being the most intensive, valuable and interesting thus far."

The results of this survey might not be typical of the views of the long-term volunteers at Corrymeela from 2002 onwards, but they do give a broad snapshot picture of the challenges, tensions and rewards of such involvement. Clearly, Corrymeela and its volunteers gave much to each other, and the overall experience was well outlined in the introduction to the Report: "The overwhelming feeling from the survey was a positive appreciation by volunteers of their Corrymeela experience. Different volunteers, of course, stressed different aspects of the experience, but all found strong positives. Negative comments were less common, and therefore harder to generalise. However, some may provide pause for thought."

The comments of one volunteer summed up some of the best of Corrymeela during some of the worst of times in the tortuous history of Northern Ireland: "Corrymeela touched my life deeply, and although an extremely busy life has stopped me making deeper contact, a visit to the Centre always brings a sense of magic back."

A more recent volunteer, from Nigeria, outlined the atmosphere in Corrymeela in the emerging 21st century. Ochanya Jane Ameh first heard about the Community from the Methodist Church in Lagos and successfully applied to come to Corrymeela. She arrived in September 2006 for a year's placement. She says, "I had read almost everything in advance about the Centre and its activities, but I was surprised to discover the range and volume of activities that actually take place. I was overwhelmed to realise that it is a safe and open space for all, and that this does not stop at reconciliation work only – it helps people with personal injuries to heal their wounds, and they feel relieved at the end of their stay here."

Corrymeela, she believes, is truly a place of refuge. "It is open to Christians, Muslims and foreigners from every part of the world, who come as a group to share ideas on how to resolve conflict, which is one of the major problems facing the globe. I've learned how to welcome people and to introduce myself, how to accept others, irrespective of the differences in religion, faith, colour or traditions."

The essence of the Community, she feels, is in service. "This will go a long way with me, even after leaving this place. I am now engaged to my long-term boyfriend, although we separated at one time because of a conflict. We are planning to get married when I return to Nigeria, and I think that it is the peace and reconciliation work at Corrymeela that has helped to make this happen. Being here has been a blessing to me in so many different ways."

SEVENTEEN

HARD TIMES

DR DAVID STEVENS, who took over from the Reverend Trevor Williams in January 2004, was the first non-ordained minister to be chosen as the Leader of Corrymeela, though he was an elder in the Presbyterian Church. He was, at the one time, the most and the least obvious candidate to take over a job which made the utmost spiritual, intellectual, emotional and sometimes physical demands on the person asked to do it.

Stevens was the most obvious candidate because he had been a long-time member of the Community, and he worked for over twenty years with the Irish Council of Churches (ICC). People were prepared to believe that anyone who could help hold together such a wide range of Church institutions during decades of community violence and deadlock would have no trouble in leading a Christian community with its own stresses and stains.

Stevens, on the other hand, might have been seen as an unlikely candidate for the post of Leader. He had no managerial credentials, or even the experience of running a parish. He looked like a bearded academic don, and he had a direct style as well as a reputation for not taking prisoners.

This was well illustrated by his foreword to John Morrow's book, *On the Road to Reconciliation*. While praising Morrow warmly for his integrity, fairness, honesty, courage, persistence, hard work and respect for words, David Stevens also noted that "like many Presbyterians, he can be an awkward customer at times – John's are not charismatic virtues, but they are the virtues of a good companion on the Way". Ironically, a number of Stevens' friends would describe him affectionately in almost exactly the same manner. It is a characteristic of Northern Presbyterians that they tend to tell the story exactly as they see it.

Stevens was not part of the smooth "celebrity" culture so suited to the intensive media exposure of the modern age, though that was a distinct advantage. Behind the image, however, David Stevens was a warm-hearted individual with a sharp mind, and one quality which – above all – would be essential for anyone taking the post of Leader in the early Nineties: this was the ability to take hard decisions in an age of retrenchment, and also the gift of being able to retain the vision of Corrymeela and to adapt it to the challenges facing it. In that vital aspect, Stevens shaped up well to the job.

In his inimitable style, he described his early background, and the factors which led him to Corrymeela, in his seminal book *The Land of Unlikeness – Explorations Into Reconciliation*. He wrote: "My family went to Dublin for a holiday in 1961, and one of my sisters got lost in Clery's store. My mother's first thought was, 'The nuns have got her.' My grandfather on my father's side played badminton with the local parish priest on a Sunday evening. I remember my aunt saying, 'The Catholics are moving into the area'; yet she was a good neighbour to the Catholic family living down the street. I remember a Catholic friend talking about her father being a commander in the IRA in the 1920s; at least one of my relatives was a 'B-Special' at the same time."[1]

Stevens describes vividly the religious and social apartheid of the Northern Ireland where he grew up. He remembers talking to a Catholic priest who came from the same town as he did: "We worked out that we must have travelled on the same bus to school. I have no memory of him, but I can remember the Catholics on the bus crossing themselves when they passed Holywood Chapel, and wondering what these strange people were doing. These people did not belong to me. They were not part of my religious or political community."[2]

His only contacts with Catholics in his schooldays were through playing chess with them. "The things that struck me about Catholic education – learned from this contact – was that pupils could smoke, and they got beat. Thick hedges screened us from each other." This was not true only of schools. "I remember the Northern Ireland of the 1950s and 1960s as being a suffocating place, both religiously and politically. Nothing ever seemed to happen. And there were the silences, the denials, the evasions, the lack of honest conversations – the 'whatever you say, say nothing' – the coasting along – a world of profound disease. I belonged, and I didn't belong."[3]

Stevens became a student at Queen's University, and at a Freshers' Conference in 1966 he discovered Corrymeela, which had been founded by Ray Davey and others the previous year. He recalled, "I sensed a world of freedom there, which I was immediately attracted to. I have been involved ever since." He relates how Corrymeela, over more than three decades, helped him to "see rare beasts and have unique adventures", as described in W H Auden's poem "Land of Unlikeness".

Even in the earliest days, Stevens could see the broad picture clearly. He stated, "Corrymeela … was still very much a Protestant world, but at least there was a group of people who were seeking to face the divisions in Northern Irish society, and were open to meet 'the other sort'. If they hadn't yet fully connected with the Catholic community, they were preparing themselves for what was to come in the 1970s."[4]

Stevens worked for Corrymeela for two years, after leaving Queen's in 1973 with a degree in chemistry. As General Secretary of the ICC from 1992 to 2003, he gained valuable experience in this role, and he worked with a number of able, courageous, high-profile, and in some cases, formidable Church figures during some of the worst of the Troubles. They included Canon Bill Arlow, Primate and Archbishop George Simms from the Church of Ireland, the Reverend Dr Eric Gallagher, a Methodist President, Dr Stanley Worrall, the headmaster of Methodist College in Belfast, and the Reverend Dr Jack Weir, the Moderator and Clerk of the Presbyterian General Assembly.

Stevens also became involved with the Dutch Northern Irish Advisory Committee, a small inter-church group with members from the Netherlands and Northern Ireland. They sometimes took themselves rather too seriously, but they had some good ideas and they also knew how to enjoy themselves. Despite their best efforts, however, the Committee was too small and under-resourced to make a significant and lasting impact.

However, it did have achievements, not least in introducing Stevens and others to new aspects of Northern Irish life as seen from an outside perspective. This included prolonged exposure to the remarkable Roel Kaptein, and his Dutch colleagues, the Reverend Aat Van Rhijn and Father André Lascaris.[5]

(The author was an active member of the group for several years, and shared many of its individual and collective faults, as well as some of its achievements, pains and pleasures.)

During his years as ICC General-Secretary, David Stevens was involved in important peace and reconciliation initiatives, including those from the Corrymeela Community and others, such as President Mary McAleese and Geraldine Smyth OP, Cecelia Clegg, and Joe Liechty from the Irish School of Ecumenics. They worked closely with church groups, among others, and Clegg and Leichty produced the important standard work, *Moving Beyond Sectarianism: Religion, Conflict and Reconciliation in Northern Ireland.*[6]

Stevens was also impressed by Frank Wright, an English political scientist who joined Queen's University in the 1970s. "He was one of the most impressive political thinkers I've ever met, and wonderful with young people and women's groups. He recognised that Northern Ireland was an ethnic frontier society where Irishness and Britishness meet, and where the forces of law and order find themselves taking sides with one community. Frank analysed this in great depth in 19th century Ulster, and described how the British state took sides with the Orange Order, because it could not maintain an authority which supported both communities."

Frank Wright wrote an important article in the 1970s about Loyalism "when everybody else was writing about Republicanism.

Tragically, Frank died at 44, but he had predicted correctly what was going to happen in Bosnia. He could see why it was going to disintegrate, out of his profound knowledge of divided societies."

He also wrote a book titled *Northern Ireland: A Comparative Analysis*. Stevens says, "Though terribly badly written, it was brilliant. When Frank encountered the work of Rene Girard through meeting Roel Kaptein, he totally rewrote the book. It ended with a quotation from St John's Gospel, which was a very interesting development, for a secular political scientist. Frank was a very bright guy, and his death was a great loss."

Though much of David Stevens' career, like that of others, was forged through the worst of the Troubles, the situation in Northern Ireland gradually improved following the Downing Street Declaration of 1993, and the messy paramilitary ceasefires which followed relatively soon afterwards. As well, the complex, deliberately ambiguous, and virtually unworkable Good Friday Agreement helped to improve significantly the political and social landscape.

The 1993 Declaration led to a tortuous "peace process" which seemed under constant threat of self-destruction by its seemingly reluctant participants. Nevertheless, it brought about, by September 2006, the still surprising but welcome admission by the International Monitoring Commission that the Provisional IRA had indeed disposed of its arsenals and had decommissioned its weapons.

However, despite the continuing paramilitary racketeering and gangsterism, it was clear that Northern Ireland was entering a period of relative peace. On 5 October 2006, a London *Times* editorial stated "Ulster Moves Forward – There is reason to cheer steady progress in the Province".[7] This new mood had set in much earlier than 2006, and it had important implications for many people and organisations, including David Stevens and Corrymeela.

He recalls, "When I was considering the post of Leader in 2003, I was aware that the situation was changing for the ICC, and for Corrymeela. A certain phase of their existence was coming to an end and they were going to have to become different sorts of bodies. The outside interest in Northern Ireland, and the funds that had been channelled into the province as a result, was coming to an end."

Stevens was then 55 years old. He says, "I realised that if I stayed on with the ICC, I would have been there until retirement. I had been around Corrymeela for a long time, and I was aware that difficult decisions were going to have to be made. I was prepared to take that on. I felt greatly challenged and renewed at the prospect of doing the job."

With characteristic candour, David Stevens admits to not knowing whether he is a visionary or a manager. He says, "I come from a family of bureaucrats, and my background is in administration. My father was a Town Clerk, and my memory was of him sitting with his legs up on his desk and reading. It wasn't that he was lazy, but this was a different era in the late 50s and early 60s, and he'd done the work."

When David's own children came into *his* office much later on, they would say, "Can I sit in Daddy's 'thinking chair'? So I don't believe that I'm particularly a visionary or an administrator. I suppose really I'm an intellectual – I analyse and I think."

There was much to think about during his early days as Corrymeela Leader, and David Stevens took over at a time of particular difficulty. The Centre Director, Frank Nealis, was on long-term sick leave, and Alastair Kilgore deputised for six months until Frank was able to go back to work. Nealis later submitted his resignation, and he departed in March 2005. Kate Pettis became Acting Director for three months, and eventually Ronnie Millar was appointed as Centre Director in June 2005.[8]

Stevens, on taking over, faced two major problems: in finding a permanent Centre Director, and also in tackling the financial challenges. He says, "The first priority was in keeping the show on the road. Within a reasonably short time we appointed Ronnie Millar as Centre Director, and that was important. He's a really good guy, and I feel that we are lucky to have him. I leave Ronnie to run the Centre, but there's hardly a day when we are not in contact, and we talk through issues that have to be dealt with. However, I don't interfere. Ronnie bears the day to day brunt of running things at the Centre."

From the start of Stevens' tenure of office, finance was a problem. He says, "The Community Relations Council announced that it was reducing our grant aid from £183,000 a year to £125,000 a year, over a three year period. It was clear that we faced financial instability, and we asked our accountants to carry out a review of the Ballycastle Centre. As a result, we had unfortunately to make redundancies, including one of our management team, as well as abolishing other posts. So my first year was a baptism of fire."

Was this difficult personally? Stevens says, "I remember a friend in an executive position in another organisation saying to me, 'If you have to do these things, do them in the first year. Don't hang about, or it will get harder. I am not a person to lose sleep or to agonise over these things. If you have to do it, you have to do it. The decisions are usually fairly clear. At Corrymeela, there was the personal angst of those involved, but I learned that it was not so difficult dealing with the people who were actually being made redundant."

What was more difficult was dealing with those people around them. "There was 'survivor guilt' and also 'surrogate guilt'. By this I mean that the people you think will be angry at being made redundant are not so, but other people are angry on their behalf. And people who are around those who are being made redundant have all sorts of feelings as well. Members of the Community, and of the Council, found things difficult."

Some of them would ask themselves and others, "How can we do these things, within a Christian community?" Stevens says reflectively, "The answer, unfortunately, is we all live within financial realities, whether we are churches, Christian communities, families, or organisations. If you don't have money, you don't survive. I don't see myself as a 'hard man', but I am willing to make cut-backs. It isn't a choice, it's a matter of survival."

This, inevitably, has been painful for Corrymeela. Stevens says, "We have a culture that likes meetings, and participation, but which doesn't like to be involved in the hard decisions. One member of staff in Corrymeela described a decision by the Community as 'simply another stage in an endless process'. This implied that decisions were not things to be taken seriously, and that's one of the mind-sets which I have tried to change."

Stevens was determined that the Community would confront the harsh realities. "I wanted people to realise that we actually were going to do these things. In most organisations there are not the same personal relationships that we have in Corrymeela. I was very much aware that some Council members found themselves making their friends redundant, and that this was not easy for anyone. I understood that, but it still had to be done."

The decision to close the Knocklayd Centre, in the longer term, was particularly difficult. This was gifted by Peter Tennant, who became involved with Corrymeela much earlier on, and it created an important niche for members of the Community – particularly with adults working in the area of spirituality. It became clear, however, that a large amount of money would be required to refurbish Knocklayd properly, and this outlay had to be measured against the needs of the Ballycastle Centre.

Stevens says, "Many people have a passion for Knocklayd, just as they had for the Corrymeela Link in Reading. Individuals become very committed, and loyalties grow up, but we are in a world where the resources are simply not as available as they were in the past."

He continues, "The Corrymeela Link at Reading had done a good job, but we concluded that we couldn't raise more from our existing sources of voluntary income, and that we needed to be more serious about fund-raising." In doing this, however, the Community could be accused of placing more importance on "fund-raising" than on "friend-raising", which had been the basic philosophy of the Corrymeela Link.

Stevens says, "The Reading connection was supporting primarily a number of groups whose members were ageing. I don't necessarily see that as a criticism, because the Churches in England and Wales have members who are ageing also, and they need to raise funds to maintain their infrastructure. We in Corrymeela also realised that, with Northern Ireland going out of the news headlines, it would be more difficult to raise funds."

Those which had been donated in earlier years were, in one sense, artificial. "If there hadn't been the Troubles we wouldn't have grown to the size we were, at one stage. In reality, we are in the process of returning to normal, so we must keep this in view as part of our long-term perspective. One might even argue that we should be supporting ourselves primarily from resources in Northern Ireland, and not from England or Wales or from elsewhere. The basic reality is that the world has changed, and we cannot support and sustain the things that we have done in the past."[9]

So what are the alternatives? David Stevens says, "It is not simple, and there is no single 'way ahead'. However, there are a number of things which we can do. We are aiming to increase the use and occupancy of the Centre at Ballycastle, and we are looking towards more inputs from volunteers to help with our work.

"We are also trying to direct our fundraising better and more economically, to reduce any costs we can, and to focus on key objectives. This includes the use of a website, and also concentrating on what we have learned and are learning from Corrymeela which will be of relevance to other people who are also facing the challenges of peace-making and reconciliation."

The key to future viability, Stevens believes, is to make the Ballycastle Centre more economical. "It is our biggest expense, and we must put more people through it. This sounds all very managerial, and my background is not in management, but whoever had come into my job would have been faced with these issues. We have done difficult things, and I think that the Community realises that we have not been doing these things because we want to, but because we need to."

The role of the Leader is not only to help secure the financial future, but also to guard and nourish the original vision and to help to adapt it to meet the challenges of the modern age. David Stevens says, "One of the difficulties about working in the whole area of reconciliation is to help give it a practical content. Ray Davey was a prophet in the 1960s. He was talking about reconciliation and relationships at a time when nobody else was doing so."

On the other hand, some of the basic issues in Northern Ireland have become clearer. "We now know more about the real price of making peace. There are at least three main issues facing the entire community and its politicians – will the conservative and non-ecumenical Protestants, like the Democratic Unionist Party, really share power long-term with representatives of the Roman Catholics, and will the Republican movement fully support the state institutions of Northern Ireland, including the police? The final issue is trust, and this is essentially the issue about relationships between the two main communities."

Part of the role of Corrymeela is to demonstrate that groups of people across the political and religious divide have shown that it is possible to develop trust and interdependence. David Stevens says, "Corrymeela has been doing this for forty years, and it is clear that reconciliation in any meaningful sense in this society is going to take at least another forty years."

Despite the ceasefires and the imperfect "peace process", the situation in some ways has become more difficult. "We have an exhausted, weary, cynical and privatised society, particularly within the middle-class, where people still think that they can opt out with impunity. In the present context, it is difficult to energise people. When there was violence, the divisions had greater clarity, and you could talk more easily about peace and reconciliation, but now we are discovering how difficult this actually is."

The price of peace is complex, and stark. "People will have to abandon deeply inherited historical patterns of living, and of course there are always reasons for not trusting Protestants to share power with Catholics, for the simple reason that they have shown historically that they have not wanted to share power. Naturally, of course, Protestants believe that they also have good reasons not to share power with Sinn Fein because they believe that this organisation has been involved in violence. There are always reasons for continuing on historic patterns of behaviour, but the reality is that you cannot make Northern Ireland work as an entity if people are not prepared to work with the other community, the other crowd, 'the other side'."

David Stevens believes that there is nothing wrong with the original vision of Ray Davey and Corrymeela. "It remains as valid as when the Community was founded, but it is very important that this vision is not grounded solely in the Troubles, or even in Northern Ireland. If we had been solely identified with the Irish Troubles, we would have had enormous identity problems when those Troubles ended, or whatever they were being transmuted into."

Significantly, the Corrymeela "vision" constantly needs to refresh itself in the light of changing circumstances. "Northern Ireland is now a more diverse society, and there are issues such as ethnic minorities and other factors. The big challenge is in having the eyes to see the new issues, and to be able to respond to them."

The answer does not necessarily lie with Corrymeela becoming a bigger organisation. Stevens says, "That would require large inputs of resources, and it is never the way that people like Ray Davey or John Morrow worked. We were into multipliers, into getting people to do other things, and we still are. If you looked at the Government's document on the 'Shared Future', this is what Ray Davey was prophesying forty years ago. Now it has become mainstream."

Stevens is reassured by the long-term influence of a large number of volunteers who come to Corrymeela. He says, "Some 40 per cent of these people who were involved with us as volunteers made significant career changes, and became all sorts of things. For example, Duncan Morrow became Chief Executive of the Community Relations Council; Brendan McAllister became Chief Executive of Mediation Northern Ireland; and Eamonn McCallion worked in Community Relations in Schools. There was a whole breadth of Corrymeela influence and involvement in our society through peace and reconciliation work."

Despite all the challenges, including the lack of funds, Stevens remains optimistic. He says, "Newness will come, though you never know where it will come from, so over the next while our task is about carrying out what we have learned – the vision and the spirituality – in such a way that the new generation will also learn from that. You need roots, and the vision provides you with a certain rootedness and seeing what this means for today and tomorrow. That's the way to go. It is not just simply to take up every passing fancy and to think that this is new and exciting.

"It's a bit like the Old Testament. The Israelites were turfed out of the Promised Land into Babylon, and the prophet Jeremiah told them, 'Terrible things are going to happen to you, but there will be newness.' The whole point of this, of course, is that Jeremiah did not tell them precisely where this newness was going to come from! In our modern context in Northern Ireland, creating newness is actually very difficult, but I do think it can happen."

Stevens was proved right, but more quickly than he and many others imagined, when the agreement between the DUP and Sinn Fein was concluded so unexpectedly in the spring of 2007. Archbishop Alan Harper, the newly-elected Church of Ireland Primate, spoke for most people when he addressed a press conference during the first day of the General Synod in Kilkenny. Speaking shortly after the historic meeting between Paisley, McGuiness, Blair and Ahern at Stormont on 8 May, he said, "The politicians now have to take full responsibility for their actions, and they have to do what they say they intend to do – to create a prosperous and equal society.

"The difficulty of their task is illustrated by the length of the engagement that has been needed to get them to this stage. They must make it work, and I believe that they have the wish to do so, but it doesn't alter my opinion about the difficulties. They have all come a huge distance, but there is still more to do."

EIGHTEEN

CHANGE AND CHOICE

RONNIE MILLAR, who became Centre Director in 2005, faced a task as formidable as any of his predecessors. He took over the job at a time of great change, due to the improving peace process, which led to a dramatic decrease in violence, but which brought financial and other challenges to Corrymeela, as has been noted elsewhere. It was becoming much more difficult to attract funding, which in turn led to redundancies and downsizing.

This was very different to the Corrymeela of earlier times, and the pain was felt by all. On the positive side, however, the new circumstances challenged Corrymeela to be more innovative and relevant.

Ronnie Millar possessed many of the important qualities and the experience needed for the job of Centre Director. His early background in Northern Ireland had given him a painful awareness of the realities of the sectarian divide, and as a successful business executive he had the experience of taking hard decisions. Most important of all, he had a deep awareness of the ethos and objectives of Corrymeela, which matched his own.

Millar grew up in a Loyalist housing estate in Antrim. His father was a Presbyterian, and his mother was a Roman Catholic. Life for a family in a "mixed marriage" situation was not easy in the troubled and sectarian Ulster. Even from his early childhood, Millar remembers the tensions. He says, "As a young boy I watched the rioting in Ballycraigy, and I saw my friends being burned out of their homes. It got to the stage where my father felt that it was not safe to stay, so we moved to another Protestant housing estate at The Steeple in Antrim, which seemed slightly safer."

However, there were still problems. Ronnie, the eldest of four children, felt very much an outsider. "All of our immediate Protestant neighbours were part of the Loyalist culture, with the flute band, and the Orange Order, and that kind of thing. The annual Eleventh Night bonfire, with the resultant Loyalist celebrations, took place only 200 yards from our house, and I was very much aware of the differences between us. At times I felt harassed and intimidated, like any other teenager who was perceived to be 'different'. I was caught up in street fights, and at times I had to run for my life."

The family moved yet again, and this time to Randalstown. Ronnie, though bright, did not do well at school. He recalls, "I went into a full phase of listening to punk music, the Sex Pistols and that sort of stuff. I even dropped out of school, but recovered this later on."

Millar also found religion, in an environment where the child of any mixed marriage could find it difficult to decide whether he or she was a "Catholic" or a "Protestant". Ronnie was baptised as a Catholic but regarded himself as a "Christian". He says, "When I was about 18 or 19 years of age, I definitely became aware of God in the sense of needing something else in my life."

He joined a small church group in Randalstown. "It was really a 'wee meeting place' with a strong evangelical approach, but also inter-denominational. Though it was small, it was remarkable, and a great experience to share. For the first time in my life, I was really aware of having a relationship with God."

In the meantime, Millar was discovering his skills in electronics, some of which he had inherited from his father, an electrician. He eventually found employment with an American computer company, and became a hardware engineer, based in Belfast. He later went on to university to complete his studies.

Although he was living the "good life" with fast cars and the material trappings of success, he was still deeply involved as a deacon and as a Sunday School teacher in the Randalstown church. He says,

"I loved sweeping the floors, peeling potatoes and that kind of thing."

Millar's connection with Corrymeela began some years later as the result of dating Kelly Matthews, an American student at Trinity College in Dublin. Kelly was from Milwaukee and with strong Catholic roots in an Irish-American family. Her great grandfather, Francis Patrick Matthews, had been a former US ambassador to Ireland. When Kelly decided that she wanted to spend a year as a residential volunteer at Corrymeela, Ronnie drove her to Ballycastle for her interview.

He says, "Initially I was wary of Corrymeela. I felt that it was a bit insular. I remember cautioning Kelly to be careful about deciding to work there! Thankfully, she didn't listen to me, and she was accepted as a volunteer. When I started coming to see her at Ballycastle, I worked as a volunteer at weekends in housekeeping and in the kitchen, and I really began to appreciate what Corrymeela was doing. It fitted in to the kind of thing I wanted to do."

Then Kelly and Ronnie went to live in the United States, where they were married. Ronnie was relocated by his computer company. He also took a degree in Human Services and Community Planning at the University of Massachusetts. Kelly, though living in Boston, was still nearer her parents in Milwaukee than if she had stayed in Northern Ireland.

The Millars spent eleven years in Boston, but they kept up their ties with Northern Ireland. Ronnie was keen to see his parents regularly, and he had also decided to leave the world of technology and devote his time to youth work. After five years in Boston he volunteered to work on "crisis hotlines", and community projects. He later went into education full-time, and started working in after-school programmes in Boston public schools.

Kelly, who had taken her primary degree at Harvard and her Masters at Trinity College Dublin, wanted to do a PhD. This would have taken up to seven years in the USA, but there were much shorter courses available in the UK and Europe. By this stage they had two young children, and they wanted to move somewhere which would provide stability for a young family. The Millars considered coming back to Northern Ireland and volunteering to work at Corrymeela for two years. Ronnie says, "I felt very strongly about reconciliation, and about working with young people, and helping them to discover what they had in common. So when the job of Centre Director was advertised, I read about it in Boston, and jumped at the opportunity to apply."

This looked like the opening which the Millars were looking for. Ronnie says, "Though I still had to apply for the job and undergo a formal selection process, I felt that this was an opportunity to come 'home' both personally and professionally. Northern Ireland is a very welcoming place, and that is what kept us coming back regularly all those years when we were living in Boston. For me, also, there was a spiritual dimension to the journey. In Boston, things were moving at a crazy pace, and I was well used to working 80 to 100 hours a week. I felt that I needed to have more space to develop spiritually, and to be in a community."

Millar was offered the job on 16 March 2005, and started work at Corrymeela in June. He says, "David Stevens had prepared me well during the intervening months. I was briefed on the management and finance issues, and I had experience in the private and voluntary sector of dealing with budgets and managing change. I was not brought in to 'downsize' as such, but the budget was stressed, and while we were looking at the next five years, we hadn't figured out how we would approach it in detail. We had a strategic plan, and my primary task was to put that into effect."

Unfortunately, this led to redundancies. Millar says, "It was not something which I would have preferred to do, but I had been through it before. I was deeply aware of the personal pain of people, and it was not easy. Some of the people involved had been with Corrymeela for over thirty years, and they were part of the fabric of the Community and the Centre."

Though Millar was the "front" man, he had the support of the Corrymeela Leader and Council. He says, "It was actually worse than I thought it would be, but I felt that I could cope even though there were many sleepless nights, and very hard things were said to me personally. All of that had an effect. I was also aware that we were dealing with people who had a combined service to Corrymeela of more than one hundred years."

From his experience Millar knew that managing the rate of change was important. "You can't rush things, and you need to build up relationships and trust." However, finance was a major priority, and there was a need to bring more people to the Centre, and to charge them more. "We made good progress just by being responsive and providing basic customer service in such things as answering the phone and replying to e-mails. The business cliché is 'picking the low-hanging fruit' – like sending out invoices and getting money in. It is paying attention to the easy stuff."

What about the "harder stuff", like programming? Millar says, "Our work has to be relevant to Northern Ireland and to young people, church groups and family groups in the 21st century. We can no longer run the kinds of programmes that were working in the Seventies, because people are bored with that kind of thing. There are so many residential centres where people can do this. The beauty of Corrymeela is that good things can happen in the programme, and also outside the programme when people get together over cups of tea or when washing up. That's where some of the real work takes place."

Some of the hard stuff is dealing with the consequences of the Troubles. This includes work with victims' groups, sometimes on a cross-community basis. As one participant from a programme involving Shankill Stress & Trauma and the Victims & Survivors Trust (VAST) from the Falls commented, "If you could massage the hand of the other, sure you could never kill them."

North Belfast is a patchwork quilt of Protestant and Catholic communities, often with walls between them. Corrymeela's Interface Worker, Susan McEwen, carries on a great deal of work with such communities. A recent residential "stay" at Ballycastle involved a strategic planning weekend for the North Belfast Conflict Transformation Forum with community activists from both sides of the divide.

Significantly the modern programming is not just about Protestant-Catholic encounter. Millar explains, "When groups come together, it is as much about living with people who are different from ourselves in terms of views or backgrounds as it is about Protestants and Catholics."

In December 2005, the Causeway Cluster Community Cohesion Project ran a "Welcome to Northern Ireland" event, specifically targeting migrant workers. Fifty people from twenty-one nationalities attended. Corrymeela was deemed the only possible venue locally, as the Community was able to offer particular resources in terms of hosting the event, and of having adequate rooms and staff who would be equipped to deal with the diversity. One of the organisers said, "I found them an excellent organisation to work with – it was hard work, crossing three borough council areas, and they took over the food/accommodation/decorative welcome banners; on the night of the event, the volunteers played an important role on standby for registration, serving, welcoming, and encouraging people on to the dance floor. We were provided with a whole team of people at no cost because they were all volunteers." The Centre has also been hosting weeks for refugees and asylum seekers for a number of years. All of this is being done in response to the increasing multi-cultural and multi-ethnic diversity of Northern Irish society.

The Youth in Community Project managed by Corrymeela staff member, Tara McHugh, is working with marginalised young people. The programme is delivered in partnership with other youth service providers, including the Nucleus Centre (Derry), Ballymena Community Forum, Springboard, Cedar Foundation (Ballymena), Indian Community Centre (Belfast), Homefirst Aftercare and Leaving Team (Magherafelt), Include Youth, RAFT Project (Armagh), Trauma Advisory Panel (Newry), and Wave (Armagh).

The residential components involved 72 young people recruited from all over Northern Ireland and from the most marginalised communities. It includes those from ethnic minorities, of different sexual orientation, some with physical and learning disabilities, and others with connections to Social Services.

The work focused specifically on identity, cultural traditions, sectarianism, and community relations issues within the context of personal and social development activities. One of the young people said afterwards, "It made me realise what the differences in culture are, and that some people hold certain beliefs which are different to others."

For Corrymeela it is important to stay with the work of reconciliation and of being together in community. As Ronnie Millar says, "This is why I like to think about the establishment of Corrymeela in 1965, and the beginnings of bringing people together from different backgrounds. Sometimes when you talk about Corrymeela it can seem very simplistic, but that's what we are about, and having the privilege to host people in this place and giving them a chance to talk. The core and very heart of Corrymeela has not changed, though we might have to adapt to the current environment and society. Different people from different backgrounds will always struggle to live with one another, and they will always need some assistance with that."

One of the important challenges facing Corrymeela is how best to help others in situations of continuing conflict. Ronnie Millar says, "The Northern Ireland I came back to in 2005 was not the place I left in 1993. It is a different ball-game completely, though there are still undercurrents of the sectarianism, racism and fear that is in each of us. The violence has decreased, but the tensions and the distrust are still there. The big challenge still is where do we move our programme and our work, and how do we remain relevant and progressive?"

Perception is important. "Someone said to me recently that Corrymeela is sectarian 'because you call yourselves Christians, which means that you are not welcoming Muslims and Jews'. That is not true. We are a Christian community in the broadest sense, and there is a spiritual dimension to reconciliation and to living together."

One of the newer projects hosted but not organised by

Corrymeela is the Young Enterprise Programme, which involves Protestant and Catholic schools from North and South. The essence is to help teenagers learn more about business and commerce, and to look at reconciliation in terms of economics. While it brings much needed revenue to Corrymeela, the programme does not necessarily share the spiritual concepts of the Community.

Ronnie Millar is aware of the inherent difficulties of this approach. "There are tensions because the project brings in money, yet those who take part are not much into the Corrymeela way of doing things. For example, we have morning and evening worship, but the teachers and the staff in the Young Enterprise Programme seem less interested in this dimension to Corrymeela's daily life.

"However we are working hard at developing relationships. We don't have any input into the Young Enterprise Programme, and that does not sit easily with us, because we are so used to facilitating the programmes ourselves. The situation is being carefully monitored and we will decide whether we want this kind of relationship to develop or not in the long-term."

Corrymeela is a Christian Community which reaches out positively and practically to people of other faiths. Ronnie Millar says, "I've had the pleasure of working with Israeli and Palestinian students at Corrymeela and to share our experience with them, and I also went with a number of our programme staff to London to help coach and to mentor the students in preparation for going back to their own countries. At Corrymeela they had a sense of being given a welcome and also of being made to feel safe.

"I believe that the experience of Corrymeela and the skills that we have developed are applicable in other places, but only so long as this is within the context of each particular situation. After forty years we have learned a great deal, and Northern Ireland is further along the road of conflict resolution than some other places. It is important to bear in mind, however, that the Troubles here have been like a kindergarten compared to the degree of conflict that has taken place in other parts of the world – including Rwanda and the Middle East."

However good the programmes are, one of the hard realities of running the Ballycastle Centre is its financial viability. Millar says, "Our total building projects for the next few years will cost more than £3 million, and that is a lot of money. We are going to reduce the number of beds from 110 to 88, partly because the groups are becoming smaller, and we are not dealing any more with groups of 50 to 60 people. Our aim is to be able to host several separate groups on-site at the same time, with appropriate meeting spaces and other facilities.

"Coventry House will be rebuilt, with appropriate accommodation, and improvements are planned for The Croi, which in many ways is the heartbeat of the Ballycastle Centre. The International Fund for Ireland is a major supporter of the work of Corrymeela, and we are applying to different foundations and trusts for more resources."

All of this is familiar to anyone who undertakes capital development on a large scale, and while Corrymeela faces financial stringencies in trying to met its budgets and development costs, there seems to be an awareness of the truth of the old cliché that "behind every visionary is a good accountant". The way ahead lies with bricks and mortar in a practical sense, but the Christian vision of Corrymeela, which has brought the Community safely through many challenges, remains the primary focus.

Yet, while Corrymeela has a spiritual dimension, it does not try to impose religion on people as such. Millar says, "Our approach to working with groups is about developing relationships, but I did not come back from America to run a hotel or a residential centre and nothing else. For me, the very core of what we are about here is our faith and our relationships with each other. We have a clearly Christian ethos, and that is central to what we do. We do not preach or lecture, but I've met people from all religious backgrounds and of none who have come to this Centre and who feel a peacefulness and a spirituality about the place."

Ronnie Millar's vision for Corrymeela is that the Community "will be doing heart work with all kinds of different people and having more of an influence in the community at large. I hope that we will be influencing most of the programmes that are here, and working for an environment where we can be honest with each other, and remaining true to the welcoming, the hospitality, and the voluntary service – not into making profit, but financially stable with enough reserves for a rainy day, and not having to go through redundancies when we hit a storm."

It will be important to continue to work with institutions "whether it be with schools, or the youth service or the churches. It is so important to work with priests and ministers, and with churches either at the institutional or the parishioner level. Corrymeela should be a louder voice to the churches, and to those marginalised or who don't feel connected to churches. There are a lot of people out there who are hungering and exhausted, and are looking for something deep in their lives in this age of commercialism and busyness."

Millar pays tribute to the many people who have been an inspiration on his journey to becoming Centre Director at Corrymeela. "David Stevens is a real leader, efficient and businesslike, and also a philosopher and theologian. Alastair Kilgore has been a great mentor, Derick Wilson has been an inspiration, and John Morrow has been very supportive."

Recently, the Dalai Lama came to Corrymeela and met Ray Davey and other members of the Community. Millar says, "It was like a meeting of two spiritual giants. They embraced each other, and there was a real heart to heart. We've hosted many visitors at Corrymeela, but nobody else could have held the moment like that. Everyone was in awe. I seldom cry, but when I saw Ray and the Dalai Lama embrace each other, I was in tears. It was just amazing.

"Ray is still a remarkable influence, and sometimes I feel that I'm doing this for him, carrying on the vision, and I think of him often, and also of Kathleen. For me it's a bit like passing on the baton – we are all part of one relay team, and it's been a great privilege to be part of this story."

NINETEEN

MORE CORRYMEELA PEOPLE

MANY PEOPLE HAVE COME to Corrymeela and have moved on. Others have stayed for a longer or a shorter time, and have made a greater or lesser contribution to the Community, but they have made a contribution nonetheless.

Some visitors have memories which even pre-date the development of the Corrymeela site. Edna Kerr, now living in Canada, says, "My first encounter was away back in 1952, when I was a first year college student, and worked there as a volunteer during the summer holidays. It was then a Holiday Fellowship Centre and it catered for people who wanted to explore the Northern Irish countryside, and enjoy more creature comforts than those offered by the Youth Hostels at that time."

Three meals a day were provided for guests: a cooked breakfast, a good evening meal and, most important, a packed lunch for the day's hike in between. Edna recalls, "The Warden was a Miss Shelly, and there was a cook and a programme director who arranged all the day trips, and social events in the evening. There was also a maintenance crew and several volunteer helpers who worked as maids and helpers and, like me, served meals and made the beds."

Even then there were chalets on the site. "The main building had more accommodation for guests. There was also a large dining-room, a common room for games, dancing and other activities, and an administration office. The helpers were given one day off each week, and they used that time to accompany the guests on their outings. This was a wonderful experience for me, as I so enjoyed hiking and exploring all the beautiful areas around the North Antrim countryside."

Edna later went to live in Canada, but she kept in touch with her roots and visited Northern Ireland regularly. She says, "I was thrilled to learn that during the Troubles, Corrymeela had become a reconciliation centre, and later had a new raison d'être. During our visits there, we were warmly received by the staff. Our Canadian friends who were with us were very impressed, and commented on the special feeling about the place. It was heartening to see so many diverse groups there, coming together for fellowship and hopefully realising that we are one people under the skin."

Desney Cromey (née Kemptson) was one of the founder-members and worked closely on the work camps. She again recalls some of the excitement of the early days: "There is something special about the beginning of any journey, and although we had nothing in material terms, yet we had everything. It was an exciting and rewarding challenge, and there was a sense of privilege and trust. I smile as I think of the great fun, but it was also hard work. For many it was life-forming, in terms of skills and faith development. I get so much pleasure remembering those beginnings, and they remind me of the lines from Wordsworth:

"Bliss was it in that dawn to be alive
To be young was very Heaven..."

Another volunteer in the early days was the Reverend Dr Donald Watts, who later became a Presbyterian minister, and eventually Clerk of the General Assembly. His introduction to Corrymeela was in September 1966 at a "Freshers' Conference" at Queen's University, and he later visited the Ballycastle Centre. He recalls that "The House had just been bought the year before and was coloured a dull green. The accommodation was basic, and I especially remember the low wooden sink you had to lean over to wash dishes, but the views from the cliff-top were as spectacular as they are today. So also was the warmth of the welcome. Corrymeela became a second home, as well as a place which gave us the freedom to ask big questions of our Christian faith at a time when our community was also beginning to ask questions, to which we are only now perhaps finding an answer. Corrymeela has been a bright light shining for many people through very dark days."

Like many others, Donald Watts took part in work camps. He says, "We weren't always very good at it! I remember trying to install a water-pipe to supply the 'new' chalet village at the cliff-edge of the site. No one had thought to tell us that it would have been easier to roll it out before we filled it with water. However, through all our mistakes, we built relationships and a confidence in discussing our faith with others who held different opinions. Those years certainly helped to form my fundamental understanding of how to live out our Christian faith in a challenging world."

When Watts finished as a student at Queen's University, he went off to study theology in Edinburgh. He says, "For some years it was possible to maintain a fairly strong link with Corrymeela, and long enough to meet my wife Fiona, who was working in the kitchen there one summer."

However, with passing time, it became more difficult to keep the ties, other than through friendships and interest. Watts says, "I still like to think that the lessons learned in those student years have not left me, but have found expression in other ways. I am certain of one thing, however – Corrymeela did not come into existence just before the Troubles by accident. It was called as a light to shine in the darkness, and the darkness would have been much deeper without it."

Though the majority of members in the early Community were Protestants, a number of Roman Catholics were involved as time went on. They include individuals who rose to high positions in the Church. One such person was Donal McKeown, who became a priest and in 2001 was appointed Auxiliary Bishop in the Diocese of Down and Connor. Within the Irish Episcopal Conference he has responsibility for Ministry to Young People and to Third Level students and Vocations. He is also a member of the Episcopal Commission for Education.

In the late Seventies he was invited by friends to take part in Corrymeela activities. He says, "The Ballycastle site offered a venue – even in the midst of difficult years – for people of energy and enthusiasm to meet and feel at home. Its informal construction and atmosphere meant that anybody could come and potter around, making a chosen part of the building the corner where they felt at home, safe, in control.

"This was very important, as people gathered from all sorts of local and international backgrounds. There was space inside and outside, at a time when we all needed such space around ourselves and within ourselves. And there was room to connect and learn. People could learn to be themselves and to trust others with that fragile, hurting self."

Worship offered opportunities for creativity. "Sitting on the floor was not my usual prayer stance, and the realities of church divisions were painfully felt by many people. However, Corrymeela offered the opportunity to be honest and consistent, despite the temptation to fudge issues and pretend that there were no differences in belief or conviction."

McKeown learned through his friends, who were members of Corrymeela, about the vision of the Community and its many struggles. He says, "Building relationships is not easy. Coping with the tensions created by outside events and by our own internal struggles – this takes big heart and great integrity. I saw that in many Community members. Through their struggles to work together, they provided an environment where others could learn hope, a listening ear, support, and a place to tell their story, whatever pain it held."

He believes that Corrymeela made a valuable contribution to inter-church relationships and understanding "as one of very many places where Church people have met and planned together, often when the political parties were studiously ignoring one another. Its main role, until now, has been on the micro level. The Community and its life helped many people to take one more step along the rocky road that they were on. That has helped to stabilise situations all round Northern Ireland, and beyond."

Corrymeela, he believes, "like so many retreat/spirituality centres, will have a future if it has core conviction as to what it is trying to do, and it can be a place to take a prophetic role. It will do well if it remains true to its searching, Christian roots. Consistent weakness and gentleness can be very strong!"

Another senior Catholic cleric Gerry Clifford, who later was appointed Auxiliary Bishop of Armagh, came to know Corrymeela in the 1980s. He says, "I remember well being involved in the discussions and debate, most of them friendly but all of them challenging and constructive. Corrymeela stood as a symbol of new opportunities and new beginnings.

"It has made the clarion call to Christians to explore the future together, and to leave behind the bitterness and divisions of the past. It has helped in its own way to build confidence in a divided community and it has been instrumental in helping us to heal the divisions of the past and to look to a better future for all."

Clifford particularly treasures the meetings in the Belfast home of Ray and Kathleen Davey. "Those were the moments for church men and women to talk out the differences between us, to respect that difference and to address the areas of division that need attention. They were always warm, friendly, hospitable and memorable occasions."

Some people like the Methodist, Professor Sir Des Rea, had a relatively brief but seminal association with the Community. He says, "I was 'in' at the beginning, although on the periphery. I greatly admired Ray in his Chaplaincy role at Queen's. In his very person he was a peacemaker, and in moving to set up Corrymeela in response to the times, it was an evolution process that in retrospect was natural, given his inclination."

Sir Desmond believes that Ray has been "more of a pastor than a leader, and that is not to minimise his role. He surrounded himself with a 'community' of people who brought their own gifts to building up Corrymeela and its role in Northern Ireland. The Community, at all times, has sought to build bridges, and it called upon its members to seek to do so in their individual lives. That was certainly true for me." Rea went on to hold a number of "bridge-building" posts in the community, including the Chairmanship of the Northern Ireland Policing Board.

A childhood and perceptive word picture of Corrymeela is painted by Duncan Morrow, the son of the former Leader Dr John Morrow and his late wife Shirley. He admits that "Somehow, Corrymeela has always been part of my life. I must have been only four years of age when I was first taken to Ballycastle, so I might not be the best person to give objective judgements!"

As a child, Duncan was aware that the Ballycastle Centre was a place "where other people wanted to be. During the summer weeks, I remember using the fact that our family arrived a day before the others came, and left only when they had got on to the bus, to boast about how I 'lived' there. I was also aware at an early age of how devastated I felt when I left the place."

However, three things left a big mark on him, as a child. "First, I met people whom I didn't know from my ordinary life; people from abroad, people who 'had to be' at Corrymeela. Secondly, I remembered a sign which said, 'Corrymeela begins when you leave'. From an early age, I suppose I imbibed its missionary content.

"Thirdly, I remember sitting in a worship tent and enjoying being there. Not that I knew any theology, but I got a clear sense that something of importance was happening to me there." Those three factors remained with Duncan Morrow into adulthood. There was the conviction that "the lived experience of Corrymeela had a wider meaning for the rest of life, and an unconditional joy, which went beyond the merely explicable, and pointed to a more important communion".

In fact, Duncan Morrow literally grew up with Corrymeela. He says, "I was there during internment when Corrymeela buses ferried families out of West Belfast. I was there on Bloody Friday and watched adults cry as they waited on people coming back from day trips to the city. I met recovering drug addicts, 'hoods', people who swore a lot, ministers, priests, church groups, North-South groups and people with disability."

He watched young adults entertain pensioners, he washed dishes, he sat on reception, he helped in the kitchen. He says, "I was a helper on family weeks and I led international work camps. I once led a camp, half of which was on the peace-line in West Belfast. I helped with the early development of Corrymeela's work in schools and with young people, and in facilitating difficult conversations around the political and religious topics which others avoided."

The young Morrow met people from around the world: "Desmond Tutu on reconciliation, Jean Vanier talking about living with people who had a disability, Jim Wallis on global justice, and Roel Kaptein talking about the core truths. And I got to work with Roel and Derick Wilson and Frank Wright, and to think and learn about understanding conflict, and finding ways out of it. Ultimately, all this was critical to my whole career, including my current job as Chief Executive of the Community Relations Council. It was a rich diet."

Other people had different, but equally rich, experiences. Louis Boyle, a Catholic who held a senior post in Social Services until his retirement, has been a member of the Corrymeela Community for over twenty-six years. He first experienced Corrymeela early in 1972 when he was working for the Community Relations Commission. He recalls, "I was struck from the outset by the ambience of the place, by a sense of being really made welcome, of a relaxed, informal atmosphere which was pleasant and comfortable but not luxurious. Above all there was the outstanding beauty of the location, with a commanding view of Rathlin Island."

He remembers a number of conferences at Ballycastle, and particularly those concerning police and community relations in some of the most difficult years of the Troubles. Boyle says, "I also remember a conference in 1976, not long after the establishment of the Peace People, who helped to release an outpouring of anger, grief and yearning for peace which could only be sustained for a short time.

"There was intense media, including international media, interest in this new movement and they for a time succeeded in taking over the stage almost entirely in relation to peace work. Some other organisations felt somewhat eclipsed by what was happening, but most activists welcomed the upsurge of feeling from the grass roots against the ongoing violence."

The 1976 conference attempted to look at peace work at that time, but Louis Boyle recalls that "it was very difficult to prevent the agenda being taken over by the Peace People. Corrymeela was one of the groups who were involved in peace work for the long haul, and while happy to facilitate and support these events, the Community did not allow the intense interest generated to detract from the ongoing and longer-term agenda."

Boyle, like David Stevens and others, was an active member of the Dutch-Northern Ireland Committee and pays tribute to the work of Roel Kaptein and his colleagues from the Netherlands: "Roel's thinking and insights had a big influence on some members, and an influence which is still prevalent to this day. Roel eventually became a member himself, possibly our only Dutch member!"

For several years Louis Boyle was chairperson of the Corrymeela Council, a position which gave him a greater understanding of the complexities of Corrymeela. "This included the ongoing tension between the Community ideal, which we were trying to create and maintain, and the organisation which we were trying to run. Holding everything together, as the staff and Council try to do, is no easy challenge. It has always struck me that the amount of voluntary work from community members, friends and others, is tremendous and that the Community and the Centre could not function without this."

The period of the Republican hunger-strikes was a particularly testing time for Corrymeela. "Quite wide differences of opinion occurred, and much heat and emotion were generated. The divisions were not just on grounds of religion, and within both the Catholic and Protestant communities there were significant differences on moral and political perspectives. It is important to note about

Corrymeela that the divisions we face do not just go down the usual political/religious lines but often cut across all the conventional boundaries."

In the 1990s Louis Boyle and John Morrow set up a current affairs group and invited leading politicians, clerics and others for private discussions. Boyle says, "I always found that in a private non-threatening setting, our political invitees were a lot more open than would have been possible in public, or indeed in their own very private party setting. Although I suspect that some politicians, especially in the extremes, saw us as 'do-gooders', I found that all of our guests treated our meetings seriously and conveyed to us a high regard for our work."

Arising from these private encounters, Boyle and Morrow organised a series of open political conferences at Ballycastle. They had no difficulty in enlisting support from the Ulster Unionists, the SDLP and the Alliance Party, but the DUP studiously remained aloof. Boyle says, "It was typical of the negative and defensive position that characterised the DUP during those years."

At the same time, Sinn Fein were still being regarded as "political outcasts". Boyle recalls, "We were not able to invite them officially, as this, if it were known, would have stopped some mainstream politicians from attending. However, a number of low-key representatives came along. It is difficult to know, with hindsight, what these conferences achieved, but at a time when political dialogue was more difficult and when little was happening on the political front, these gatherings made some contribution to the situation."

Arising out of the first meeting with Sinn Fein, and in response partly to a veiled invitation, Corrymeela held meetings in Clonard Monastery with some of their leading figures over a series of months. Boyle says, "Sinn Fein saw us as a channel to the Protestant and Unionist community, and it took us a little time in getting them to realise that while we could hope to articulate the Protestant-Unionist viewpoint, we did not represent that community. As members of Corrymeela we represented a range of political and religious perspectives, and we emphasised the independence of our stand."

Boyle was struck by Sinn Fein's clear analysis of the situation, though only from their own perspective. "They saw the problem in Northern Ireland essentially in terms of the British presence, and once their military and political apparatus were out of the way, the Unionist community would come to accept their part in a new Ireland. For our part, we conveyed to them that there was a substantial majority of the Protestant-Unionist community who in effect *were* the British presence, and who would have to be negotiated with, irrespective of what any Westminster Government might do."

Louis Boyle also recalls that Sinn Fein were unhappy with any attempt to raise the issue of IRA violence. "Whenever this was put up front in dialogue with others, it became a block to further discussion. I am aware that around this time there were other contacts and dialogue initiated with Sinn Fein, and this preceded the Hume-Adams talks. Both Sinn Fein and ourselves took the dialogue seriously. It extended for several months and contained some straight talking. We certainly conveyed to them the huge difficulty, if not impossibility, of any political progress or serious political discussion involving them with the ongoing violence of the Provisional IRA and of their links with them."

Louis Boyle's recollections provide clear insights into the extent to which Corrymeela was prepared to take risks in reaching out to groups like Sinn Fein, with whom it was not politically correct to be in touch at that time. However, Corrymeela had its own difficulties in making meaningful and permanent contact with the Protestant evangelical churches. David Porter, Director of the Evangelical Contribution on Northern Ireland (ECONI) – now called the Centre for Contemporary Christianity in Ireland – charts his own steps to greater understanding with Corrymeela.

He first heard of the Community as a young man growing up in East Belfast. He says, "Being of the Mission Hall persuasion in that Church, Corrymeela was not perceived or received as a good thing. It was where they were being 'ecumenical'. My first sight of the place was during a school weekend at the Scripture Union bungalow, just along the coast from the Ballycastle Centre. A few months later we actually went up the hill to Corrymeela and joined in an evening at the Centre. But then other things were happening – the Peace People were established, as was the 'charismatic movement', with nuns and priests at Cecil Kerr's meetings at Queen's. Developments in the late Seventies were certainly moving my teenage boundaries."

Porter knew that some of his fellow Evangelicals, including Derek Poole, Maurice Kinkead and Joe Campbell, were actively involved with Corrymeela, and he also met John Morrow and David Stevens. "I found them to be fellow-travellers. I had read some of the work of the Faith and Politics group, and was now getting to know the members, and sharing a common concern and conviction in relation to the ongoing impasse in Northern Ireland."

David Porter's first "real" visit to Corrymeela – actually attending an event – was in 1989. He says, "By then ECONI had come into being, and I had just been appointed to the British and Irish delegation to attend the San Antonio World Mission Conference of the World Council of Churches. John Gladwin, the Evangelical social justice guru, was speaking at the clergy conference, with Bishop Cahal Daly. It was designed to bring Evangelicals into the conversation. We went along to Corrymeela, with others from The Bridge, a Baptist-based urban mission project in East Belfast. Gladwin was the attraction, and a new relationship with Corrymeela was the outcome."

Porter also recollects that some years ago he had "a very heated conversation" with a leading member of Corrymeela in the bar of a hotel in Washington DC. He says, "There was anger at the Evangelicals, and particularly with some of the older figures associated with ECONI, who in the late Sixties and Seventies, when Northern Ireland was in freefall, kept their distance from Corrymeela and others. They knew that the community situation required at least a conversation together, but they were wary of the ecumenical dimension."

Porter admits freely his doubts that he would have been any different from his older colleagues. He says, "The Northern Ireland conflict did not necessarily negate all other concerns, and our journey in reconciliation required us to be authentically evangelical. Some resent the time we have taken, but that is not to understand the Evangelical community in its wide context, and the significant impact of the 1974 Lausanne Covenant in creating the space for social justice alongside evangelism and a world-affirming Biblical faith. Within a decade this was reforming Evangelicalism in Northern Ireland, and this made the dialogue with Corrymeela and others possible."

Part of the story of the community conflict in Northern Ireland is the fact that the Evangelicals pursued their own course. Porter says, "Now that journey has brought them along the same and parallel paths to Corrymeela. In a context where ecumenism and political compromise are perceived by some as dangerous rocks for the ship of faith, we still take a different tack as we navigate the winds of the peace process. But we are all in the same convoy."

Porter stresses, "It is to Corrymeela's credit that, as our journeys have brought us together, they have welcomed Evangelicals to the conversation. Since the early Nineties I have found the Community a place of welcome and of listening. Space has been provided for the Evangelical voice to be heard and respected, and my colleagues and I have spoken at Summerfest, both as main contributors and in seminars."

David Porter also associates Corrymeela with individuals who have made an impact on him. "It was through a Community seminar that I forged my friendship with President Mary McAleese. Trevor Williams was a good friend before he became Leader, and it was in regular meetings with him for coffee, as leaders together, that I became most familiar with Corrymeela. The two people who have had the most impact and who remain among my closest professional colleagues are indisputably Corrymeela people – Brendan McAlister and Duncan Morrow."

Porter also pays tribute to the Corrymeela Leader, Dr David Stevens. "He is a wise man full of good counsel and astute analysis, and with that most uncommon of gifts, common sense. More than most, as General Secretary of the Irish Council of Churches, and moulded by the Corrymeela ethos, he has ensured the space for Evangelicals to be at the table when others did not have the patience or the inclination to do so."

Despite the developing relationship, Porter points out that the conversations with Corrymeela have not always been easy, and he retains reservations about some of its inter-faith dialogue. He says, "Evangelicals have strong views, and we are not afraid to speak them. I still differ with many in the Community on the true nature of the ecumenical enterprise. Politically I have been surprised at how Unionist some members of Corrymeela actually are – and that is not the stereotypical expectation. I am also concerned about Corrymeela's future as a Christian community of reconciliation as the ecumenical dialogue extends to include inter-faith dimensions."

However, David Porter acknowledges that one of Corrymeela's strengths is that it was not born out of the Troubles. He says, "Its vision preceded that period. Like all of us, it has been shaped as a Community by those events, and must now recast itself to make a major contribution to our shared future. Part of that must involve recapturing the original founding vision and drawing from it the core values that must shape any Christian witness for reconciliation in the new context in which we now find ourselves."

An important insight into the work of Ray Davey and of the Corrymeela Community is provided by the Reverend Dr Mark Gray, who recently became minister of Cooke Centenary Presbyterian Church on the Ormeau Road in Belfast. He graduated from Queen's University and taught at Coleraine Academical Institution and then in Malawi. He studied in the United States before taking up an assistantship at Gilnahirk, and he was later the minister of Carnone and Convoy in Donegal, before coming to Belfast. He is a member of the Corrymeela Community and, as convenor of the Presbyterian Church's World Development Committee, he has an international view about social justice and development, as well as peace and associated issues.

He believes that it is significant that Ray Davey saw the need for the Corrymeela Community prior to the outbreak of the Troubles. He says, "Ray had the vision to see that the division and brokenness in Northern Ireland were part of a wider global context. The terrible reality of the traumatic rupture in the human family he experienced during the Second World War helped him to see more clearly than others what was really going on beneath the surface in Northern Ireland when he returned from the war. This pointed to the need for deep reconciliation, allied to and dependent upon the search for peace with justice."

Mark Gray quotes the prescient lines by the poet Seamus Heaney, who wrote about Northern Ireland before the outbreak of the Troubles: "Life goes on, yet people are reluctant to dismiss the possibility of an explosion. A kind of double-think operates; something is rotten, but maybe if we wait, it may fester to death."

Gray comments, "Ray indicated that he too knew there was something rotten in Northern Ireland, but he did not participate in the double-think. Instead, he took the action he could to begin to address the situation. He could see that, contrary to the story we still like to tell ourselves, this was not 'a grand wee place where most people got along just fine, and sure everything would have worked out in the end if it hadn't been for the trouble-makers'. Ray lived and acted out of this insight."

Mark Gray recalls a story that illustrates how Davey challenged and motivated others. He says, "This was told to me by Addie Morrow [the brother of John Morrow], who said that at the start of the Troubles, some Corrymeela people met each week to pray about the deteriorating situation. Ray announced at one meeting that he was going to an area of Belfast where Protestant vigilantes were attacking Catholic homes. He said that he needed to be there in solidarity with his Catholic neighbours and asked us who would accompany him. Addie Morrow recounts that at that moment he realised there was a cost to faith, and that faith must find expression in action."

Mark Gray believes that "Ray Davey was the most important, prophetic and visionary Irish Presbyterian of his generation and perhaps of the 20th century." Gray also notes that there is much talk at Corrymeela currently about reconciliation taking some thirty years and becoming an inter-generational process. He warns, however, "While there is, no doubt, truth in this, if the Community allows itself to become too narrowly and closely defined by one aspect of life in Northern Ireland, it will have lost something of its visionary source and inspirational depth."

He adds, "The search for reconciliation, peace and justice in Northern Ireland is part of, and must be connected to, the journey of the whole of humanity as it struggles and limps towards the new heaven and the new earth."

It is a point, however, about which Corrymeela has remained very much aware.

TWENTY

THE POLLEN OF PEACE

ON A SUNDAY AFTERNOON in November 2005 the Dalai Lama made history by visiting the Corrymeela Centre in Ballycastle. There was an air of anticipation as Corrymeela members and friends crowded into The Croi, and they were not disappointed. The Dalai Lama, accompanied by Ray and Kathleen Davey, entered together and were given a warm reception.

Due to language difficulties, the Dalai Lama relied on an interpreter, but his support for the work of Corrymeela was made clear. He said, "My spirit is with you and please carry on your work tirelessly. You can consider me as a member of your Community." However, the occasion was one for symbolism as much as for words.

The presence of the Dalai Lama together with Ray Davey, both wearing white scarves, was indicative of the stature of both men in their different ways, and it also underlined the international outreach and reputation of the Corrymeela Community. It was also interesting to note how both men, who had achieved so much spiritually, were modest and self-effacing. There was a natural affinity and respect between both leaders.

The Dalai Lama confirmed to a reporter later on how much he had been impressed by the quiet spirituality of Ray Davey. He also told the journalist a story which could easily have come from Ray himself. He said, "A friend of mine was released by the Chinese authorities in Tibet after a long period of imprisonment and torture. He said to me, 'There is only one thing I now fear. I am afraid that I will not be able to forgive my captors. If I go on carrying a

resentment against them, that will not do any harm to the Chinese
authorities, but in the long-term that resentment will destroy me.'"[1]

Incidentally the Dalai Lama's two-day visit to Northern Ireland
attracted considerable media attention, and an inter-faith event at St
Anne's Cathedral in Belfast was so well attended that the Church
authorities had to lock people outside due to fire and safety
regulations. It must have been one of the rare occasions in recent
times when any Cathedral's doors had to be locked due to the
numbers of people attending.

Although the Dalai Lama's visit to Ballycastle and his meeting with
Ray Davey had been unique and symbolic, it had not been a day for
words from either of them. However, there were a couple of eloquent
set speeches from the Corrymeela Leader, Dr David Stevens, and
from Community member Norman Richardson.

Stevens, as ever, put his point succinctly. In outlining the history
of Corrymeela, he told the Dalai Lama that the vision for the
Community came out of Ray Davey's experience of being a prisoner
of war outside Dresden when the city was bombed by the Allies some
sixty years ago.

David Stevens underlined how Corrymeela had been deeply
shaped by the local conflict, and spoke of its mission to be an
ecumenical community of Protestants and Catholics, in order to seek
"the mending of relationships within the Christian family". He
added, however, that in today's world there was a tougher challenge.

He said, "It is the challenge of building bridges between different
faith communities. Religion is now a major presence on the world
stage in a way that would have been inconceivable some two decades
ago. If communities are to stand effectively against the perversions of
religion that lead to terrorism and violence, we shall need to stand
united as human beings. Such unity will not gloss over the differences
of creed or truth claims, but will celebrate the strength that properly
integrated diversity can bring."

Stevens reminded his audience that "Religious traditions bring
words and worlds of strangeness, difference and transcendence to the
places of political power and to those who see the world confined to

the economic and the material. They speak of a 'beyond' of truth, most clearly seen in our Christian tradition in Jesus' dialogue with Pontius Pilate. All religious traditions can bring messages of truth to power. You, like us, have been prisoners of hope. Corrymeela has sought to be a place of hospitality, an open village where the grace of meeting can bring surprise."

Stevens' message was not only a well-crafted welcome to his distinguished guests but also a powerful reminder to everyone of what Corrymeela was essentially about. This was followed by another eloquent welcome from Norman Richardson, who was the then Acting Secretary of the Northern Ireland Inter-Faith Forum.

He talked about the need for a "wider ecumenism" and the obligation of pursuing a "global ethic". He warned that "In Northern Ireland we are still too easily drawn in to the simplistic approach that defines everyone as either Catholic or Protestant. We neatly divide each other into 'us' and 'not us'. But this was never accurate, because it denied the significant diversity within those traditions, and often completely ignored the wider diversity."

He said that Corrymeela had to learn from the lessons of reconciliation that it had largely applied to the Catholic-Protestant divisions. He underlined that "Corrymeela must never become just a holy huddle of Christians congratulating each other on being able to share our Catholic and Protestant traditions. We must build on the strengths we have gained from this in order to challenge these new barriers, expressing our broader universal responsibility."

He said that, as a Community and as individuals, Corrymeela members had learned lessons "that apply just as much to our relationships with those who come from less familiar faith and ethnic backgrounds. We have begun to understand the power of listening to the other, encouraged by the old Jewish rabbis who taught that if God gave us two ears and only one mouth, we should listen twice as much as we speak."

His message, and the visit of the Dalai Lama, were timely reminders of the wider challenges facing Corrymeela in an age of multi-faiths which was overtaking the older Protestant-Catholic divisions. It was a reality which Corrymeela had already been trying to address.

Dr John Morrow makes the point strongly that the Community never regarded reconciliation as simply being about Protestants and Catholics. He says, "Our whole concept is about dealing with difference at every level – between men and women, between people of different race and culture, between industry and labour. In fact, with people at every level. Right from the beginning our approach has been to deal with crossing the divides. We have been working with a concept which is global. Ray Davey, in coming from the Second World War, was bringing a perspective which was about 'How do you create a world where we can learn to live together?' That is the massive question for everyone today."

Morrow believes that Corrymeela was "dragged back" to face one particular facet of that question, but that the Community never let go of the other dimensions. He says, "We will now, hopefully, be able to give them more space in the future, though a number of people – including myself – have already been heavily involved in some aspects of inter-faith work."

John Morrow was a founder-member and co-chairperson of the Council of Christians and Jews and a member of the Inter-Faith Forum, of which Norman Richardson has been a leading member. Morrow says, "A lot of work in that area is being done by Corrymeela, and in recent years our volunteers have been coming from Bosnia and other places, and we have had Muslim volunteers as well as Christians and atheists."

Like others, he believes that Corrymeela has learned lessons which could be helpful to others. "There are very few examples in the world where people of two national identities have got to live within one nation. The models for that are very few, and if we were able to work out something here, it would have significance for many other places. Increasingly we began to realise that once the troubles of eastern Europe began to make the headlines, Northern Ireland was not half as unique as people thought it was. They used to think that we were just some kind of backward place, a leftover from the 16th/17th century, but we are discovering that this type of ethnic conflict is now widespread, and that Britain is going to face it increasingly as racial minorities grow."[2]

In practice, Corrymeela has long been part of a global network as friends of Coventry Cathedral, but it has also been making new friends as well – including the St Ethelburga's Centre for Reconciliation and Peace in London. This was one of the oldest medieval churches in the city, which survived the Great Fire of London and the Blitz.

Sadly, however, in April 1993 it was devastated by a huge Provisional IRA bomb in Bishopsgate which was targeting the business sector of the city. The Church was almost completely destroyed but, significantly, a decision was taken to rebuild it as a peace and reconciliation centre. The Bishop of London, Dr Richard Chartres, said, "When I first saw St Ethelburga's, it was a heap of rubble, the victim of a violent quarrel in which religion had played a part. I thought it would be an ideal place to create a centre for preventing and transforming conflict, especially conflicts with a religious dimension."

With imaginative backing from a wide range of people and institutions, the vision became a reality. Today the Centre is a focus for important multi-faith meetings and dialogue and other activities, and Corrymeela speakers have contributed on a number of occasions. Simon Keyes, the Director, says, "When I came to the centre some two years ago, I found that there was a willingness for the two organisations to work together. Since then, the relationship has developed in a number of ways."[3]

Keyes says, "What I like about Corrymeela is that it's not just a theoretical policy, but actually about creating a community that lives out and protects simple but very powerful principles. That is something I would like to emulate at St Ethelburga's. We are a very different type of organisation, but I do think that the idea of a community which lives out religious ideas – and is not a traditional religious community – is a very powerful force in contemporary society."

An example of this interaction between Corrymeela and St Ethelburga's was seen in a Conference held in December 2006 on "The Nature of Reconciliation". David Stevens, and others with a wide experience of the work of Corrymeela, shared with the others the important concept that reconciliation often requires both parties to learn to deal with the loss of an aspiration – in a situation where, to create agreement, both sides do not necessarily get what they want. It was abundantly clear to observers, including this writer, that the lessons which had been hard won by Corrymeela in Northern Ireland could also have a national and an international implication.

Keyes says, "I think that Corrymeela has some good, well-proven, and well worked-through models of how to get people to talk across fundamental differences. Those kinds of facilitative human skills are in short supply, and Corrymeela could be enormously helpful in this respect. I'm always slightly wary of the idea that the specifics of peacemaking can be exported from one situation to another, and I don't believe it works like that, but I see Corrymeela as a kind of beacon."

He believes, however, that this experience needs to be distilled, so that people can see its relevance. "In dealing with Corrymeela, I've always been impressed with the reflectiveness of its people. They have that quality in spades, and that is one of the secrets. There is a wisdom and an experience that other people could relate to, if it is presented in the right way. Certainly we are going to continue to invite people from Corrymeela to come here and to contribute to our events. We also have our own Gullion Project in South Armagh, and I think that there could be some direct collaboration in Northern Ireland with Corrymeela. People in England often don't know what to make of the Northern Ireland situation, and they can't really work out what a peacemaking organisation actually does. Corrymeela has to lift itself out of that specific historical context and offer its experience, which can be relevant to the world now. I believe that it really has something to offer."

Corrymeela, though small in numbers, has already made a name for itself within the international peace and reconciliation network.

Dr Geraldine Smyth OP, is a lecturer in the Irish School of Ecumenics, and was formerly its Director, a position which she relinquished voluntarily when she became Head of her Order.

She says, "People *know* about Corrymeela. I go to conferences in Europe and the United States and they say, 'I'd like to see that place.' Somehow the message has got out there, and it has a credibility, if you look at people like Derick Wilson, Duncan Morrow and Doug Baker.

"These are the people I tend to meet from time to time, and they are all fired with a kind of pastoral vision, but they are also intensely practical. If Corrymeela doesn't have anything to say when the rubber hits the road, then it is just people talking to each other. So how do they sustain that? You have had people there from the very beginning, and yet they have always had the capacity to attract new members. They have volunteers every year, and I've spoken to one or two, and they have been changed by their experience."

Geraldine Smyth first encountered Corrymeela when some of her boarders at the Dominican College in Portstewart attended events at Ballycastle. However, she really got to know Corrymeela when she was a speaker at a two day ministry conference in the early Nineties. She says, "I found it a profound experience to be drawn into the different concentric circles. It was my first encounter with the notion of a dispersed community, because I am a member of a religious community. It was interesting to see the commitments and the bonds, and the thinking environment that was there, which was sustained by a relatively small core group, with these concentric circles."

She was particularly impressed by the atmosphere of The Croi. "It was, as the name suggests, a place of the heart, a core place. There was a sense of going in under the earth, and yet you had a sense of the sea around, and sitting on the floor, and of levelling, and of people coming into the place with simplicity, and openness and receptiveness. There was also a sense that a lot of pain had been shared there, and that journeys had begun and had been sustained there."

She remembers going for walks on her own "and looking out, and the sense of the land behind me with all the Troubles, and this Community which was being embedded – and the amazing work I was seeing in people who turned up to do the dishes and drive mini-buses, and the Community spirit of helping with the washing-up and engaging people in bringing something to it, as well as receiving back. There was also a concept of all that was behind it, but it was also in some way turned outwards."

Geraldine Smyth was also impressed by the range of people who came to Ballycastle, and not least the international volunteers. "It was Janus-like, with two faces. There was a face turning back into the Community and the land of Ireland north and south, and the different communities that came there, and yet with a sense of horizon. It was full of paradoxes like that."

As others have noted, there was also the sheer beauty of the place. "It was a rugged beauty on a harsh day, and yet some of the Summerfest experiences were sun-blest. The pain, the beauty, the community spirit, the prayer, it struck me as a place of hospitality, but it was a very non-judgmental kind of hospitality. Corrymeela created that kind of space. I'm sure that like any other community it had its fair share of eccentrics, and maybe some people who were dependent on Corrymeela rather than just being altruistic themselves. If the truth be told, many of us have that two-way relationship with any group we belong to – we both get and we give, but there was a sense that Corrymeela did not exist for its own sake."

She confirms the concept that Corrymeela has a high reputation in the national and international peace and reconciliation "industry". She says, "I can only speak for myself, but I think that our Director of the Irish School of Ecumenics, Alan Falconer, would not have continued to work with Corrymeela if he didn't have the sense that not only was their standing good, but that we had something to learn from them. We are a Research Institute and at the same time we are keen to stay in touch with some kind of a lived reality, where we won't just get lost on the wrong side of academe."

Corrymeela, she believes, is extremely important for theorists and also academics. "It is not about putting all the eggs into one basket, but theories need to be tested, and they need to be informed by experience, and experience also needs to give rise to it. I often think of the Reformed French theologian, Paul Ricoeur, and his phrase that the symbol gives rise to thought. Something that Corrymeela symbolised and stood for, the way that it embodied its vision – I think that this gave rise to new thinking."

Dr Smyth believes that Corrymeela's long-term sustainability is extremely important. She says, "I'm not in a position to judge how that would work out, but I am aware that peace groups come and go, and a lot of them lack sustainability. Roger Williamson is an Anglican who has been very involved in peacemaking and arms reduction, and he once told me that in his experience these groups have a life span of about eight years – in terms of people's tenacity, their ability to cope with disappointment, to negotiate crises, demoralisation, others just drifting off, getting married , moving elsewhere.

"However, in contrast to all of that, whoever conceived the Corrymeela 'formula', whether it was Ray Davey totally or the first group, there is still that sense of a dispersed Community. It seems to me that Corrymeela has all these concentric circles, the image of the different levels of community and participation, and some if it very intense. Yet somebody is directing it, somebody is leading it, somebody is constantly referring back to the founding vision, and at the same time grappling with changes in society and political structure."[4]

One of Corrymeela's basic strengths, she believes, is its adherence to its core values. Dr Smyth says, "When you go into The Croi, there is the Celtic Cross, the candle and the Bible. They are sustained and sustaining core symbols which call you back to the Christian message, and the fact that you can be a light in the darkness, or that sometimes the darkness creates its own light."

She feels that it would be a mistake for Corrymeela to stray from its core beliefs. "There is a huge temptation for people to do that today, because of all the worries about faith schools and Muslims and Hindus. There's this 'blessed rage for sameness' and a feeling that we've got to iron out all the differences. Let's celebrate the feast of Aedes with the Muslims. Let's celebrate Hanukkah. It's like settling for this hollowing out of the different stories, systems of meaning, symbols, rituals that shape who we are and motivate us, inspire us and hold us together. There's a way of doing this and I think that Corrymeela has the right balance, that is not apologetic and not exclusivist, and which isn't obliging people to conform to it."

Despite the strengths, however, there is always an economic reality, and Corrymeela has had to undertake serious financial heart-searching. Geraldine Smyth says, "I don't know a lot about that inner examination, other than seeing the anguish at times on David Stevens' face, and knowing that he had radical cuts to carry out in order to make the whole thing a leaner operation. There is also the challenge of trying to deal with the pain of the shift from the volunteerist model into another well-managed, professional, sustaining organisation, because I've been on that journey myself. How do you hold the best of both and, at the same time, knowing that if you are not sustainable, all the volunteerism in the world is not necessarily going to pay for the oil bills?"

She believes that "living with limits" is the core of the Incarnation. "I wish I could live it better myself. We over-extend ourselves and we think we should never say, 'No.' I think that the leadership of Corrymeela, especially the current one, is good at doing that." The secret of sustainability, she believes, is to keep reflecting on failures as well as successes.

She says, "If you are up there and flourishing, the only way is down because the very fact that you've got it up there means that you've developed out of a vision, set a direction, policies and structures, but structures won't sustain a vision. So it occurs to me that Corrymeela is not afraid to let a structure die, and allow the space to be filled with perhaps something new. You can't put your energy into everything. I become suspicious of organisations that try to branch into all kinds of things. If you want something to be sustainable and deep, you need to keep asking what it is that we can do, that if we don't do, nobody else will, and I don't think there is another Corrymeela in Ireland, or probably not anywhere that I know of."

Despite the success of Corrymeela, is there validity in the argument that the Community might some day decide that it should be allowed to die off? Is there a danger that every institution, given a long enough period, might begin to believe more in its own publicity and past achievements than in an evolving mission based on its unchanging core values?

Geraldine Symth says, "If you are talking about peace and reconciliation, there is a way of merely using that as a shorthand for being into community relations, but there's always been a bit more rigour and substance to the way Corrymeela tries to think about that. In terms of the new hard-edged questions like racism and providing an hospitable place for people who are here in Ireland to make a second home or trying to help their families into a more decent mode of survival back at home, there is going to be a need for places like Corrymeela that have gained enough experience in dealing with difference, and being welcoming, and celebrating diversity.

"You can't get to that unless you deal with the hardcore issues of human rights and social justice, and you are able to think self-critically about your own assumptions, prejudices and ways of viewing 'church'. Corrymeela has a lot of experience, and I would hate to see it being lost."

The continued existence of Corrymeela, she believes, is a sign of hope. "It's a prophetic space and a place that is not afraid of failing. That to me connects into the very core of the Christian message which is in the heart of violence that was the Crucifixion – in the heart of betrayal, failure to understand, something radically different and evoking and drawing out of people who were broken and lost, the capacity to begin to change the world.

"Christianity has its history of all kinds of other oppressions, with a Cross in one hand and a sword in the other. Corrymeela understands that in some deeply human and Christian way, and at the same time – being mindful of our motto in the Irish School of Ecumenics which is 'Flourish in order to perish' – when the time comes when it is no longer needed, that people will be willing to let it die to the root and see what will emerge from it, trusting this pollen of peace idea, in the sense that pollen is scattered by birds and the wind.

"However I hope that this will not happen just yet! I hope that Corrymeela will be there for a long time to come, because we still have a steep journey of justice, reconciliation and of peace-building ahead of us."

TWENTY–ONE

BEGINNING
– WITHOUT END

IT IS ONE THING TO CHART the story of Corrymeela from its very beginnings, but it is quite another to predict the medium-term or long-term future of the Community. Despite its shortcomings, perceived and real, it has a considerable record of achievement to its credit, and the plaudits have largely been deserved.

The Irish President Mary McAleese has been a long-term supporter of the Community, from which, by her own admission, she has "learned a lot". She said in December 2005 that Corrymeela "taught us that change was possible but you had to commit to the long, arduous labour. You had to put the work in, so Corrymeela taught us the gift of patience and also, I think, the gift of respect."[1]

She also said that Corrymeela could take enormous credit "for the fact that so much has changed in Northern Ireland in the relationship between north and south, and in the relationship between these islands. Corrymeela set a standard. It set an agenda and was uncompromising in what that agenda was. It was an utter belief in the capacity of the human person to change for the better."

The Community, she said, "was always infused by a very strong Christian ethic. It was driven by the determination to love one another, no matter how unloved some of the people might have been by others, and even sometimes by themselves. For me, Corrymeela stands for the Gospel lived, and lived through very hard times, and through almost impossible times, but lived through authentically. It was a place that never allowed itself to be driven back by the forces of despair or the overwhelming forces sometimes of the awful events like Enniskillen or Omagh that drew so many people back into their bunkers."

Those things, she said, had never driven the people of Corrymeela into any bunker. "They just completely harnessed their determination to continue working even harder, to work even more determinedly to make the future a better future. So I think that what we enjoy today, we enjoy thanks to Corrymeela, and the many other organisations that are committed to doing that very difficult work."

Similar praise was expressed by Church leaders in Ireland and elsewhere, even though some of the Community's sharpest thinkers were critical of the lack of support from the organised churches – despite the fact that many individual church members had given strong and practical support to Corrymeela.

The complexity of living with diversity – a challenge facing the Churches and many other groups – was underlined by a former Presbyterian Moderator, the Very Reverend Dr John Dunlop, who spoke at a Corrymeela Sunday service in Westminster Abbey on 14 March 1993. He said, "Churches have not been particularly successful at accommodating difference and diversity. Denominations and congregations in Britain, as in Ireland and the United States, are often culturally and ethnically homogeneous."

When this happens, he said, it was easy for the Church to become, perhaps unwittingly, the servant of exclusive and excluding theologies. "It then betrays its vocation to be a community which crosses ancient lines of rupture. When that happens we denominationalise, nationalise or privatise God. Some ministers then become prison chaplains to imprisoned communities, while others become the chaplains to the warders."

Dunlop added that "Jurgen Moltmann in *The Trinity and the Kingdom of God* suggested that we should contrast notions of divine monarchy which can provide justification for earthly domination requiring servitude and dependency, with the Doctrine of the Trinity 'which corresponds to a community in which people are defined through their relations with one another and in their significance for one another, not in opposition to one another in terms of power and possession'."

Dunlop claimed that "therein is a challenge for the diverse peoples within the European Community; for the peoples of Ireland and the United Kingdom; for the people in the whole of Ireland and those within Northern Ireland". He also said that realism and vision were needed.

He concluded, "We need friends who take the trouble to discover that Ireland is a country significantly marked by difference. People who cannot do that are not friends of Ireland. We ourselves need to be people who can recognise and face difference and positively accommodate it. In this matter the Corrymeela Community has been a sign of the Kingdom of God, and a challenge and a help to the Churches."

The work of Corrymeela was also recognised outside, as well as inside, Ireland. Archbishop Desmond Tutu, the South African peace campaigner, was appreciative of the work of Corrymeela and said that the Community "was a practical witness of peacemaking in Northern Ireland".

His senior Anglican colleague Archbishop Robin Eames, the former Church of Ireland Primate who had served during some of the worst years of the Troubles, said that Corrymeela "broke new ground" at the right time because it was doing what in another sense the Ballymascanlon Inter-Church Conferences were trying to do for the organised churches' leadership.

"Corrymeela in breaking the mould was also saying, 'Here is a place in beautiful surroundings where it is safe to be yourself.' I once met a German who said that he had never been to a place like Corrymeela where the silence had spoken to him. That stuck in my memory." [2]

The Irish Roman Catholic Primate, Archbishop Sean Brady, who shortly after his appointment was a guest speaker at a Corrymeela Sunday in Portsmouth, said that he also had a high regard for the work of the Community. There was a danger, he said, that as the violence in Northern Ireland decreased, the work of the peacemakers might seem less urgent. He underlined, however, that the behaviour would not change "unless the attitudes which underpin the behaviour have changed. Obviously there are attitudes of suspicion and distrust going back quite a while but they are beginning to change. That's heartening, and it's bringing people along. The challenge is also to say, 'We can't leave it to the leaders, it's not fair to leave it to them', because all of society must be transformed and not just individuals."[3]

Cardinal Cormac Murphy-O'Connor, the Roman Catholic Archbishop of Westminster, gave an insight into the work of the Community in his keynote address at the 40th anniversary service for Corrymeela, in St. Martin-in-the Fields in London on 13 March 2005. He said, "Corrymeela is a place where the scales of distrust fall from people's eyes, where they always seek that which is fully human. More than a place, it is a spirit, one which constantly points to bigger horizons in defiance of structures and values and fears which cause horizons to shrink."

Other, non-clerical, accolades have underlined the general regard for Corrymeela and its work. Two of these came from well respected figures in the communications and artistic fields in the United Kingdom. Nick Ross, the broadcaster, had attended Queen's University in Belfast as a student, and as a young BBC television reporter later on he had covered some of the worst of the violence in Northern Ireland.

He said, "I realised how decency has to be fought for as tenaciously as others wage war for extremism; but, sadly, fanatics are more highly motivated than fair-minded people. Throughout the worst of things, Corrymeela has been an island of activism for reasonableness and reconciliation. If only there were more like it."

Simon Callow, the actor, was a Queen's student in Belfast, when the conflict erupted so suddenly and so violently. He says, "Whenever I go back, what I'm struck by is the will to build on the peace, however imperfect it may be. Corrymeela helps people to build and re-build."

This kind of praise, apart from being useful for Corrymeela's promotional literature, is fully deserved, partly because of the authenticity of the comments by people who are successful in their own fields, but who also spent part of their formative years in the cauldron of Northern Ireland.

So much for the best and worst of the past, but what about the future? Indubitably the situation has changed dramatically from the mid-Sixties when Corrymeela was established, though despite the political advances and the decrease in violence in recent years, there is still one factor in common – namely, that the long-term solution for Northern Ireland has still to be made to work. In the past forty years, it often appeared that peace would never be possible, but recently a number of dramatic developments have begun to enfold.

For example, the Reverend Ian Paisley and senior figures from his Democratic Unionist Party had a constructive official meeting at Stormont in late 2006 with senior Roman Catholic clergy, led by Archbishop Sean Brady. Such an encounter would have been politically impossible only a few years ago. Equally it would have been hard to envisage the possibility of the Republican movement giving its support to the police forces in North and South – even if some political analysts interpreted this as a calculated attempt not only to secure power-sharing with a sceptical DUP at Stormont, but also to add to Sinn Fein's political power-base in the Irish Republic.

Some of these tortuous political machinations were neatly summed up by the Church of Ireland Bishop of Clogher. Dr Michael Jackson, in a Christmas Eve sermon in December 2006, when he referred to the politicians carrying out "a dance routine of very complicated footwork and being ever so polite in insisting that someone else jumps first". In the end, they all jumped together.

However, beyond the political posturing, there has always been the spiritual question, which was outlined by David Stevens in his book *The Land of Unlikeness*, as to how much the people of Northern Ireland really want peace. There will always be the die-hards, on both sides, who want peace only on their terms, which (as history has shown) is not possible.

Stevens, in his book, refers to the story of the man at the Pool of Bethesda who has been ill for some 38 years and is asked the loaded question by Jesus, "Do you want to be healed?" As Stevens points out, this must have raised many questions in the man's mind, including "What am I going to be without my illness? How will this change my relationship with other people? How will I cope?"[4] As Stevens suggests, these questions can also apply to ailing communities, like Northern Ireland.

He asks, "Do people in societies riven by conflict really want to be healed? People who have lived their whole way of life with violence know where they are with conflict and violence. Having enemies gives identity....Like Tom and Jerry (the cartoon characters) we are always fighting, but we really need each other, and it would be rather boring without the conflict."

Change means taking responsibility and finding a new way of living with other people, as Stevens indicates. "The story of the man at the Pool of Bethesda suggests that Jesus would answer, 'Just do it.' Then we might have a miracle and surprise ourselves. That might make us interesting – and healthy – people."

Thus far, the hard-headed observers in Northern Ireland would point to the absence of such a cross-community "miracle", though literally miraculous spiritual transformations have been witnessed in the lives of some individuals who have been scarred by the violence, either as victims or perpetrators. It could also be argued that, given the despair and dehumanisation of nearly four decades of violence in Northern Ireland, what has been happening more recently is nothing short of "miraculous".

Indeed, one of the aspects of Northern Ireland which perplexes insiders and outsiders alike is how such hospitable people can also produce such violence, and equally how a population which wants peace can so regularly vote for deadlock at the ballot-box? Even after so much upheaval, Northern Ireland still stands at a crossroads as its people face the question "Do we want to be healed?", with all the losses as well as gains that this implies.

Assuming, optimistically, that the answer is in the affirmative, the work of Corrymeela will appear more and more relevant. If, however, due to reasons beyond the control of peacemakers and politicians alike, a political breakdown occurs, it is hardly conceivable that the situation could regress into the near civil war of the recent Troubles. It is worth remembering, however, that few people, including those who founded Corrymeela in 1965, would have foreseen the re-occurrence of the Troubles, and their continuation for over thirty years.

Dr John Morrow is hopeful, but realistic. "We are far from out of the woods as yet, and if we try to settle this problem with some form of benign apartheid, it will simply break down again. Unless we go on the journey of a shared society, we will be back in the circle of conflict. I am not pessimistic, however, and I believe we have sown the seeds which can grow into the kind of fruit that I hope they will. But an awful lot of nurturing of that seed has to be done if it really is to bear fruit."[5]

A similar point was made by Joseph Liechty and Cecelia Clegg in their definitive study *Moving Beyond Sectarianism*. They write: "To commit oneself to the journey of moving beyond sectarianism is to find oneself, along with the Magi in T S Eliot's poem 'The Journey of the Magi' no longer at ease, here in the old dispensation. While the road towards a new dispensation will undoubtedly pass through hard places, we are confident that those who make the journey together will find it rewarding, at times even joyous."[6]

Another significant factor in the story of Corrymeela, as mentioned before, is that the decrease in violence may lead to decreased funding which may not necessarily be a bad thing for Corrymeela as it may require the Community to be even more inventive. Nevertheless, it will not make life any easier for the leaders and the members.

Corrymeela has remained a small organisation, and current economic trends indicate that it may become even smaller. Small can be beautiful, but notwithstanding Corrymeela's impressive reputation, is it large enough to make a significant contribution to a problem which now has a global dimension – and which involves a large number of other well-funded government and non-governmental agencies?

The Community is aware of such challenges, as members and friends have indicated earlier, but one of the major problems which will continue to face Corrymeela is in trying to work out its core values in an increasingly difficult economic climate. This theme has been a constant feature of David Stevens' stewardship of the Community since he became Leader.

In his annual report in November 2006, he stated bluntly, "We are in a place of change, and change is happening to us. Lots of resources – both Government and voluntary – were put into Northern Ireland from the early 1970s, and we have had our fair share. Some of that is ending, and there is nothing we can do to stop it. We are reverting to normality; there are going to be less sources around. This is not about failure and blame, but about facts and living in reality."

Re-adjusting, he said is often hard and painful. "No one can say how many staff we will have in five, ten, or twenty years' time. What you can reasonably ask, however, of a Leader, a Management Team, a Council, is that they face reality, make the changes that have to be made, look for new possibilities and, if possible, find new ways." Recent redundancies and decisions affecting Knocklayd and Reading had caused "hurt, anger, pain and anguish to different people".

Some Corrymeela members strongly see their commitment as integrally linked to their involvement in Knocklayd, and others see Knocklayd as fully part of Corrymeela. After much discussion recently, a decision was taken to move towards closing Knocklayd. David Stevens says, "This decision was taken in view of the need for Corrymeela to concentrate our efforts, and the financial pressures in relation to the core business of the Community which, it is felt, is not that of Knocklayd. The decision was *not* taken around the value of what Knocklayd was doing."

Turning to the general picture, Stevens in his 2006 Annual Report reminded the Community that "Reality is a tough taskmaster, and an avoidance of reality and delay simply makes it worse. We want things to carry on as before, but reality – often through economics – is telling us they cannot. There is no easy way to do these things. Hurt, pain, grief and anger come with this territory because we are talking about real endings. It is a sort of death, and things – particularly relationships – are not going to be the same again."

Typically, David Stevens reminded the Community that even the meaning of "Corrymeela" in the Gaelic had been revised from "the hill of harmony" to "the lumpy crossing-place". He said, "That more truly expresses the reality. We have to deal with the reality of imperfection, and recognise that things are often simply lumpy. And Corrymeela is still a crossing-place, and there are few of them in Northern Ireland."

Equally realistically, he forecast a period of uncertainty in the political life of Northern Ireland. He said, "We need to understand what the restoration of devolution means and will do. It is another step in a long journey. It is not the end of the journey. At best it may be a sort of half-resolution, and there are huge uncertainties hanging over it. How it will work – if it works at all – will be through trade-offs and clientalism, and it will not be a pretty sight."

As well as the realism in Stevens' message, there was also a renewed challenge, and a sense of hope. He said, "There is still a need to look beyond tiredness, self-absorption and money pressures to what we are called to be and do in new times. This is a long-term business and we need to think how we can inspire the new generation – the people who are really going to carry us into a promised land."

He also referred to James Alison, the Catholic theologian, who claimed that there can be "an apparent heaviness in reconciliation work. But he goes on to say that from a Christian perspective this is profoundly wrong, that we should start from 'the extraordinary sensation of being in luck, of having fallen, despite ourselves on our feet, in the midst of ridiculously good fortune'." Stevens also asks, "Is not that our actual situation is Corrymeela? Have we not, despite ourselves, despite all the nonsense we find ourselves in at times, fallen on our feet in the midst of ridiculously good fortune?"

Perhaps another way of putting it, with Biblical undertones, would be to observe that for the true Corrymeela the "yoke is heavy but the burden is light". The future for the Community will depend not only on outside and internal factors but also on the spirituality, strength and vision of the members themselves. It will also depend on Corrymeela's ability to remain endlessly flexible, as its founder Ray Davey has advised, and to know what lies in its own heart – even to the point of disbandment or a total re-grouping, if that ever seems necessary.

After more than forty years of existence, what has Corrymeela really achieved? Duncan Morrow, who has spent so much of his life within, and contributing to, Corrymeela says that he is unnerved by the word 'achievement', which speaks to him of actions, set goals and effectiveness, or of deliberate actions for specific purposes.

He says, "I am very clear that if Corrymeela had defined its purposes in terms of 'key performance indicators' or 'targets' then they would have been a catastrophic distraction in 1969 or 1985. However, the challenge for a Christian Community is not to deliver targets, but must be to bear witness to the reality of love in the world, whatever the circumstances, and through staying close to this faith, to transform the world for all those who then come into contact with that reality. And the test of 'achievement' is how well, through testing circumstances, did we keep the faith?"

For Morrow the knowledge that "there is a love for each and all of us, which survives longer than every challenge, including death, makes all the difference. When this was real to me, I found myself living with other people who were officially my enemy, but who were now my friends, bringing new dimensions of insight and experience to my own life."

Corrymeela has been 'a big part' of his experience of what this theology might mean. Morrow says that "In its best moments, Corrymeela is a community of people who are 'on to something', something utterly important and hardly open to description – but it matters. Of course most of the time we found ourselves failing, and we are forced to learn each time how utterly dependent we are on forgiving and being forgiven to have a future at all. What we did, especially what Corrymeela is known for, by being a place of openness and acceptance in a Northern Ireland consumed by fear and hatred, depended – and still depends utterly – upon being open to what was given to us, what came to hand."

He believes that it was not up to the Community to evaluate "the practical contribution that witnessing to love makes, but I am sure that it remains and acts in very strange ways. Most importantly, in the Northern Ireland context, it was part of the evidence that hatred and fear did not define, or contain, all of reality. And that mattered at a very difficult time, in very complicated ways."

What made the witness of Corrymeela possible in the 1970s and 80s "was ultimately not the Community's ecumenical nature, its 'Hill of Harmony' image or its willingness to talk to all when other avenues seemed closed; but through all of those activities, in sustaining a practical and slightly credible witness to the God of all the victims, who loves all of His children, and grieves for every lost sheep in the midst of a veritable whirlwind of bitterness, violence and hatred."

In the Northern Ireland of the Troubles, this translated into a task of welcome, of human meeting and contact, of worship and of eating together and of mutual service, but not primarily one of "speaking at" or "preaching to" people. Duncan Morrow says that Corrymeela's inevitable calling was to be a contrast to the culture in which it lived, but not as another "angry culture" to the "surrounding culture".

He says, "No matter how much killing there was, it was made up of our brothers and sisters in whom we also repeatedly recognised ourselves. We couldn't condemn or 'win over' this world, but we could try to point to a way out, on the basis that we already knew that it was our redemption too."

So what was the achievement? Morrow says, "The achievement, if there was one, was to give credible and practical meaning to reconciliation in a world which had lost any sense of it, except through victory over others. And much of that vision was carried out by people and groups and organisations who were not directly Corrymeela, but were either directly or indirectly made safe or given confidence by what Corrymeela was grappling to do."

However, Corrymeela had failures, and these were in many ways the underside of its achievements. Morrow says, "So often we were hypocritical, doing to members and in our pompous judgement of others, exactly the same things as we condemned others for doing. There are too many stories of personal injury, which belie our self-congratulation as a Christian community, to be comfortable about. There is truth, too, in the accusation that Corrymeela in Ballycastle was an unreal fairyland, too disconnected from the real challenges of inter-community violence to make a lasting difference. There is also more than a grain of truth in the accusation that many issues were ignored, or not given due weight."

Duncan Morrow believes, like others inside and outside the Community, that Corrymeela was far from perfect. He says, "That imperfection was the vital grit in the oyster which taught us the paradoxical truth, that without forgiveness and mercy we are all lost. This was a Community who were on to something more important for human life than killing for national sovereignty or religious purity, and that *was* and *is* important."

Corrymeela was a candle in the darkness, when it was especially dark in Northern Ireland. Morrow recalls that "The task was to bring reconciliation to life in a world which did not believe in it, and was not sure whether it wished it. Sustaining a commitment to reconciliation while a civil war rages may be extremely difficult, but it does not create a clear boundary and clarity of purpose and mission."

There are paradoxes. "At a time when reconciliation has become a 'buzz word' of a whole political class, and central to a wider British and Irish concern to bury the enmities of Northern Ireland in common pursuit of success in the modern economy, the particularity of an ecumenical Christian Community is less. The result may well be that Corrymeela has to become less visible, less famous. It may even be that the Community which was Corrymeela eventually disappears."

However, Duncan Morrow, like others, believes that this need not be so. He says, "The task of Christian communities is endless, to witness for real reconciliation, to demonstrate real openness to all, and to search for the practical meaning of inclusion in the modern world. Corrymeela was never a meeting place for Catholics and Protestants as representatives of institutions, but as a place where Catholics and Protestants met, and found each other's humanity, and learned something important about what it meant to have life together."

In all of this, the story of the past is a strength and not a weakness, "but only if it is a model of the spirit with which we engage in the issues of this age, rather than a practice which has to be carbon-copied, even though the challenges have changed. Yet a contrast to the exclusions which the world puts up is as needed as ever."

Reconciliation, Morrow believes, is not an "event". He says, "In Northern Ireland, the legacy of the past is huge, and it will continue. Trust will never be learned by inciting people to trust one another, but only by making it possible through generosity and openness to meet and learn. As Northern Ireland changes, so the people who live here will change, and the challenges of meeting and learning will become more, rather than less, complicated."

Duncan Morrow believes that Corrymeela can find an ongoing role in it all. He says, "Finding justice without revenge, making peace with real enemies, meeting people after deep injury, seeking to make faith meaningful and real – these are all tasks requiring urgent attention. They just have a different colour and order now. Corrymeela's experience of practical engagement with the unknown in faith is as central as ever. And if it is not Corrymeela, it will have to be reinvented."

EPILOGUE

THE POLITICIANS IN NORTHERN IRELAND, and its people, have travelled a long way in recent months. The elections in early 2007 gave the politicians a mandate to get on with the business of governing. Despite all the odds, they duly obliged by forging an unlikely agreement, and by starting to tackle the issues, such as housing, education and the economy, which people on all sides had wished for a long time to be addressed by local representatives.

The words of the political leaders, some of whom were previously not talking to one another, underlined the long road that had been travelled, but with commendable speed, towards the end. Dr Ian Paisley said, "Today, at long last, we are starting upon the road – I emphasise *starting* – which I believe will take us to lasting peace in our Province... Northern Ireland has come to a time of peace, a time when hate will no longer rule."

Martin McGuinness said, "We know that this will not be easy, and the road we are embarking on will have many twists and turns. Ian Paisley, I want to wish you all the best as we step forward towards the greatest, yet most exciting, challenges of our lives." It was, indeed, a day which no one thought would ever arrive.

Corrymeela has travelled a long way since 1965, but it has kept at its heart the core values of its early vision which has sustained the Community through so much change and turmoil. That vision, shared with others, has been best expressed in the life and leadership of Ray Davey himself, whose moving and life-changing experience of the destruction of Dresden, and its renewal, is so symbolic of a powerfully inspiring message in the Book of Revelation, "Behold, I make all things new."

Today the city of Dresden, only a short rail journey from Berlin, has emerged from a long historical winter, symbolised by the magnificent Frauenkirche, which has been rebuilt to its former glory after its almost total destruction by the Allied bombing during the Second World War. In that city also stands the historic Kreuzkirche with its Cross of Nails, where Ray Davey brought his message of hope and reconciliation, some forty years after the destruction of Dresden.

It is appropriate, therefore, that the first and last words of the Corrymeela story to date, belong to Ray Davey himself. In his *War Diaries* he describes how, as a prisoner just outside Dresden, he visited the devastated city after the Allied bombing. In an entry dated 20 March 1945 he wrote: "Today, I went down to Dresden and saw it all for myself. All the buildings I had come to know so well – the Zwinger, the Hofkirche, the Frauenkirche, the Neus Rathaus, the Semperoper, the Schloss, etc, are now at best shells and mostly rubble. Postplatz is unrecognisable, the Zwinger is burnt out and looks like an ancient monument just unearthed. In the streets there is an unusual silence, few people about; scattered groups of British or Russian POWs leisurely working on the ruins. I felt strangely uncomfortable walking around the sorrows of this once beautiful city."

Some forty years later, Ray Davey returned to Dresden as part of a group from the British Churches Council, and he spoke at a service in the Kreuzkirche. He recalls, "I spoke very simply and directly as to how I felt about being back, how the last time I had been a prisoner and indeed an enemy in their city. I described something of the pain and hurt we prisoners had felt at the loss of many of our comrades who had died because of forced marches from the east, and others who had been cruelly treated

"Then I went on to describe how I and my fellow prisoners had felt about the terrible air-raids, and all the death and suffering that followed. But now today we were meeting at the one table and sharing the one Bread, and were mutually forgiven and reconciled by the one Lord. I felt very much that I was not only speaking for myself, but for all my fellow prisoners who had been with me away back forty years ago.

"But it wasn't only for them, but also for all those in our own country who today pray and yearn for peace and healing among nations. I believe that we in that service together were being visible signs of that peace and reconciliation and oneness that God wills."

The service led to a remarkable coincidence. That night Ray and Kathleen went to the famous Semperoper (Opera House) that had been so badly damaged in the air-raids and had just re-opened on 13 February 1985 – the fortieth anniversary of its destruction. On that terrible night in 1945, Carl von Weber's opera *Der Freischutz* was being performed, as it was during the re-opening night. Ray recalls that, during the interval, a lady sitting next to Kathleen started talking to her. She and her husband had been to that day's service in the Kreuzkirche, and she had recognised the Daveys.

Ray recalls, "She went on to explain just how much it had meant to her husband and herself. They had come over from Munich in West Germany, and had decided to go to the Kreuzkirche because her husband had been confirmed there. At the time of the air-raids, her husband, although he was only sixteen, was in the army and staying in barracks."

During the air raids, his mother, his six-year-old brother and both grandparents were killed. "Ever since, he had been filled with hatred and bitterness against the British and Americans, and simply could not forgive. But being present at that service and seeing what happened, he felt something speak to him and he broke down in tears and realised that now he could forgive."

Back in 1945, shortly after the Dresden bombing and as the war drew to a close with the defeat of Germany, Ray Davey reflected in his *War Diaries* about the meaning of Easter. He was joyful, and yet he remembered the ashes of Dresden; so many people had died, including his former comrades. He felt like leaving Easter to "the ancient Festival of Spring" but he concluded, "Somehow I can't do that. For me, it means that I want God and when I interpret Easter in terms of God, then I get peace."

Easter, he reflected, was not an escape from the mystery of evil and pain. "It's God's answer to it. It's not an attempt to take us from the grimness of our 20th century world, but a call to face it and see through it and see God. Like our world, the drama moves down into the valley of death and destruction, but it climbs up the other side into life and victory over death. Here God sets His stamp on the real inward qualities of life's character of love, joy and courage, and shows us that these are the final things of life."

And that is all that needs to be said.

NOTES

CHAPTER ONE
1 From Little Gidding.
2 In an interview with Judith Cole in the *Belfast Telegraph*, October 3, 2005.
3 *The War Diaries*, published by The Brehon Press, Belfast, 2005.
4 Ibid Page 101.
5 Ibid Page 147.
6 Ibid Page 198.
7 Foreword to Ray Davey's book *Take Away This Hate*, published by The Corrymeela Press.
8 In an interview with Alf McCreary for *Corrymeela Connections* Volume 5 No 2.
9 *Journey of Hope – Sources of the Corrymeela Vision* by John Morrow, published by The Corrymeela Press, Page 14.
10 In an interview with the author.
11 *The Corrymeela Story*, page 11, published by the Community.
12 Ibid.

CHAPTER TWO
1 Corrymeela pamphlet, page 4.
2 Dr David Stevens, Leader's Address, November 2004.

CHAPTER THREE
1 Leader's Report 1965-78.
2 Corrymeela Introductory Paper.
3 *A History of Ulster*, published by the Blackstaff Press, pp 622-623.
4 In an interview with the author.
5 In an interview with the author.
6 In a conversation with the author.

7 *Lost Lives* by David McKittrick, Seamus Kelters,Brian Feeney, and Chris Thornton, published by Mainstream Publishing, page 61.
8 Recollections of Alf McCreary, who was then a senior writer on the staff of the *Belfast Telegraph*.
9 Corrymeela Leader's Report, November 1979.
10 Ibid.

CHAPTER FOUR
1 Quoted in *Corrymeela – The Search for Peace* by Alf McCreary, published by Christian Journals Ltd, 1975, page 18.
2 Ibid.
3 Ibid.
4 In an interview with the author.

CHAPTER FIVE
1 Quoted from *Tried By Fire* by Alf McCreary, page 87, published by Marshall Pickering, London, 1986, and earlier by Christian Journals Ltd, Belfast.
2 Ibid pp 89-91
3 Ibid page 92.
4 Ibid page 94.
5 *A Channel of Peace* by Ray Davey, pp 18-19, published by Marshall Pickering, 1993.
6 *Profiles of Hope* by Alf McCreary, pp 43-52, published by Christian Journals, 1981.
7 Ibid.
8 Ibid.
9 *Take Away This Hate* by Ray Davey, published by Corrymeela.

CHAPTER SIX
1 *Corrymeela – The Search for Peace*, pp 30-31.
2 In background notes prepared at the request of the author.
3 In a lengthy background note, prepared at the request of the author.

CHAPTER SEVEN
1 These figures used to be easily obtainable from the security forces, but this has been less so in the recent years of relative peace. The figures quoted were contained in the appendices of one of the most valuable reference works covering that period, *Northern Ireland – A Political Directory 1968-89*, complied by Dr Sydney Elliott and WD Flackes, with John Coulter, and published by the Blackstaff Press.
2 In conversation with the author on 21 July, 2006.
3 Ibid.
4 *Take Away This Hate*, published by The Corrymeela Press, pp 108-9.
5 Ibid.
6 Ibid.
7 In conversation with the author on 21 July, 2006.
9 Ibid.
10 *Corrymeela Connections* Vol 5, No 2, page 5.

CHAPTER EIGHT
1 *Journey of Hope – Sources of the Corrymeela Vision*, published by the Corrymeela Press, 1995, page 14.
2 Ibid.
3 Ibid.
4 Ibid.
5 In an interview with the author in late 2005.
6 Ibid.
7 Ibid.
8 Ibid.

9 *Journey of Hope*, page 51.
10 Ibid.
11 In an interview with the author.
12 Ibid.
15 Ibid.

CHAPTER NINE
1 In an interview with the author in early 2006.
2 Ibid.
3 Ibid.
4 Ibid.
5 The work of Summerfest will be covered in a later Chapter.
6 Evangelical Contribution on Northern Ireland.

CHAPTER TEN
1 *Northern Ireland – A Political Directory*, pp 681-89
2 *On The Road of Reconciliation*, published in 2003 by the Columba Press, pp 58-9.
3 Op. Cit. page 58.
4 The important work of Edmund and Maura Kiely has been mentioned earlier.
5 In an interview with the author.
6 Op. Cit. page 59.

CHAPTER ELEVEN
1 In an interview with the author.
2 *On the Road to Reconciliation*, page 77.

CHAPTER TWELVE
1 In an extended interview with the author in 2006.
2 *Northern Ireland – A Political Directory 1968-99*, pp56-64.
3 *Nobody's Fool* by Alf McCreary, published by Hodder and Stoughton, London, 2004, page 176.
4 This issue is also discussed in *The Land of Unlikeness – Explorations in Reconciliation* by Dr David Stevens, published by the Columba Press, 2004

5 Some of these matters will be discussed in a later chapter.

CHAPTER THIRTEEN
1 As described by the Reverend Doug Baker in a paper on Summerfest, prepared at the request of the author.
2 Ibid.
3 *On the Road To Reconciliation*, pp 60-61.
4 Op. Cit. pp 54-55.
5 *The Land of Unlikeness*, page 11.
6 *On The Road To Reconciliation*, pp 56-57.
7 *The Land of Unlikeness*, page 11.
8 *On the Road To Reconciliation*, page 56.
9 In an interview with the author.

CHAPTER FOURTEEN
1 Quoted from *An Unfinished Journey* by Ray Davey, published by The Corrymeela Press.
2 Op.Cit.
3 Ibid.
4 In a conversation with the author in Reading.
5 In an interview with the author in Reading.

CHAPTER FIFTEEN
1 The author is indebted to the editors of the Corrymeela worship book, *Celebrating Together*, for information about The Croi and its contents.
2 In a paper prepared for the author.
3 In an article in *Corrymeela Connections*, Vol 5, No2, pp 23-24.
4 The background was explained by Norman Richardson in an article for *Corrymeela Connections* in January 2006.
5 *Corrymeela Connections* op.cit.
6 In notes prepared for the author.

CHAPTER SEVENTEEN
1 Published by The Columba Press pp 7-8.
2 Ibid.
3 Ibid.
4 Ibid.
5 The Dutch were later to make an important contribution to Corrymeela, as has been noted elsewhere.
6 Published by The Columba Press in 2001.
7 Op.Cit Page 19.
8 Ronnie Millar's contribution to Corrymeela is outlined in a later chapter.
9 Unless stated otherwise, David Stevens' remarks in this chapter were during a recorded interview with the author.

CHAPTER TWENTY
1 The conversation took place with this writer just before a Press Conference in Belfast on the day after the Dalai Lama visited Corrymeela.
2 In an interview with the author.
3 During an interview with the author in St Ethelburga's in August, 2006
4 In an interview with the author in Belfast in December 2006.

CHAPTER TWENTY-ONE
1 In an interview with Dr David Stevens, the Leader of Corrymeela, which was published by the Corrymeela Magazine P 16, No 1, December 2005.
2 In an interview with the author in mid-summer 2006.
3 In an interview with the author in 2006.
4 *The Land of Unlikeness*, published by The Columba Press pp 72-73.
5 In an interview with the author.
6 First published in 2001 by The Columba Press, page 346.